THE SHAPING OF 19th CENTURY
ABERDEENSHIRE

THE SHAPING OF
19th CENTURY
ABERDEENSHIRE

Sydney Wood

SPA BOOKS

ISBN 0–907590–05–5

The publishers express their thanks to ABERDEEN UNIVERSITY
LIBRARY and NORTH EAST OF SCOTLAND MUSEUMS SERVICE
for their kind permission to reproduce photographs in this volume

The publishers acknowledge subsidy from the Scottish
Arts Council towards the publication of this volume

Published by SPA Books Limited
PO Box 47
STEVENAGE
Herts

Printed in Great Britain by
Paradigm Print, Gateshead, Tyne and Wear

Contents

List of Illustrations

Introduction

The visitor to North East Scotland cannot fail to notice one of the distinctive features of its man-made landscape – the area is dotted with numerous large villages and small towns. Few of these places exhibit significant visible evidence of a past stretching back beyond the late eighteenth century; most have a strongly Victorian character. The solid grey properties that line the main streets include shops, churches, schools and, in many cases, homes that do not have front gardens. These communities of populations ranging upwards from 200 people to as high as 12,000 would seem to have occupied an important place in the past. Historians have commonly concentrated their attention on large towns and cities, especially those with a predominantly industrial character. Accounts of smaller places have tended to be the work of local ministers determined to list previous worthies of the kirk, or local authority employees bent on doing the same for past officials and councillors. Yet in North East Scotland, away from the City of Aberdeen, smaller communities constitute the predominant way of life. It is necessary to travel south to Dundee and Perth or north west to Elgin and Inverness to find centres playing a wider regional role.

The study of smaller places poses problems. Those of burgh status generated their own records, places big enough to adopt the Police Acts of the nineteenth century produced a rich source of evidence. But, for many places, the past lies buried in the broader archives produced by parochial boards, school boards and turnpike trusts as well as in the papers of private landowners and the occasional reminiscences and histories recorded by inhabitants. Sizeable places acquired their own newspapers in the nineteenth century; smaller places had to be content with brief references in publications aimed at a wider area. This study attempts to make a tentative way towards a picture of smaller community developments and difficulties during the nineteenth century. Since inland and coastal places differ so markedly an example of each has been studied in depth. Inverurie lies at the heart of the prosperous farming district of the Garioch; Fraserburgh clings to the exposed north east tip of the Aberdeenshire coastline. These two towns indicate the importance of the twin themes of farming and fishing in the area's past and present.

Affecting their fortunes to a varying degree looms the dominant community of the area, the City of Aberdeen.

Part I

THE SHAPING OF ABERDEENSHIRE COMMUNITIES

Chapter One

THE GROWTH OF SMALLER COMMUNITIES

The communities of the late eighteenth century

Most inhabitants of late eighteenth century Scotland lived in settlements that rarely exceeded a population of a thousand.[1] Aberdeenshire fitted into this picture with but two places (other than the burgh of Aberdeen) that were clearly well over a thousand inhabitants in size. Neither of these places – Peterhead and Huntly – challenged the importance of the burgh of Aberdeen. The census of 1801 showed that of a total population of 123,082 recorded as living in Aberdeenshire, 27,608 dwelt in the burgh. Smaller settlements (whose populations exceeded 100) accounted for but 10 per cent of the County population living outside Aberdeen.

The figures provided by ministers contributing to the Statistical Account show a County in which significant areas lacked any kind of local village centre.

Inland community populations of the 1790s				
a) Pre 1700 settlements		b) Planned villages, post 1760	
Ellon	190	Cuminestown	404
Huntly	2,000	New Byth	195
Inverurie	360	Strichen	200
Kincardine O'Neil	100		
Kintore	228		
Old Meldrum	783		
Tarland	150	Source O.S.A.	
Turriff	701		

Inland settlements included places of some age and also a cluster of recently established communities sited in the bleak interior of Buchan. Not all of these planned villages were an immediate success. New Pitsligo, established in 1787, had but a dozen feus occupied in a decade by hardy settlers prepared to cut peat in their own back-gardens and take animals half a mile away to the only patch of land suitable for grazing.[2] The planned settlements are evidence of efforts to up-grade an area: the older communities lay amid fertile farmland. The clustering of Kintore, Inverurie and Old Meldrum offers clear evidence of the well-established fertility of this district.

Aberdeenshire Communities of the 1790's

The importance of farming

Farming in eighteenth century Aberdeenshire still followed such soil-exhausting procedures that fertile naturally-drained environments were most likely to be the site of communities. Upland areas and lands liable to flooding were less likely to be well-populated.[3] The bulk of the countryside's population lived in kirktons, cottar-towns, milltowns etc of around fifty people.[4] These randomly-shaped clusters of properties, traversed by unpaved tracks and dotted with dunghills located before the houses, were the despair of improvers.[5] The planned settlements were not only a sign of landowners' efforts to improve the farmland of the area, but also of their belief that communities needed re-designing.

By the 1790s a few parish ministers glimpsed signs of decreasing poverty among the peasantry. In King Edward the minister noted that whereas in the 1750s only two people in his congregation had been able to afford hats, by the 1790s every ploughman owned one.[6] He observed, too, the spread of tea drinking. But most Aberdeenshire people had little to spare for buying imported or specialist-made goods. The part-time craftsmen of the townships managed the making of footwear and clothing, the construction of housing and the processing of grain. Most ministers agreed with the judgement offered by the Alford incumbent, 'all the old-fashioned prejudices of husbandry are still looked upon as sure and infallible rules of good management'.[7] The endless cropping of the high crooked rigs of the infield with bere and oats, the poor returns of outfield and the primitive agricultural implements attracted repeated notice. So too did the interminable hours spent in cutting, drying and carrying off peats. As New Pitsligo's minister commented, 'it is barbarous and expensive work and detains them long from the improvement of the land'.[8] Moreover many sub-tenants lacked the incentive of a secure lease.

Thus the signs of improvement in the late eighteenth century were still limited. Landowners sought to modernise their home farms with tree-planting, ditch digging and dyke building, crop improvements and fertilizing of the ground. Some tenants emulated their example and the tilled acreage of the County increased in the second half of the eighteenth century by 30,000 acres.[9] A sizeable cattle trade had developed since the early seventeenth century and, by 1800, involved the movement of thousands of beasts to great fairs like Aikey near New Deer and St Lawrence, near Rayne and from thence to southern Scotland.[10] The droving traffic had no significant impact on the growth of Aberdeenshire communities, though. Animals wandered the countryside along routes which drovers knew would sustain them. As long as agriculture followed its old ways the growth of communities able to offer specialist services and skills was not likely to be impressive. When James Anderson surveyed Aberdeenshire in 1794 for the Board of Agriculture he gloomily noted the marshy and treeless appearance of the County, the general use of the old Scots plough, the flail and winnowing by 'letting down the corn in the wind between two barn doors.[11] Travel difficulties dogged inland Aberdeenshire in 1794 to such an extent that the fruitful corn country of the Garioch was outstripped in production by coastal areas better able to get fertilizers.[12] Country people lived in little cottages of rough stones, turf and bits of wood roofed with a turf and heather covering that had to be lashed down with straw ropes to prevent devastating storm damage. They warmed themselves by open peat fires, cooked on them with a few simple iron utensils and lit their dwellings with the dim light of dried and peeled bog-fir torches. A life at this level generated little to spare for spending in village shops, or the workshops of village craftsmen.

North-East farming was undoubtedly changing. As in the rest of Scotland the key figures were the lairds. In the 1770s aristocratic land-owners owned over half of Scotland's agricultural wealth and lesser lairds around 40 per cent.[13] Aberdeenshire lairds were active and generally aware of the desirability of stimulating community growth. But their farming improvements alone were insufficient to sustain such a development.

Coastal places

By 1800 fishing was a well-established activity along the Aberdeenshire coast. James Anderson decided the people of the fisher communities prospered sufficiently to live 'in easy circumstances'.[14] Certainly the activity of sea-fishing was likely to lead to community growth, Dr J. R. Coull has shown that the origins of pre-1800 fisher places owed much to the activity of the landowners upon whose lands they were sited.[15] Lord Pitsligo developed Rosehearty in the late seventeenth century, providing boats, a quay and seatown properties in return for a fifth of catches.[16] By 1793 42 fishermen worked seven boats from Rosehearty. Fishing itself involved crews of six or seven to a boat: the work of finding bait, preparing the lines, making and mending nets, drying and salting the catch and selling it drew in a whole community. By the 1790s even a small fishertown like Pittulie was sending salted fish to the Firth of Forth and lobsters to London (at twopence each).[17]

The location of communities depended not only on the enterprise of landowners but the geography of the shore-line. The Aberdeenshire coast consists of sections of rocky cliff, sweeps of sandy shore and areas of shingle beach. Sandy areas were difficult places on which to build houses and awkward to traverse for fisherman dragging their boats ashore. Though many fishermen still worked from open beaches, the more successful communities of the late eighteenth century were those places that had provided themselves with harbour works. Both Fraserburgh and Peterhead were busy with this problem and at Rosehearty Lord Gardenston was greatly concerned that the pier failed to shield ships tied up at the quay from the lash of North Sea gales.[18]

Coastal community populations in the 1790s (Source O.S.A.)			
Boddam	192	Newburgh	c.170
Broadsea	200	Peterhead	2,959
Fraserburgh	1,000	Rosehearty	213

Fraserburgh's fortunes will be considered in Part III. Peterhead's remarkable size warrants further comment. It lay at a point where ships were likely to seek refuge in foul weather, between the Moray Firth and Firth of Forth. It was also the first landfall for many vessels from the Baltic.[19] Its early harbour was financed by the superiors of Peterhead, the Keiths. The latter's Jacobite loyalties lost them their control but their successors, the York Building Company and then the Merchant Company of Edinburgh were pleased to see further harbour work. Early eighteenth century harbour repairs were paid for by the feuars and the Scottish burghs. A substantial harbour extension of the 1770s was financed by a loan secured on town funds, money from the Commis-

THE TERMS OF ADMISSION

FOR THE

LADIES AND GENTLEMEN

ATTENDING THE

MINERAL WELLS AND *BATHS* OF *PETERHEAD.*

For the Use of the ROOMS . . . . 10s. 6d. *for the Season.*

Gentlemen, for the Use of the NEWS-ROOM . . 10s. 6d. *each, for Do.*

The OPEN COLD BATH . . . . 1s. *per Dip,* or 21s. . . . . . . *for Do.*

The HOUSE COLD BATH . . . . 2s. . . . . . *per Dip.*

The COLD SHOWER BATH . . . . 1s. . . . . *per Do.*

The WARM SHOWER BATH . . . . 1s. 6d. . . . . *per Do.*

The PROJECTING BATH . . . . 1s. . . . . *per 100.*

The VAPOUR BATH . . . . 6s. . . . . . . *per Dip.*

The WARM WATER BATH . . . . 3s. 1s. 6d. & 1s. *per Do.*

The MEDICATED BATH . . . . 3s. . . . . *per Do.*

The WARM AIR BATH . . . . 3s. . . . . . . *per Do.*

Dances.

TO SUBSCRIBERS.

Gentlemen . . . . 1s. *each.*

Ladies . . . . 6d. *do.*

TO NON-SUBSCRIBERS.

Gentlemen . . . . 2s. 6d. *each.*

Ladies . . . . 2s. . . . *do.*

Card Parties.

Ladies and Gentlemen . . . . 1s. *each, per Night*

Pleasure and Fishing Boats.

From 5s. to 10s. 6d. *per Day,*

Exclusive of the Wages of the Men who may be employed in conducting these Boats.

Chalmers & Co. Printers, Aberdeen.

sioners of the Annexed and Forfeited Estates and a lesser sum from the Convention of Royal Burghs.

The harbour enabled Peterhead to develop a coasting trade in coal, iron, building materials and food (inward); grain, butter, salted fish and meat flowed from the port. The burgh housed three thread, two wool, one linen and one cotton manufacturing enterprise.[20] A small number of fishermen worked from the shelter of the harbour. The town's appearance was improved in the later part of the century with locally-quarried granite used to create solid properties, and imported slate to roof them. The main streets of Peterhead, unlike those of Aberdeenshire communities were regularly cleared of dung and were free of peat stacks. The town had good reason to make itself look attractive for it had become a health resort.

Local springs produced a strong-smelling yellowish water exploited as a health cure by a town druggist, James Arbuthnott. He claimed it was so effective that 'the feeble, dispirited, without appetite and without strength, return home hearty and well'.[21] Arbuthnott inspired the creation of baths for men and for women, a pump room, apartments for billiards, tea and coffee, and a hall for dances. For three or four months, an optimistic contemporary noted, 'all the beauty and fashion visited the healthy clean town of Peterhead ... the whole town was given up to gaiety and bustle'.[22] This trade encouraged the building of decent inns, and accommodation for the summer visitors. Ordinary local people were, however, prone to grumble that the invasion of outsiders pushed up the price of provisions.[23]

Peterhead's success impressed Fraserburgh sufficiently to persuade it to try and copy its development as a health resort. But both ports were on the brink of embarking on the herring business. Peterhead was increasingly involved in whaling and the smells that floated up from the harbour quays and curing yards and especially from the sites where blubber was boiled down to produce oil, were offensive to a degree. The improved travel facilities of the nineteenth century soon enabled the wealthy to make their way to more attractive resorts.

Fishing was sufficient to sustain a small village by the late eighteenth century, but no more. Scottish fishermen still concentrated on white fishing and operated in a small-scale fashion. Peterhead and Fraserburgh's locations, harbour works, trading and manufacturing activities pushed up their populations above those of other coastal communities. Their harbours, in particular, helped them to deal with one of the great constraints on community growth before 1800, the difficulty of travelling.

Travel

Inland communities occupied a position less fortunate than Peterhead's; the shifting of goods to and from them was a real problem. The older inland communities all lay on routeways, four of them at river crossing points. But the inadequacies of Aberdeenshire roads attracted repeated complaint in the Statistical Accounts. In Logie Buchan 'the badness of our roads in general and particularly to the port of Newburgh from which we get our lime and which is a general market for our grain has hitherto been and still is a great obstruction to the improvement of the County'.[24] James Anderson echoed this widely held view, 'till good roads be established, agricultural and internal improvements can never proceed with energy'.[25]

Roads still depended primarily upon statute labour. Legislation of 1699 obliged the labouring population to turn out for six days a year, bringing horses and carts if they possessed them, to labour upon the roads. Upon proprietors a tax of ten Scots shillings per £100 of valued rent was levied to pay for the necessary materials.[26] James Beattie's grumble in his diary entry for March 1790 – 'paid for myself and son something called road money, a premium perhaps to the Commissioners of Supply for keeping the roads in bad repair'[27] reflects the feelings of the better off towards the results of this system. When statute labour went to work in Rothiemay it made the roads worse by heaping the soil and clay contents of ditches in the centre of the road.[28] The system remained in force till 1845 but increasingly labour services were commuted and hired workmen replaced resentful locals who 'not sensible of the great advantage of good roads go to the labour with reluctance and perform it in an awkward and slovenly manner'.[29]

Yet this unsatisfactory system of 1790 was an improvement over early eighteenth century conditions. Landowners had been busy clearly marking out roads and shifting boulders. New Deer had three or four carriers by 1793; fifty years earlier the district's solitary carrier had either used packs on horseback or had staggered along with a creel upon his own back.[30] In Oyne parish there were around fifty carts but – typically for the travelling difficulties of the time – they could not be fully laden. The uneven and poor-quality road surfaces wound up and down over the natural contours of the County, clinging to awkward higher ground in order to avoid marshy land.[31]

To some travellers these problems were not important. Drovers moving south followed routes from Spey and Deveron basins across the hills of the Mounth to the glens of Angus and Kincardine. Few bridges helped them negotiate the Dee, though Braemar possessed one by the early seventeenth century and another was built at Ballater in 1783.[32] But communities suffered. People needing to ford rivers to reach places like Inverurie or Turriff faced a hazard that was always a nuisance and occasionally dangerous. Several lost their lives attempting to ford the Deveron before Turriff obtained a bridge in 1826.[33]

Improving lairds concerned to ease the passage of wheeled traffic were prepared to find extra money of their own. The road north-west from Aberdeen, for example, was improved in 1776 at the point where it negotiated the awkward obstacle of Tyrebagger Hill. From April to September gangs of workmen between five and twenty-two in number laboured six days a week for eight pence a day each. The wages bill of £61 rose to £77 when the purchase and frequent repair of picks and barrows was added. This bill was met primarily by local heritors together with £10 from Aberdeen burgh.[34] But the road and bridge building activities were insufficient for local lairds and business men. Well-established communities lay on well-used routes; road improvement would undoubtedly encourage their growth. But newer planned places were not necessarily so fortunate. Cuminestown, for example existed to serve its immediate locality and did not straddle a significant route. Yet even here improvement was needed; if landowners wished to see their villages develop they would have to make it easier for trade to flow.

Industry

Industrial activity in the North East of the 1790s tended to cluster in Aberdeen. But small communities and the countryside itself supported a range of small-scale activities. In this respect the poorly-developed travel systems of the period, compared to those of the later nineteenth century, helped sustain the country enterprises by excluding the products of urban areas. However where bulky goods were produced activity tended to be confined to coastal areas. In Aberdeenshire's case this meant granite quarrying and shaping. The major quarries lay by Aberdeen, Peterhead and Fraserburgh, employing around 600 men.[35] The stone met not only local needs but supplied material for surfacing London streets.[36] Sailing ships bringing coal found stone a convenient return cargo.[37] But the potential of inland granite quarrying remained unexploited: the industry aided existing communities, it did not stimulate new ones.

Aberdeenshire's most significant industrial activity, the textile trade, retained a partially rural character before 1800. Its machinery used water power rather than steam.[38] Small enterprises like lint and waulk-mills were encouraged by landowners developing their estates. Even though landowner activity in these enterprises peaked in the 1780s, development was continued by farm and mill tenants. The planned villages were commonly intended to contain textile workers. Linen production was meant to occupy people in Cuminestown and Strichen; New Byth tried to attract weavers by offering crofts and peats.[39] In New Pitsligo Sir William Forbes spent £1,000 on creating a bleachfield.[40] Communities housing manufacturers were a magnet to people of the nearby area. Cairnie's minister bewailed the way his parishioners were drawn to Huntly by the opportunity to find work in the Duke of Gordon's expanding settlement.[41] Methlick's minister felt that manufacturers 'draw a great many hands from the country into towns so that servants for agriculture are scarce'.[42] In his view farm workers looked for treatment from manufacturers that would be less harsh than that they were accustomed to from farmers. Huntly's success owes much to its development as a textile centre. The Duke of Gordon overhauled and re-shaped the town in 1770, making vigorous efforts to attract textile workers. By the 1790s both nearby rivers, the Bogie and the Deveron, had been bridged. Huntly housed 52 flax dressers and 209 weavers and contained a bleachfield and cotton manufacturing.[43] No nearby community challenged Huntly, it lay on the main Aberdeen-Inverness route and was a focus for a sizeable sweep of farmland. Peterhead, too, was strengthened by the presence of textile trades employing over 400 people. The importance of the port facilities was shown by the presence of two shops in Peterhead that only sold goods manufactured in Paisley and Glasgow.[44]

Huntly's success in attracting textile workers was exceptional for a smaller community. In general inland places relied on their small-scale services to justify their existence. Old Meldrum had acquired a brewery and a distillery by the 1790s, yet its minister preferred to attribute the importance of the place to the fact that its weekly markets were the best for provisions north of Aberdeen.[45] The role of the smaller places can be seen by looking more closely at Tarland and Kincardine O'Neil.

Tarland was a burgh of barony made up of forty homes housing 150 people. It lay on a sheltered slope by the meandering unbridged Tarland Burn, serving the people who lived in the relatively sheltered bowl of the Howe of Cromar. The village was primarily a focus for trading. Its weekly markets enabled local people to buy meal, wooden goods for domestic and working use, and 'all things necessary for country consumpt'.[46] At six fairs during the year livestock was bought and sold. Four shopkeepers traded from their homes, an inn and three or four alehouses supplied local people and drovers passing south, whilst the village craftsmen included a shoemaker, a saddler, a dyer, a carpenter, a blacksmith, a farrier and a wheelwright.

Several miles nearer to Aberdeen, on the north bank of the River Dee, lay Kincardine O'Neil. Its site had been of significance for centuries: here the route up the Dee Valley intersected the important way north from the Cairn O'Mounth. At the village travellers could choose to cross the river by either a ford or a ferry. The village served its surroundings with smiths, masons, carpenters, weavers, shoemakers and millers but the importance of its position to travellers was indicated by the presence of three inns.[47] A doctor and a schoolmaster and no less than ten shop-keepers also lived there. Although Kincardine O'Neil did not have the six major fairs Tarland possessed, it was the site of a single fair far bigger than any at Tarland. In late September Bartle Fair dominated the village. Visitors to it were able to buy 'moss fir used for light throughout the winter evenings, shoes, home-made cloth, shirting, horn spoons, wooden pails, caps and plates, harrows, wheels'.[48] The fair spilled out into the kirkyard to the annoyance of the kirk session. Traders allowed their horses to wander among the graves, or chained them to the church wall whilst they used the flat-topped gravestones to display their goods. Rowdy behaviour, fighting and drunkenness sometimes so alarmed local people that they scrambled up on to the thatched roofs of their homes and from there peered down in safety at the jostling throng below.

Aberdeenshire communities offered a service role to their neighbour-hoods; they busied themselves with fishing, trading and industrial work in varying degrees. The travelling difficulties limited the impact upon them of the wider economy and of the dominant settlement of Aberdeen. Ministers in Deeside and Donside can be found, complaining of country people drawn to work in the city. Many country women worked at a hosiery trade controlled by Aberdeen businessmen. The County was beginning to feel the impact of what was going on elsewhere in Britain. Ideas for agricultural improvements, urban areas with growing de-mands for food, the rise of manufacturing, all these were forces beginning to touch the north-east. The fortunes of smaller communities in the nineteenth century were to vary according to their ability to play both a role useful to their immediate locality and also a part in a wider economy.

Factors shaping community growth

The varying fortunes of Aberdeenshire communities in the nineteenth century stemmed from the effect upon them of several factors which will be separately studied but which in actuality interacted with one another. By the end of the century many communities had expanded in size and new communities had been established (see Appendix 1).

Improved farming
The growth of communities designed to serve the rural neighbourhood and absorb some of its surplus population was one aspect of a farming revolution. The French Wars of 1793–1815 did much to stimulate output at a time when a transport revolution was making it much easier to bring in fertilizers as well as shift bulky produce. Between the 1790s and 1811 rents for infield land doubled and outfield rents quadrupled as production was overhauled and prices rose.[49] When George Skene Keith compiled a second Agricultural Survey in 1811 he was able to describe a scene far more optimistic than Anderson had seen seventeen years earlier.[50] He particularly noticed how the growing of turnips helped farmers who had formerly had to manage with oat-straw as a winter feed for cattle. And acreage in turnips of 2,522 in the 1790s had risen to 28,893 by 1811 and continued to climb, reaching 82,316 by 1859.[51] Lime, bone, guano and shell-sand fed the land; farmers near Aberdeen and along the Aberdeenshire Canal found it worth buying Aberdeen's night soil – a community service that other sizeable settlements were to offer later in the century.

Early nineteenth century tenants set to work transforming their homes. Sizeable stone and slate structures with proper floors and chimneys began to appear in large numbers; such fortunate farmers were increasingly the possessors of leases of nineteen years – occasionally longer. Their leases often required them to improve their land. Such was the interest in experiments that Sir Charles Forbes even attempted to settle kangaroos in Strathdon. The pair he sent over from Australia thrived – but were both of the same sex.[52] One of the simpler improvements was to adopt the scythe instead of the sickle; when Alexander Murray began farming near Peterhead his pioneering use of the scythe brought crowds of interested spectators to peer at the marvel, wonder at its speed, and contrast it with their own 'rustic and home-made' implements.[53] Whereas it took $4\frac{1}{2}$ to 5 days for a worker to harvest an acre of wheat with a sickle, a man with a scythe could accomplish the task in 2 to $2\frac{1}{2}$ days.[54] In some ways the sufferers on all this were the poorer subtenants. As landlords re-organised their estates they often broke up the old townships, preferring larger single-tenant farms. Yet the improved farming needed many workers, especially for work on turnip fields and at times of seasonal demand, like harvesting. Thus the growth of villages as places where some farm-workers and their families lived, was encouraged. In Cairnie the Duke of Gordon created larger farms in the forties (like Newton, built from seven former holdings). The result was that many of those engaged in agricultural pursuits moved to villages and towns or emigrated.[55]

The change that came over the County in the early nineteenth century struck George Cruden especially forcibly. In the 1790s he had been parish minister in Old Deer; by 1840 he was at Logie Buchan, one of the few men who lived to contribute parish portraits to both the original and new Statistical Account. 'When I look around me', he wrote in 1840, 'I seem to live not only among a new race of men but in a new world. Cultivation has changed the face of the earth'.[56] Not only the incentive of profits and the determination of landlords, but a quite staggering effort by ordinary people had brought about this change. Before the wire-fencing of the later nineteenth century, enclosure usually involved stone-dyke building whilst ditch and drain-digging, clearing great boulders from farmland and cutting down broom and gorse added up to a most wearisome work load. In 1877 the tenant of Drumdelgie in Cairnie parish recalled that he and his father had reclaimed 450 acres of waste, built eleven miles of stone dykes, and laid endless tile drains.[57]

The land drainage systems improved during the century. Tile drains replaced earlier stone ones and tile works emerged to supply farmers' needs. As compensation for the Corn Law repeal of 1846 Sir Robert Peel offered Scottish farmers half a million pounds to be tapped for loans at $6\frac{1}{2}$ per cent.[58] Effective drainage not only brought into cultivation land hitherto felt to be too wet and heavy, it enabled the old system of drainage through rig-building to be scrapped. Upon the newly-levelled fields of Victorian Aberdeenshire small horse teams could readily tug iron ploughs and machines for sowing and reaping too. A flurry of water and horse-mill building provided power for threshing; by 1840 in Oyne parish few farms of over thirty acres were without one of these devices.[59] Thus machinery spread whose complexity of construction was beyond simple rural craftsmen. In the latter part of the century even more elaborate gadgetry became common such as the numerous portable steam threshing mills widely used over much of the County.[60]

The County produced great quantities of oats. By 1872 from its 585,299 acres of arable, Aberdeenshire devoted 191,880 to oats, 18,930 to barley and only 1,357 to wheat.[61] This helped protect the area from the severe impact of agricultural depression in later years of the century. Average wheat prices between 1870 and 1900 fell by 4/5d a hundred-weight but oats by only 1/9d and barley by 2/7d.[62] Cattle prices held up well too and the 95,091 acres of turnips and swedes grown in 1872 were clear evidence of the effort devoted to cattle raising. Several County farmers worked at improving cattle stock, notably William McCombie of Tillyfour and Anthony and Amos Cruickshank, so that the County's 157,960 cattle of 1872 were generally of high quality. McCombie observed 'steam navigation and the use of bone dust being both introduced at the same time shortly produced a complete revolution in the cattle trade'.[63] Drovers had plodded around ten or twelve miles a day, across country. From the 1820s it became more sensible to take cattle to a coastal community and ship them by sail or steam. Sail offered lower prices – a little over half those charged by steamer services – but its reliability was suspect. McCombie himself watched sailing vessels laden with cattle attempting to beat out of Aberdeen harbour only to be driven back.[64] The railway building of the later nineteenth century further eased the movement of cattle and encouraged their gathering at the communities stimulated by a convenient location on a line. Thus as the century progressed the cattle trade tended, as a result of steamship and railway development, to be sucked into Aberdeen, though sizeable ports like Fraserburgh and Peterhead remained actively involved too.

The increased affluence of farmers provided them with money with which to improve their life-styles. Farm and steading rebuilding continued during the century, creating more substantial properties. The tastes of farmers' wives expanded, requiring diet more varied and clothing more sophisticated than the country folk could provide. The expansion of shopping and leisure facilities in many County communities was one of the features of the nineteenth century.

The farming changes of the nineteenth century contributed very significantly to the growth of communities in the County. In small towns and large villages lived labourers who could dig drains, build dykes and help with farm work: there were specialists able to create the farms and steadings appropriate to an improved estate. When the Hatton Estates were transformed in the 1850s and 60s it was Turriff people who were able to benefit from the money spent – over £700 on drainage and nearly £28,000 on new buildings between 1851 and 1886.[65] The coming of railways increased the importance to farmers of the rail depots in towns and villages, for here gathered suppliers of animal foods and of fertilizers; here clustered buyers of farmers' produce too. Closely related to farming changes, then, were changes in travel, and changes in industry too. When combined they encouraged the development of specialist services in sizeable communities. The growth of horse power during the century led to the increase in associated trades often housed in villages and country towns like blacksmiths and wheelwrights. In 1841 the County contained 1,289 blacksmiths, a number that had risen to 1,648 by 1901. So important did this development seem to many Aberdeenshire lairds that, in the later eighteenth century, they began to deliberately foster the creation of villages. In 1811 George Skene Keith surveyed this process with approval, arguing that 'neat villages which contain from 100 to 500 inhabitants are in many respects preferable to cottages which are scattered over the country in all directions . . . at least two blacksmiths, two ploughwrights or house carpenters and two sets of artificers' shops in a village are most beneficial'.[66]

Skene Keith was merely expressing views already put forward by Sir John Sinclair. To Sinclair whereas manufacturing towns were places that eroded the moral and physical well-being of inhabitants, villages were of an ideal size for social and economic purposes. They could house tradesmen, offer goods, services, markets and schools and could accommodate textile workers. Yet they were sufficiently small to remain in touch with their surroundings, to be genuine communities and to be free from the pollution of urban life.[67]

The pages of the 'Aberdeen Journal' in the late eighteenth century contain advertisements for communities seeking to attract inhabitants. A 1798 issue urged people to consider coming to Strichen (then known as Mormond Village) a planned village of the 1760s for which many merits were claimed, 'The situation of this village is dry and healthy, moderately elevated with an extensive tract of deep moss adjacent, a great command of fine spring water and a sufficiency for driving mills and machinery, lime-stone and abundance of excellent stones for building to be found on the spot . . . The proposed turnpike road from Aberdeen to Fraserburgh passes near said village.

NB: An excellent situation for a Brewery with great command of fine water to be let in Mormond village'.[68]

The factors that induced landowners to deliberately stimulate village development have been surveyed by Christopher Smout[69] and studied by D. G. Lockhart.[70] Several contributors to the old and new Statistical Accounts offered their interpretation of developments, as at Cuminestown the creation of 'Joseph Cumine of Auchry, observing his tenants were frequently at a loss for a market he determined to establish a permanent one on his own estates. For this purpose he planned a regular village upon the moorish part of a farm which in whole yielded only £11 a year. For a while he felt in silence the sneers of his neighbours who reprobated his scheme as wild and impracticable, but these temporary sneers soon gave way to lasting esteem. He prevailed on a few to take feus, he assisted the industrious with money . . . Settlers flocked annually to Cuminestown and the village soon assumed a flourishing appearance. In connection with some neighbouring gentlemen he established in his village a linen manufacture'.[71]

This picture of a community created to serve the surrounding countryside and to provide industrial employment applied to other places too. These new rural communities were to have a more than rural function. New Pitsligo emerged in the 1790s on an area formerly occupied by a couple of farms, each feu having a piece of land for farming and with an apparently inexhaustible moss nearby.[72] Lumsden's establishment on the low watershed between the rivers Don and Deveron led to the sudden increase of the population. It attracted individuals from a wide area including ... 'Traders, blacksmiths, carpenters, masons and tailors'.[73] These communities helped absorb surplus rural population, offering alternative employment (especially in textiles) to some, and providing homes for others who might still be farm workers, but had lost their old homes with the break-up of the townships. Some developed a satisfactory role, serving the area around. The newspaper advertisements for villages show the importance lairds placed on markets and fairs in these places as a means of linking the community to its hinterland.[74] By 1859 over half of Strichen's workers were active in various crafts and services and a third busied themselves in shops and inns. The decline of the domestic textile industry did bring setbacks, and not all new settlements flourished. New Pitsligo developed a successful bobbin-lace industry in the later nineteenth century, but New Leeds failed to become the textile success its name promised. By the mid seventies it was 'but a poor place with only eighteen dwelling houses ... and a small United Presbyterian Church and manse. It was at one time much larger and it was then called 'the city of sin and misery', but once smuggling was suppressed and poaching almost abandoned and honest labour substituted ... a great change has taken place'.[75]

   To some extent the success or failure of planned villages depended on their situation in relation to the transport network. Mintlaw was established in 1813 by that busy improver, James Ferguson of Pitfour, at the junction of the Aberdeen-Fraserburgh and Banff-Peterhead roads, Ballater was laid out at the beginning of the nineteenth century by William Farquharson of Monaltrie to serve as a health resort, its houses 'built on a regular plan and neatly fitted up for the accommodation of summer visitors'[76] as well as a market centre. It grew slowly during the turnpike era, then expanded rapidly once a rail link enabled tourists and holiday-makers to escape to the Dee Valley.

   The coming of the railways helped put a stop to the further creation of villages as rural centres, for the rail network reduced the need for a further development of local market centres. Community development in the later nineteenth century depended more upon proximity to the railways, though this was but one of the factors shaping the growth prospects of Aberdeenshire communities in the nineteenth century. The enhanced role of communities that the transformation of farming encouraged was inevitably intertwined with many other factors. In areas of more marginal farmland it was harder for the environment to bear a heavy expansion of population. The upper reaches of the Dee and Don were areas of considerable population migration in the nineteenth century. Where communities were successfully established here it was because extra factors – usually tourism and holiday business – operated. Farming alone seemed unable to sustain significantly sized places and communities like Braemar, Ballater and Aboyne are marks of the greater success of Deeside over Donside in attracting visitors. In fact whilst Ballater's population was increasing in the second half of the nineteenth century, the population of the parish in which it stood fell by over 300.[77] In this Deeside was greatly helped by one of the features of the transport revolution – the coming of a railway. Moreover the setbacks sustained by farming in the later nineteenth century jolted the ability of the countryside to sustain the services of ever-expanding smaller local centres of population. By 1901 the County's population of agricultural labourers had shrunk, compared to 1841, from nearly 16,000 down to just over 13,000. Rural communities like Longside, Mintlaw, New Byth, New Deer, Stewartfield, Strichen and Tarland experienced a population fall in the last two decades of the century (Appendix 1).

Transport

A comparison of the census returns of 1841 and 1901 demonstrates very clearly the growth of transport services in the County (see Appendix 1). The 1841 schedules are the earliest in which householders had to make individual returns.[78] Though the categorising of occupations in 1841 differs considerably from that of 1901, by adopting the latter's categories and working backwards it is possible to see considerable changes. (In any case 1841 as a date offers particular opportunities in examining the North East's economy for it pre-dates the collapse of textile production). By 1901 the County contained over 1,700 railway workers (over a thousand of these lived in the City) and 3,266 people involved in horse-drawn transport (2,224 of these lived in the City). In 1841, of course, the County did not house any railway workers; its horse-vehicle workers numbered 1,506. Increased numbers of seamen, boatmen, porters and messengers all demonstrated the improved transport amenities obtained by the end of the century.

The turnpike road system spread rapidly through Aberdeenshire after the passage of an act in 1795. An Edinburgh surveyor, Charles Abercrombie, was employed to plan the County's roads. The lines he laid out were designed to produce speedier travel and satisfy the economic requirements of those who provided the funds. It was in the landowners' interests to ensure that new roads ran conveniently by their estates. It also suited them to agree with the merchants (who sometimes helped fund turnpikes) that new roads should pass through communities and thus benefit their trade by greatly easing the movement of carts, coaches and carriages. The turnpikes fanned out from the City connecting up the County's communities. To people in places like Old Meldrum and Tarland the development was most welcome. The network focussed trade far more on the City. The old North-South routes (over the Mounth) that lay further inland began to decline.

The first turnpike to be built within the County, the Deeside Road, opened up in 1798 from Aberdeen to Drum. The route was pushed on up the Dee Valley by the Charleston Turnpike, in 1801. This run of road shows some of the costs that were involved in turnpike building. The actual road surface had to be levelled off and a trench around fourteen feet wide and fourteen inches deep taken out. Granite stones around two inches in size were poured in and the surface finished off with gravel or with sandy soil. The cost per mile of this on the Charleston Road ranged from £150 to £270, according to the difficulty of the terrain.[79] (In fact this was rather lower than the average cost per mile of the County's turnpikes calculated by Dr Skene Keith as being £350 a mile.).[80] A number of bridges had to be built ranging from one at Aboyne costing £215 to the small bridge at Burn of Bennie costing £60. Tollhouses and gates had to be provided at six mile intervals. The Deeside Road had made do with simple thatched edifices; the slated tollhouse at Aboyne on the Charleston Road cost just over £73.[81] The Old Meldrum Road cost £8,000 and needed £400 p.a. just to pay interest charges on money borrowed to create it. Ellon's road came to almost double the figure Charles Abercrombie estimated it would cost, finally totalling £9,400.[82]

Turnpike roads spread rapidly. By 1811 there were 300 miles of them in Aberdeenshire[83] and by mid century 449 miles. Eighty seven toll bars lay across them, often to the indignation of local people. Only brief 200 yard trips were exempt from tolls, but much depended upon where the traveller came onto and left the road. They proved to be a fertile source of annoyance, dispute and litigation. People living near a gate and using only half a mile of the road paid the same as those using five or six miles; others used miles of turnpike road and never had occasion to pass through a gate.[84] It took travellers a little while before they learned to use them safely. On the Ellon Road at first most of the carters and even some of the chaise drivers and people on horseback did not know on which side of the road to travel. The trustees decided to put up printed placards giving directions as to this at each end of the road.[85] The roads needed constant repair, not only from wear and tear but from abuse by local farmers who drove on to them across ditches, ploughed up to the road edge, and in both cases clogged up the drains at

Turnpike Roads

By 1865 the network of turnpike roads was extensive, linking up all major communities and focussing on Aberdeen.
(Source, 1865 map of turnpike roads in Aberdeen City Library)

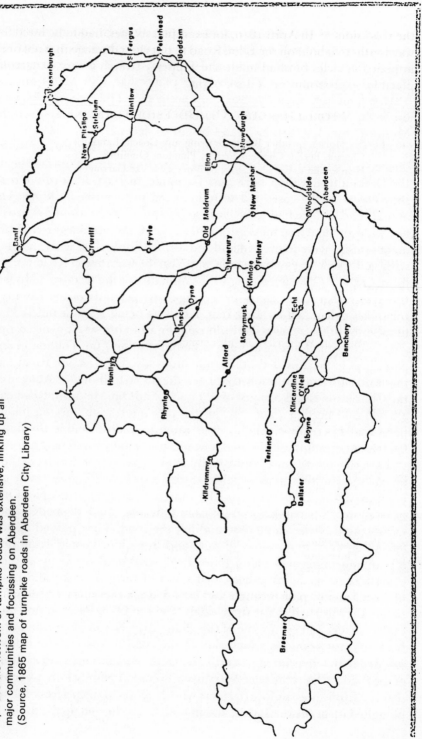

the road sides.[86] In April 1816, for example, six men had to be hired for six months to labour on the Ellon Road to put right damage that not only impeded vehicles but had made the Tipperty stretch a very dangerous place for pedestrians on a dark night.[87]

TOLL CHARGES ON THE DEESIDE TURNPIKE

	£	s.
1.—For Six Horses, or other Beasts, drawing any Coach, Landau, Chariot, Berlin, Chaise, Curricle, Phaeton, Omnibus, Hearse, Chair, Calash, Litter, or other such like Carriage, with Four Wheels, ··· ··· ··· ··· ···	0	6
2.—For Five ditto ditto ··· ··· ···	0	4
3.—For Four ditto ditto ··· ··· ···	0	3
4.—For Three ditto ditto ··· ··· ···	0	2
5.—For Two ditto ditto ··· ··· ···	0	1
6.—For One ditto ditto ··· ··· ···	0	0
7.—For Two ditto, drawing any Curricle, Chaise, Gig, or other such like Carriage, with Two Wheels, ··· ···	0	1
8.—For One ditto ditto ··· ··· ···	0	0
9.—For every Horse, or other Beast, drawing any Carriage, commonly called a Taxed Cart, ··· ··· ···	0	0
10.—For Six Horses, or other Beasts, drawing any Van, Caravan, Waggon, Wain, Cart, or other such like Carriage, with Six Wheels, ··· ··· ··· ··· ··· ···	0	8
11.—For Five ditto ditto ··· ··· ···	0	6
12.—For Four ditto ditto ··· ··· ···	0	5
13.—For Three ditto ditto ··· ··· ···	0	4
14.—For Two ditto ditto ··· ··· ···	0	2
15.—For One ditto ditto ··· ··· ···	0	1
16.—For Six ditto ditto with Four Wheels, ···	0	6
17.—For Five ditto ditto ··· ··· ···	0	5
18.—For Four ditto ditto ··· ··· ···	0	4
19.—For Three ditto ditto ··· ··· ···	0	3
20.—For Two ditto ditto ··· ··· ···	0	2
21.—For One ditto ditto ··· ··· ···	0	1
22.—For Six ditto drawing ditto, with Two Wheels, ···	0	4
23.—For Five ditto ditto ··· ··· ···	0	3
24.—For Four ditto ditto ··· ··· ···	0	2
25.—For Three ditto ditto ··· ··· ···	0	1
26.—For Two ditto ditto ··· ··· ···	0	0
27.—For One ditto ditto ··· ··· ···	0	0
28.—For Two ditto drawing any Cart belonging to a Farmer or Proprietor of Land, the same being empty, or conveying the produce of their own farm or land only, Coals, Lime, or Manure, or conveying anything else under a Cwt., and not travelling for Hire, ··· ··· ··· ···	0	0
29.—For One ditto ditto ··· ··· ···	0	0
30.—For every Stage Coach, Long Coach, Diligence, or such like Carriage, Licensed to carry Ten or more persons, including the Coachman and Guard, the above tolls, and one-half more in addition thereto.		

31.—For every Coach, Barouche, Berlin, Chariot, Landau, Chaise, or other such Carriage, or any Stage Coach, Long Coach, Diligence, Omnibus, or other Carriage of the like kind, drawn or propelled by Steam, or otherwise than by animal power,when such Carriage and the loading thereof, taken together, shall not exceed Twenty Hundred Weight, ···	0	2
32.—For every Van, Caravan, Waggon, Wain, Cart, or other such like Carriage, drawn or propelled by Steam, or otherwise than by animal power, when such Carriage and the Loading thereof, taken together, shall not exceed Twenty Hundred Weight, ··· ··· ··· ··· ···	0	1
33.—For every Horse, Mare, Gelding, or Mule, with or without a Rider, laden or unladen, and not drawing, ···	0	0
34.—For every Drove of Oxen, Neat Cattle, Asses, Horses, or Fillies, unshod, *per Score*, and so in proportion for any greater or less number, ··· ··· ··· ···	0	0
35.—For every Drove of Calves, Hogs, Sheep, Lambs, or Goats, *per Score*, and so in proportion for any greater or less number, ··· ··· ··· ··· ··· ···	0	0

Improvements came in other ways too. The Parliamentary Commissioners of Highland Roads and Bridges, set up in 1803, paid half the cost of bridge building at Ballater (1809) Alford (1811) and Potarch (1817).[88] These works helped sustain the old North-South routes; when the Bridge of Alford opened the Aberdeen Journal looked forward to the benefits 'to the north country as it will render the driving of cattle both safe and expeditious if compared with the old way of ferrying and driving across, when they were frequently detained by floods in the rivers'.[89] Where statute labour was turned into a money levy commutation roads (generally surfaced with gravel more thinly than turnpikes) were built. The commutation road that continued up the Dee Valley from Aboyne in 1831 was so smooth it was claimed to be as comfortable to travellers as gravelled walks in the parks of great houses.[90] By the 1850s there were 1800 miles of commutation roads.[91] There still remained, though, places like Old Deer, Glenbucket and St Fergus where poor roads were felt to be a severe brake on economic progress.[92]

To comtemporaries the new roads seemed to have a considerable impact. Newspapers were peppered with advertisements for farmland, houses and quarries whose merits were thought to be much enhanced by close proximity to a turnpike. In Milltimber, for instance, the Binghill estate's attributes when offered for sale included the fact that 'the turnpike road leading to this property renders it a very desirable purchase'.[93] Turnpikes were seen by a committee of 1857 reviewing their condition, to have been of great value 'Without easy means of intercommunication no agricultural progress would have been made, improvement would not have been remunerative either to landlord or tenant, and in many cases would have been physically impossible'.[94] In the mind of one elderly inhabitant, at least, Old Meldrum developed rapidly once the turnpike had been built. Certainly the road meant 'farm produce can be carried for sale to Aberdeen at every season of the year . . . and a far greater intercourse is also enjoyed with the neighbouring districts. Hence a great stimulus has been given to industry and improvements of an extensive nature have been undertaken and completed'.[95] However it is as well to remember that travel on the turnpikes was costly and, for bulky goods, slow. The roads made a considerable difference but they did not, perhaps, tie inland places into wider market areas as dramatically as the later railways.

If towns and villages were to profit from the improved network, then better services were needed for moving goods and freight. By 1804 Alexander Scrogie was operating a two-wheeled conveyance, carrying people and goods between Aberdeen and Huntly, which did well enough for him to buy a four wheeled vehicle three years later. In it six people could be accommodated, whilst two more could travel on top.[96] In 1811 mail coach services began along this road. In the next few years the local press was filled with advertisements for coach services connecting all sizeable communities in the County, like this one of March 1819 for a coach 'from William Gray's, Frederick Street, Aberdeen, and from Mr Jaffray's Hotel, Peterhead, every lawful day at 12 o'clock noon. For better accommodation of the public the proprietors will have elegant new coaches called "The Earl of Errol" ready about mid April. Parcels carefully forwarded at a moderate rate'.[97] Not only major centres like Fraserburgh and Peterhead were served by coaches, but smaller communities like Methlick, Rhynie and Old Deer. The coaches encouraged inns, stabling and other services in these places, and at stages along the way. The New Inn at Park, freshly finished in 1808, was offered for sale with optimism since it stood by a busy road especially heavily used in summer and autumn.[98] Equally important were the numerous carriers' waggons that rumbled slowly along the new roads. It is possible to build up a picture of their services from the pages of Directories. The maps are the result of working through the entries in two Directories. The first, dated 1837, gives a glimpse of the carriers at work before the railway network was constructed. The second, in 1877, shows the situation by the time a network of railways had been established. The system of carrier services that developed tended to focus on Aberdeen, though Huntly and Peterhead were magnets too. In the 1820s Huntly possessed eight carriers who made journeys every week into Aberdeen. Their vehicles

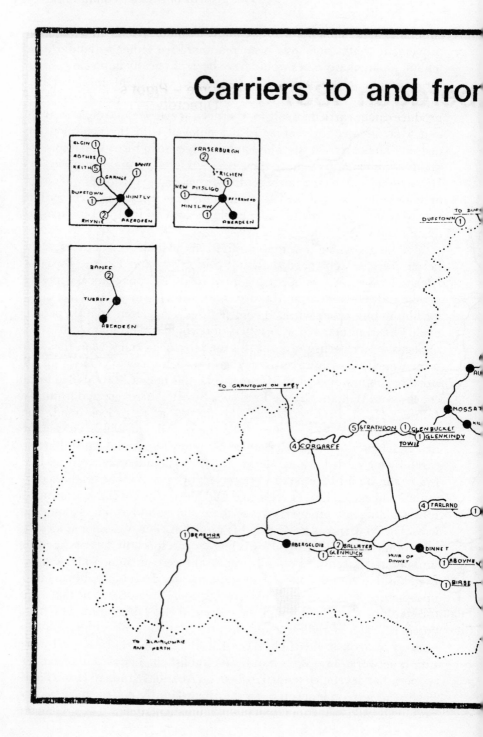

Carriers to and fror

berdeen 1837

(Source – Pigot's Directory.)

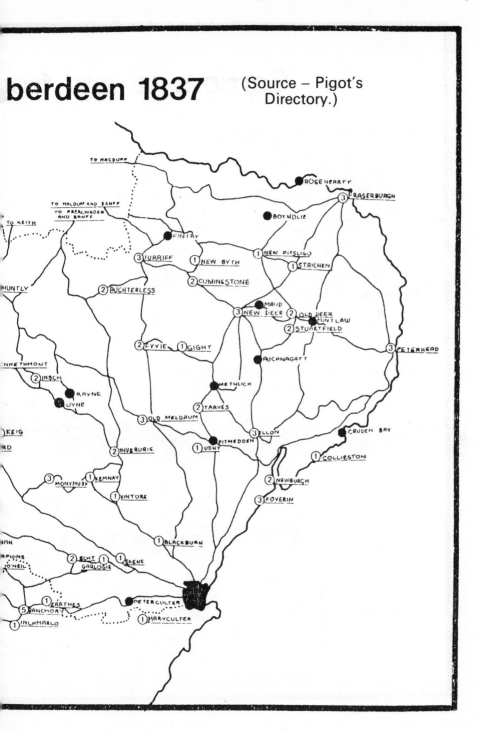

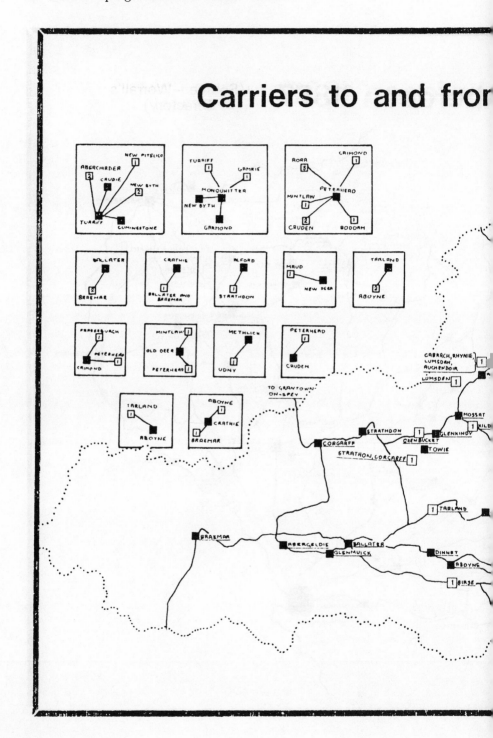

Carriers to and fror

Aberdeen 1877 (Source – Worrall's Directory)

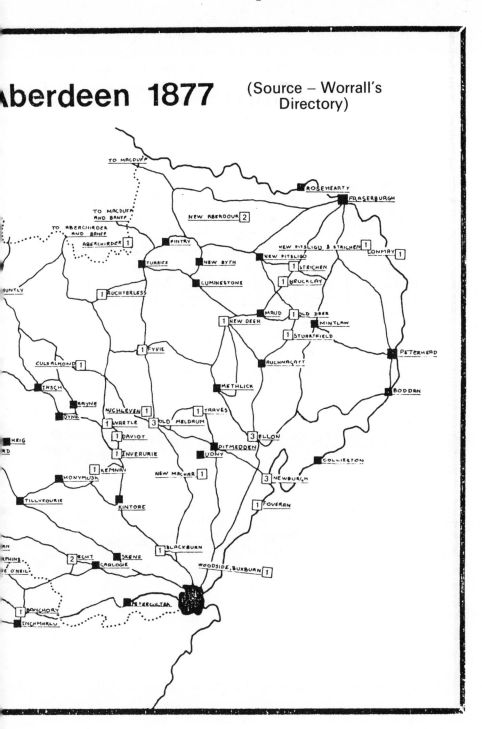

carried on average, a five-ton load of cloth, leather, meat, butter, eggs, cheese and whisky into the city. Return loads of up to ten tons consisted chiefly of iron, lint and merchants' goods to supply the expanding shop services the turnpikes stimulated in the County's smaller towns.[99] Turriff's carriers of the 1830s operated weekly services to Aberdeen too, specialising particularly in great box-loads of eggs.[100] Carriers went considerable distances, and communities placed at convenient stopping places along the way benefitted from the services they offered the carriers. Ellon, for example, was a focus for carriers going into and out of Buchan and became a regular stopping place where men and horses rested and fed.[101] Carriers plodded into the City from the County's outer fringes, even from Strathdon and Braemar. Most communities were involved; in 1841 Alford had five carriers, Echt four, New Pitsligo two and Tarland four, for example.[102] The carriers provided, in effect, a local bus service. They sustained village shops with all sorts of items, supplied towns with the products of the countryside and acted as purchasing agents for villagers. Without their services many villages could not have flourished.

The Directories of the period give a glimpse of these services but may not be comprehensive and do not usually show whether carriers served places along their route, as well as their place of origin. Nor is it easy to say whether this work provided a fulltime occupation, for the shorter runs, and less formal services these men offered are not shown. In Aboyne, Alexander Watt also ran a six acre croft, retiring eventually from his business to work the croft fulltime and leaving his carrier trade to his son George.[103] The carriers travelled slowly; the Aboyne run, still operating in 1865, took twelve hours to reach Aberdeen.[104] The carriers worked not only from towns and villages, but also from rural areas. Birse's solitary carrier of 1837 had been joined by two more five years later.[105] Tiny hamlets like Towie, Corgarff and Auchendoir all supported carriers. Where a number were gathered, however, there was usually a sizeable settlement. Huntly supported six carriers in 1837, a mark of its importance in the area. It thus had twice the number of the far bigger Peterhead and similar-sized Fraserburgh where the schooners and steamers operating the coasting trade made carrier services to Aberdeen far less vital. The County was well-covered by the services. Even the upland areas supported carriers as the numbers in Upper Deeside and Donside indicate. Farming in these upland areas was less well advanced and less profitable than in the Garioch, but the Garioch possessed a canal and thus Kintore and Inverurie needed fewer carriers. Monymusk – some distance from the canal basin – supported as many carriers as Kintore and Inverurie combined. Kemnay enjoyed the services of a carrier who could not read but 'with the help of a good memory and the setting of the goods he carried in methodical order on his cart he managed to execute his communications with wonderful correctness'.[106] By 1842 the entries in *The Bon Accord Directory* show a small increase in the number of carriers. Tarland supported an extra one, Aboyne and Alford two more. Corgarff and Strathdon continued to have as many as in 1837, showing the real importance of carriers to these remote upland communities. The most lightly served sweep of lowland ground continued to be that around the Buchan coast where alternative sea-going services existed. Many services focussed on Aberdeen. Whereas Glasgow became a hub for carrier traffic from major centres like Perth, Dundee and Edinburgh, Aberdeen attracted short runs from less sizeable centres.[107]

By 1877 the railway network was well established. Yet carriers continued to flourish. A far greater number of short-run services had emerged, focussing on communities other than the City. Carriers obviously could not match the speedy service by rail, but they could perform useful short journeys and cross-country runs where no rail link existed. Along the line of a flourishing railway, carrier services dwindled. In 1842 Banchory had nine carriers, by 1877 only one. Aboyne had lost its carriers entirely and even Kincardine O'Neil had suffered a drop despite the fact that the railway by-passed it, sweeping north through Torphins instead. The route north passing through Inverurie to Huntly saw a similar shrinkage. Only one carrier now worked from Huntly to Aberdeen. The harbour improvements coupled with the rail link demolished the carrier services working from Fraserburgh, Peterhead and Collieston.

The effect on the Glasgow area was very similar, short run traffic predominated and long runs by carriers became far less frequent. This, indeed, was the widespread consequence for carriers of the coming of the railways. By the end of Victorian times *Slater's Directory* still identified 40 different carriers operating into and out of Aberdeen. Many worked in areas without a railway (like upper Donside, Birse, Lumsden, or the Cabrach). The number contrasts with the 96 listed in *Pigot's Directory* of 1825. In 1903 at least 10 more services ran between smaller places connecting, for example, New Deer and Maud, Whinnyfold and Peterhead, Cuminestown and Turriff, and Fetterangus and Mintlaw. Nevertheless a shrinkage of services had clearly taken place. In so far as the Directories are a guide this shrinkage contrasts with the expansion of English carrier services in the railway age identified by Alan Everitt.[108] Around Newark for example, services to the railhead there expanded. Everitt has built his picture on Directory evidence too. It may be that the very elaborate rail network of Aberdeenshire meant more villages could use this network directly in a way not necessarily possible elsewhere. In Kent and Leicester only one village in eight or nine had a station.

Many carriers no doubt found plenty of work travelling to and from the new railway stations. Some flourished because customers felt the charges of the Great North of Scotland Railway were too high. Even in 1893 three carriers travelled twice a week between Old Meldrum and Aberdeen because of the railway's excessive charges.[109] Traction engines tugged loads of coal from Newburgh because of high rail charges and stagecoaches still operated in Strathdon and Braemar-Ballater, where the railway did not reach. But the railways did damage road traffic. By 1857 the Aberdeenshire Turnpike Trust was worried that their revenue from tolls was down to £14,000 a year.[110] Six years later it had plummetted to just over £9,000. Only the Inverurie Road showed a profit, the others were burdened with debts and struggled to meet repair bills (1857s repairs came to about £7,000).[111] In 1865 the Turnpike Trust admitted defeat and in 1866 the toll bars came down. The roads had played an important part in helping business in towns and villages develop. They had strengthened existing communities but had not really created new ones. The improved commutation roads reached out to remote and scattered townships and farms. Thus the roads did not have quite as dramatic affect upon communities as did railways. Nevertheless the road system emphasised the importance of Aberdeen. Until hit by railway competition most carriers made their slow way to the city to buy and sell. Whereas Leicestershire's carriers rarely travelled above fifteen miles, the carriers of Aberdeenshire were prepared to plod at least three times the distance. Leicester faced the attractions of other nearby major urban centres, Aberdeen did not and the distances covered by the carriers of the pre-railway age emphasise this point.

The roads could not match the Aberdeenshire Canal's ability to shift huge quantities of bulky farm feeds and products as well as building materials. This enterprise had a powerful impact upon the fortunes of Inverurie and will be dealt with in Part II. It was Aberdeenshire's only effective canal. The six mile St Fergus canal south of Peterhead created by James Ferguson of Pitfour did not enjoy a lengthy life. But the Aberdeenshire Canal brought benefits to a wide belt of inland Aberdeenshire. 'The canal is believed to be a very indifferent speculation in respect of profit' wrote Dyce's minister in 1840, 'but is found exceedingly convenient by those living near it for the conveyance of coals and lime at a reasonable rate'.[112] The canal attracted custom from some distance. Kennethmont farmers preferred to trundle their produce in carts to Inverurie to be shipped to Aberdeen rather than going the much shorter distance to Huntly.[113] But Dyce's minister was right; the canal's largely

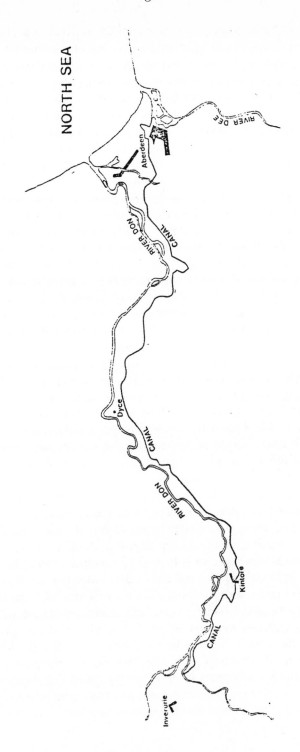

agricultural traffic did not produce enough profit. It was, by 1840, insufficient to pay off the mortgage.[114] Nor could the passenger craft – the
'fly boats' – match the stage coaches' speed.[115] The shareholders were
glad enough to see their investment sold off for £36,000 to that powerful
contributor to the County's fortunes – the Great North of Scotland Railway. During its life the canal did do much for the growth of Inverurie,
Port Elphinstone and Kintore; the railway was to have a far wider
impact on community fortunes.

The ability to move bulky goods with speed and throughout the year
made railways a powerful influence on the Victorian economy. Between
1852 and the end of the century work went ahead in Aberdeenshire
creating a network of lines that spread into quite remote corners of coast
and countryside. It was in 1846 that legislation approving the Great
North of Scotland's plans to build northwards from Aberdeen, through
Huntly to Inverness, received the royal assent. Financial problems
delayed work until 1852.[116] Contractors began operations on Westhall,
part of the estate near Oyne owned by Sir James Elphinstone who had
moved from playing a prominent role in the canal company, to enthusiasm for railway expansion. Single track line, with passing places,
was constructed only as far as Huntly, and the light nature of the track –
pinned at the joints instead of being fishplated – contributed to the slow
services with which the line began.[117] Goods trains required three hours
for the Huntly trip, passenger trains managed it on two. In the later part
of the century services speeded up: by 1884 the run to Keith was taking
two hours.[118] The G.N.S.R. was not over-attentive to its early passengers. The branch line to Alford involved a connection at Kintore for
travellers wishing to proceed beyond that point; there they had to wait,
confined within the station yards, for up to an hour.[119] Once William
Moffat became General Manager in 1880 the efficiency of the line and
the consideration shown passengers improved greatly.[120]

Despite its defects, the coming of the G.N.S.R. made a considerable
impact. It encouraged places not connected up to its early lines to
clamour for railways too. In July 1856, a meeting of frustrated railway
supporters in Fraserburgh gathered in great numbers to hear a visiting
railway-champion address them. They hung out of windows, bran-
dished banners, some had blacked their faces, others were dressed in
white robes with coloured trims.[121] The tentacles of a railway system
spread to link up sizeable population centres. In 1856 traffic began to
flow from Old Meldrum to Inverurie, by 1862 Peterhead had a railway
connection and three years later Fraserburgh joined the system. The
Alford Valley line (1859) reached into an area of inland Aberdeenshire
that did not already have a sizeable settlement: there it sought to tap and

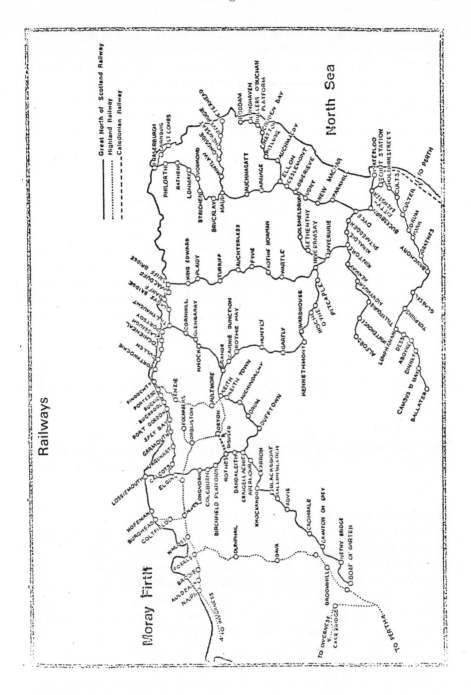

GREAT NORTH OF SCOTLAND RAILWAY.

TIME TABLES FOR THE USE OF THE COMPANY'S SERVANTS, ON AND FROM THE 1ST OCTOBER, 1857.

DOWN TRAINS. Trains will not Depart From	1 Goods.	2 Pass.	3 Mixed & Perl.	4 Goods	5 Pass. & Mail	6 Mixed	SUN. DAY. Pass. & Mail		UP TRAINS. Trains will not Depart From	1 Goods.	2 Pass. & Mail	3 Goods	4 Mixed & Perl.	5 Mixed	6 Pass.	SUN. DAY.
	A.M.	A.M.	A.M.	P.M.	P.M.	P.M.	P.M.			A.M.	A.M.	A.M.	A.M.	P.M.	P.M.	A.M.
Aberdeen before	4·25	8·0	11·0	12·40	3·0	4·50	3·0		Keith before	3·0	7·5	—	10·5	1·20	4·20	7·5
Kinybrewster	5·15	8·9	11·9	1·5	3·6	4·59	3·6		Grange	3·17	7·15	—	10·18	1·23	4·34	7·15
Buxburn	5·20	8·16	11·10	1·20	3·15	5·8	3·15		Rothiemay	3·30	7·23	—	10·27	1·32	4·44	7·23
Dyce	5·45	8·23	11·30	1·26	3·24	5·16	3·24		Huntly	4·0	7·33	—	10·42	1·45	5·0	7·33
Kinaldie	6·2	8·34	11·41	1·51	3·33	5·28			Gartly	4·20	7·40	—	10·49	1·54	5·14	7·40
Kintore	6·20	8·42	11·53	2·8	3·40	5·37	3·40		Kennethmont	4·25	5·0	—	11·10	1·45	5·24	5·0
Pen Elphinstone	6·25	—	—	2·18	—	—	—		Wardhouse	—	8·5	—	11·16	2·8	5·20	8·5
Inverury	6·50	1·59	12·0	2·30	3·48	5·50	3·48		Insch	5·0	8·15	—	11·27	2·41	5·40	8·15
Oldmeldrum Trains	—	8·58	11·45	11·45	3·6	5·30	—		Buchanstone	5·10	8·22	—	11·37	2·42	5·47	—
	9·14	8·14	12·12	4·10	4·10	6·44	—		Oyne	5·19	8·25	—	11·42	2·57	5·42	—
Inverury (Ter. Jan.)	7·15	1·4	12·25	2·45	—	5·8	—		Pitcaple	5·34	8·34	—	11·52	3·0	6·2	—
Turriff Trains	—	7·55	10·45	—	—	4·50	—		Turriff Trains	—	7·5	5·20	10·45	—	4·50	—
	—	10·28	1·23	4·25	—	7·23	—			—	10·15	—	1·25	—	7·23	—
Pitcaple	7·24	9·21	12·29	—	4·1	6·13	4·1		Inverammsay (Ter. Jan.)	5·42a	8·50	5·8	11·43	—	6·8	—
Oyne	7·35	9·21	12·30	—	4·11	6·23	4·11		Oldmeldrum Trains	—	8·23	8·28	11·45	3·5	5·50	—
Buchanstone	7·50	9·25	12·43	—	4·14	6·27	4·14			—	9·14	12·55	12·53	4·10	6·45	—
Insch	8·15	9·23	12·51	—	4·20	6·35	4·20		Inverury	5·58	8·51	9·30	12·9	3·47	5·22	8·51
Wardhouse	—	9·40	1·2	—	4·50	6·47	4·50		Pen Elphinstone	6·6	—	9·50	—	—	—	—
Kennethmont	8·31	9·42	1·8	—	4·25	6·53	4·50		Kintore	6·20	8·59	9·55	12·22	3·55	6·20	8·59
Gartly	8·47	9·27	1·27	—	4·46	7·2	4·46		Kinaldie	6·28	9·7	10·7	12·32	3·49	6·41	9·7
Huntly	9·6	10·23	1·20	—	5·0	7·17	5·0		Dyce	6·42	9·16	10·21	12·43	3·59	6·51	9·16
Rothiemay	9·24	10·27	1·42	—	1·18	7·28	5·12		Buxburn	7·10	9·20	10·35	12·54	4·8	7·0	9·20
Grange	5·56	10·37	1·52	—	5·24	7·39	5·24		Kinybrewster	7·25	9·23	11·0	1·5	4·16	7·10	9·23
Keith before	9·50	10·50	2·5	—	5·40	7·50	5·40		Aberdeen before	7·40	9·47	11·20	1·15	4·25	7·20	9·47

NOTE.—A Line across the Column denotes the Stations appointed for the Trains to meet and pass each other; and in no case shall a Train passing in one direction leave the Station where a Train coming in an opposite direction has to pass, until the said Train has first arrived and passed into the Station clear of the Points.

On Mondays and Fridays, First and Third Class Carriages will be attached at Huntly to the 3·0 a.m. Up Goods Train, which arrives in Aberdeen about 7·40 a.m.

No Two Engines in steam, unless coupled together, are to be between any two of the undernoted adjoining respective Stations, at any one and the same time, viz:—
  ON MAIN LINE.—Waterloo, Kinybrewster, Dyce, Kintore, Inverury, Inverammsay, Insch, Kennethmont, Huntly, Rothiemay, Keith.
  ON TURRIFF BRANCH—Inverammsay, Rothie, Fyvie, Auchterless, Turriff.
  ON OLDMELDRUM BRANCH—Inverury, Oldmeldrum.

further stimulate the agriculture of the area. The village of Alford, a tiny straggling hamlet, which had consisted of only an inn, a Friendly Society house and hall and a few thatched houses,[122] expanded rapidly as a railhead service point and housed 634 people by 1901. At Dyce the laird exploited the coming of the railway by creating a village on what had been a bleak moor.[123] In 1865 he offered ground to feu at 'The New Village of Dyce Station. It is six miles distant from Aberdeen and being at the junction of the Great North and Formartine and Buchan Railways has the convenience of more passenger and goods traffic than any other station in the North'.[124] Railway junctions were always likely to be a magnet for development; when the Parochial Boards of Buchan were searching for a suitable site for their new Buchan Union Poorhouse, it was upon the junction at New Maud that they settled, thus adding considerably to the population of this hitherto tiny hamlet.

The effect of railways on rural areas seemed to one contemporary observer at least, to be a mixed blessing. 'The railways themselves employ large numbers of young men from rural districts' wrote Cairnie's

Railway Stations provided local employment and served local communities and encouraged their expansion. Around Torphins a place grew up where once there had been few houses.

historian, James Pirie, 'Tradesmen such as shoemakers, tailors and blacksmiths are not now employed in rural districts to the same extent as they were 20 or 30 years ago. Ready-made shoes and clothes are brought from distant places and ... agricultural implements so that local tradesmen have been deprived of much of their former employment'.[125] To be a railhead – as Alford found, was especially fortunate. To one local inhabitant of the period, Turriff prospered more when the railway ended there than when the line was continued on to Macduff.[126] Areas that failed to attract railways tended to suffer population fall, lacking an effective means of building up sizeable communities as a counter-weight to the tendency of rural population to fall in the latter part of the nineteenth century. Between 1851 and 1891 Strathdon suffered a 22 per cent fall in population.[127] Railway stations built along the new lines became focal points for inns, houses and storage facilities. Gartly station became the centre of a developing hamlet leaving the old kirkton, two miles off, stranded and stagnant. Thus the village developed distant from its church.

The railways not only helped fresh fish, meat, fruit and vegetable trade, the shifting of grains, fertilizers, building materials and shopkeepers' goods, they also shaped people's travelling habits during their leisure time and thus stimulated particular kinds of community growth. Holiday outings by train developed in the nineteenth century and took individuals and organized groups to seaside and rural centres that already served a working function. But in two areas in particular, railway companies made a conscious effort to stimulate holiday trade. The G.N.S.R.'s Hotel committee, decided to stimulate tourism in remote and scenic Buchan. In 1897 the opening of a line to Cruden Bay helped inject a new kind of life into the fishing village of Port Errol.

Two years later the G.N.S.R. opened there a hotel that the Aberdeen Journal thought 'picturesque in site and surroundings, beautiful in design and substantial in construction'.[128] Tourism developed in the area and helped the fishing community grow from a population around 490 (1881–91) to 681 by 1901, and this at a time when smaller fisherplaces were stagnating, or shrinking before the growth of the major centres.

The Cruden Bay line had less significance for community growth than an earlier venture that edged, in a series of developments between 1853 and 1866, from Aberdeen westward along the valley of the River Dee. The valley already contained small communities in the pre-railway age, notably Banchory (in the County of Kincardine) Kincardine O'Neil, with 288 inhabitants in 1841, Charleston of Aboyne where 260 people lived in 1841, and Ballater with 317 inhabitants in that year. The beautiful natural scenery attracted a considerable number of visitors up the turnpike road. In 1850 an Aberdeen accountant, R. R. Notman, reckoned that 30 carriers and several coaches were plying the route, and that royal interest in Balmoral would further stimulate the growth of the Dee Valley's popularity. Moreover, he argued, the railway could cut the costs and improve the farming efficiency of the valley. Timber was being floated down the Dee in rafts at twenty one shillings a raft – railway transport could halve this bill. He reckoned that a two-hundred acre farm fifteen miles from a market town had to carry an annual burden of travel costs of £142: with a rail link the bill would be a mere £40.[129]

Two years after Notman had argued his persuasive case, the first turf was being cut that inaugurated line-building as far as Banchory. The Aberdeen Journal rejoiced that the line would enable 'citizens to escape at least occasionally from the stifling influences of a town into the fresh air of the country; and it will give an impulse to the agricultural population of the whole district ... agriculturalists will be enabled to bring their produce to market at an immense saving.[130] By 1854 the line had reached Aboyne. This village was able to attract agricultural and leisure traffic and expanded to a population of 561 by 1901. A few miles further north, the village of Tarland, once far more important than Aboyne, but now denied a rail link, stuck at a figure between 316 in 1861 and 367 in 1901. Even more seriously hit was the village of Kincardine O'Neil. The community had flourished at a key river-crossing point where east-west and north-south routes intersected. Once by-passed it remained virtually stagnant,[131] 'left out of sight and out of mind'[132] according to a contemporary. In 1841, 288 people lived there; by 1871 its population had fallen to 227. Meanwhile a whole new village had emerged round a station at Torphins where hitherto there had been negligible housing accommodation. By 1901, 409 people were living in Torphins. In 1866 a new stretch of line – to Ballater – opened to traffic. The Aberdeen Journal noted that the line would help cope with growing passenger traffic as well as helping local farmers and the iron producers of Corgarff. Land rentals went up substantially with the coming of a railway line.[133] The rapid growth of centres to cope with holiday traffic was epitomised above all by the village of Ballater. In 1841, 317 people lived there: by 1901 it housed 1,247. A more detailed examination of this phenomenon will be provided later in this section, but the rapidity of Ballater's expansion contrasted to the stagnation of Kincardine O'Neil provides an outstanding instance of the impact railways had on community growth.

The transport revolution in Aberdeenshire went hand in hand with an agricultural revolution, a huge boom in fishing and a big growth in the

The village of Tarland, by-passed by the railway, stagnated in the late 19th century.

granite trade. Its effect on Aberdeenshire communities was to stimulate the expansion of certain places which served as centres for markets, shopping, educational and leisure services, processing of produce and craft skills. It made it easier for farmers and fishermen to concentrate wholly on production, obtaining other items that they needed from specialists who were increasingly housed in towns and villages. But the type of location best suited to exploiting improved transport changed. Old communities lying on natural routeways at river crossing points were no longer guaranteed growth and prosperity once the railways arrived. Through the railway system men re-shaped the landscape. Like the turnpike roads, the railways emphasised the importance of Aberdeen, focussing in on the City and offering only a limited number of cross-country links. The road system did not conjure up new communities into existence, but in under half a century that is precisely what the railways managed to achieve.

Shipping services improved too. In 1819 a paddle steamer began a run between Aberdeen and Edinburgh and by Victorian times these vessels were travelling down to London. In the late nineteenth century more fuel-efficient screw-driven steamers came into operation. Shipping offered inexpensive bulk transport that was especially welcomed by dealers in bulk farm produce, fuel, and granite. The growing size and sophistication of vessels made adequate harbour facilities essential and increased the advantages of Fraserburgh, Peterhead and Aberdeen over smaller places.

The effects of transport changes on the North East have been surveyed by R. C. Michie.[134] Better transport helped town and village shops to stock a wider range of sophisticated products and of preserved and fresh foods. The area's granite quarries – especially those inland – benefitted greatly and so too did trade in fish, cattle, grain and processed foods. But the opening up of Aberdeenshire exposed rural crafts and industries to the competition of goods from Aberdeen and further afield. After the early 1870s the County's food producers faced competition from abroad. The keeping of sheep shrank sharply; the County's wheat acreage fell from 8,962 acres to under 800. Fortunately cattle-rearing did well and barley and oats growing (the latter helped by the huge horse population) continued to prosper. Rural crafts and industries were not always able to adapt, however. Some craftsmen were able to shift to the repair of products made elsewhere but activities like tanning and hosiery production dwindled. Even fishing nets were increasingly imported from Fife and the Lothians. Above all transport changes emphasised the advantages enjoyed by the City of Aberdeen and focussed activity even more firmly upon the North East's major centre.

Industry and commerce

Aberdeenshire lacks the natural resources to underpin heavy industry and is some distance from the major urban areas of Britain. Nevertheless it supports a range of activities including fishing, food processing, textiles, paper making, brewing and distilling. At the beginning of the nineteenth century the rather isolated character of many parts of the County enabled small local enterprises to survive. Moreover there were part-time activities that helped many rural inhabitants earn valuable extra income.

The fishing industry occupied a leading place in the County's economy. Its fortunes have been clearly depicted by Malcolm Gray.[135] During the century the industry expanded in both size and sophistication. Boat ownership was established in the hands of the fisherfolk themselves, replacing an earlier system in which lairds provided boats and insisted upon taking a share of the catch. As boats grew in size they required even more extensive safe anchorages where they could float in a sufficient depth of water. Fishing villages that depended on beaches up which boats had to be dragged were bound, eventually, to suffer from competition from better developed ports. Moreover as boats became more sophisticated so their cost rose. A fully equipped boat for herring fishing cost around £50 to £60 in the forties, by the eighties the cost had risen to over £300.[136] This tendency for larger places to pull in the business of the fishing industry was further stimulated by the herring boom of the nineteenth century. Herring landed in quantity required speedy gutting and salting, needed the work of gutters, coopers and curers, carriers and dealers. Gathering a large workforce, organising and financing the operations, shifting the fish to their markets, all these were activities that favoured bigger places. So too did the growing demand for fresh fish in urban Britain. A flourishing fisher-place needed a rail link.

The herring boom did not obliterate the older line-fishing for white fish. This activity continued as an occupation pursued from many small communities, where processing was also carried out. In 1871 there were 533 people living in the village of St Combs, for example. They caught and processed cod or sold it fresh in the locality: when it came to the herring season however, the inadequacies of their shingly beach for boats landing big catches led St Combs fishermen and their families to move, temporarily, to bigger ports.[137]

Places that developed harbours were also equipping themselves with a facility of wider value in attracting business to their community. Steamer services and sailing vessels carried agricultural produce and livestock, coal, building materials, fertilizers, metal goods and items for household purchase. By 1837 Peterhead had two companies running fortnightly sailings to London, another providing weekly sailings to Lerwick and a fourth offering occasional journeys to Leith and Aberdeen.[138] This helped develop Peterhead into a community that, in 1877, supported the manufacture of woollen goods, breweries, an iron foundry, saw mills, timber yards, agricultural implement works, boat building yards and establishments where cattle feeds and farm fertilizers were prepared.[139] The town also played a part in whaling. In 1788 a Peterhead vessel joined two from Aberdeen in this activity. The trade expanded in the early nineteenth century, eight Peterhead vessels were involved in 1815, whilst on-shore men worked at the evil-smelling task of boiling down the blubber to make soap and oil for lighting. The town turned to sealing too. In the 1850s the average catch for a Peterhead ship was 3,305 seals. Three steamers ventured into the trade, only to be crushed by ice. The last Peterhead ship to participate in the whaling and sealing trade sailed in 1893, the activity had become more hazardous and the attractions of herring fishing offered seamen a profitable alternative occupation.[140]

By 1800 fishing had created a number of coastal villages and had contributed to the expansion of two towns, Peterhead and Fraserburgh. Between the 1790s and the 1860s the population of the fisher villages and towns doubled, trebled or (as in Rosehearty's case) even increased five-fold. In the later part of the century the coming of the railway to certain coastal places, the need for harbours, and the challenge of Aberdeen were some of the factors that slowed or halted village growth or even turned it into shrinkage. St Combs reached a peak (614) in 1881: by 1901 its population had fallen to 530; Collieston, Inverallochy and Carinbulg reached their highest point in 1871. A large safe deep harbour and a rail link were essential for late-Victorian prosperity in fisher towns and places like Whinnyfold that lacked these amenities could not match more effective competitors. When a rail link was finally run from Fraserburgh to St Combs at the end of Victorian times it came too late to rescue this harbourless place. Some places, such as Port Errol and Collieston, were able to develop as holiday centres as well as fishing villages; the former was thus able to grow in the last three decades of the nineteenth century.

At least the fisher communities did not face fierce competition from Aberdeen for most of the century. When that competition came, how-ever, it had a severe impact on several small coastal places. Until the 1880s Aberdeen contented itself with the small-scale off-shore line-fishing activities of the people of the tiny settlements of Fitty and Torry. In the 1880s Aberdeen businessmen moved into steam trawling and triggered off an expansion that helped to make Aberdeen Scotland's fastest growing city between 1881 and 1901. The advantages enjoyed by Aberdeen included its fine large harbour, its focal point in the railway system, its large population and the wealth of its businessmen. They were able to afford the high cost of steam trawlers and of coal and ice; the wages paid the crews became a magnet to men from smaller north east communities. Associated businesses like fish-smoking, and box and barrel making were established. The profits attracted banks (especially the North of Scotland Bank), to invest in the industry. In 1889 Aberdeen obtained a fine fish market close by the railway and fish trains to London came into operation. Even the growth of fish and chip shops in the late nineteenth century proved helpful, for here was a market able to take some of the more unusual fish caught by the trawlers.[141] Like Fleetwood in England, Aberdeen pulled in the fishermen from nearby coastal villages attracted by higher, more reliable, wage levels.[142] Peterhead and Fraserburgh were sufficiently well equipped, well-established, distant, and skilled at herring fishing to be able to withstand the pull of Aberdeen, but smaller places both south of Peterhead and north of Montrose suffered. By 1905 over 9,000 Aberdeen people earned their living in connection with the fishing industry in ways other than fishing itself.[143] The tonnage of fishing boats using Aberdeen as their home port exceeded Fraserburgh's by 1,500 and Peterhead's by 5,000 tons.[144]

In textiles, too, the century witnessed dramatic changes. In the 1790s spinning and stocking knitting in particular were widespread part-time country activities. But by 1840, as Stewartfield's minister noticed, 'the state of the country, especially as it affects infirm or aged females, is altered much for the worse by the introduction and extensive use of machinery for spinning flax and knitting stockings'.[145] In Premnay earnings from such work dropped by the 1840s to a shilling and one and sixpence a week for a woman working full-time.[146] The period also saw changes in the fortunes of the widely scattered mills established in connection with the linen industry. Here too work fitted in with farming, was encouraged by landowners and suited an area with a large rural population.[147] The transport revolution hit these activities hard. Small water-powered mills and domestic hand workers found it difficult to compete with the steam-powered factories of industrial areas since the latter's products could be easily shifted throughout Scotland. Yet many villages had relied on textile production to sustain a flourishing existence. It is not surprising that places like Longside, Cuminestown, Old Deer or the ambitiously named New Leeds did not experience vigorous growth in the second half of the century. With their textile business ruined they were reduced to a very limited local service role. The County also contained water-powered wool-spinning enterprises, usually near large population centres, though the one at isolated Garlogie in 1840 employed 120 and was even lit by gas. As textile production became a

larger-scale activity so it shifted into the hands of merchants and manufacturers unconcerned with estate improvement and inclined to base
their enterprises in urban areas with good travel connections and, in the
steam power age, near coalfields.[148] Even Aberdeen suffered in these
changing circumstances, losing a number of textile works in a late forties
collapse. Here the figures in the 1841 census suggest the importance of
caution in dealing with this source. According to the City's New Statistical Account the numbers working in and around Aberdeen in wool,
cotton and flax were about 2,500, 2,200 and 7,600 respectively. Yet the
1841 census shows figures of 840, 1,445 and 3,712 for these occupations in
the whole County including the City. Even allowing for 932 spinners and
weavers unidentified as to a particular fabric, this is a marked difference.
Part-time and domestic workers may account for some of the gap and
N.S.A.'s own estimates may be a little generous. But doubts about over-
reliance on the 1841 figures still remain. Old Meldrum, ever a great focus
of the stocking industry, achieved a population peak in 1851 and thereafter declined.[149] By 1903 textile mills continued to operate in Aberdeen, Peterhead, Huntly, Montgarie (by Alford) Old Deer and Fintray,
but only those in or close to the city were sizeable.[150] The number of
drapers selling clothes increased greatly in the century, over 1,200 people
were involved in these businesses by 1901; the goods they sold however,
were often likely to have been made elsewhere.

The County's rural character produced industries concerned with
food processing and preserving. Food preserving was developed in
Aberdeen by John Moir as early as 1822.[151] By 1869 Peterhead too had a
food-preserving factory and by 1877 in Turriff 'provision and fish-curing
is successfully carried on'.[152] Numerous little corn mills were dotted over
the County and were to be found, especially in country towns and in
villages. The general tendency in the 1880s and 90s in Britain was for
milling to concentrate in ports and major urban centres where large
businesses used the new roller process to turn American hard wheat into
flour rather than the British wheat which was less suited to this process.[153] But Aberdeenshire grew little wheat in the late nineteenth
century; and few of its country communities of 1900 were without at least
one little corn mill. In 1901 three quarters of the County's 434 millers
lived outside the City.

The making of various types of drinks occupied a number of people. At
the beginning of the century the illicit distilling of whisky provided a
further source of revenue for inhabitants of inland Aberdeenshire. Then
came a new law in 1823 allowing whisky to be distilled that was as strong
as that illegally produced.[154] This act, coupled with more vigorous
enforcement and better transport destroyed the old illicit activities. By

1877 distilleries operated in Insch, Huntly, Old Deer, Old Meldrum and Peterhead.[155] Brewing, too, continued to operate from various small centres: in 1877 breweries were to be found in Cuminestown, Huntly, Port Elphinstone, Old Deer, Old Meldrum, Peterhead and Strichen. Ian Donnachie has argued[156] that the 1820s were very much the heyday of the country brewer and that thereafter transport improvements enabled urban brewers to seek out and win the country trade. A bulky item such as that produced by brewers was likely to have a very localised sale until the railway age, but certainly Aberdeenshire in 1900 still contained several small country brewers. By 1900 the County also possessed several manufacturers of aerated water; Huntly, Inverurie, Strichen and Ellon contained such businesses, for example and at least 157 people were employed in them.

The growing demand for paper from nineteenth century businesses, retailers and educational institutions was partly met, in Aberdeenshire, by expanding local enterprises. By 1900 the Mugiemoss and Culter mills of eighteenth century origin had been joined by mills on Donside by Inverurie and nearer to Aberdeen. More than half of the workforce of over 2,000 were to be found in County not City mills. The Culter mills developed in the later part of the century, the workforce increased from 200 in the seventies to 500 by 1897.[157] Output rose in this period from around a thousand tons to over four thousand. Other small businesses were scattered over the County too. There were, for instance, a bone mill and a boot and shoe factory (employing eighty people) in late nineteenth century Ellon.[158]

The towns and villages of the nineteenth century were, too, a focus for craftsmen. The desire to attract crafts had been one of the factors that led lairds to encourage the establishment of villages. Blacksmiths, tailors, wheelwrights, saddlers, and bakers, for example dwelt in Aberdeenshire communities. The little evidence available from England suggests that Aberdeenshire communities contained such craftsmen even when quite small. In 1840 English villages needed to be over 350 strong to support a blacksmith, a wheelwright and a tailor, whilst saddlers and bakers were usually found in towns, not villages.[159] Yet in 1837 Pigot's Directory shows Ballater (population 317) had a blacksmith, Aboyne (population 260) had a blacksmith too, and a shoemaker, a tailor, and a millwright, whilst Kincardine O'Neil (population 288) housed a shoemaker, 2 blacksmiths, 2 wrights, a shoemaker and a tailor. By 1900 factory-made products easily moved by road and rail threatened the County craftsmen's business, yet the number of County tailors living outside the City rose 1841–1901 from 781 to 1,236, whilst in the same period bakers increased from 127 to 577. The number of saddlers altered little in the

County. Country communities in Aberdeenshire may have been a disappointment as textile centres, but they showed great resilience as focal points for craftwork. Certainly this resilience contrasts with evidence found in parts of England. The numbers of tailors and millers in Aberdeenshire living outside the City increased a little 1841–1901. In Rutland, for example, both crafts fell sharply during this period.[160]

The century saw a remarkable growth of the granite industry. By 1900 the County was producing well over 300,000 tons of granite and workshops were busy with the labour of men cutting, shaping and polishing the building blocks, paving stones and memorials for which this stone was used. In 1800 the granite trade centred especially on the ports of Peterhead and Aberdeen employing over 600 men.[161] Farmers earned helpful extra income using their carts to trundle the granite from quarries to the shore. The demand for granite and improved methods of quarrying and shaping the stone came at a time when inland transport was improving. The Aberdeenshire Canal encouraged quarries in the Dyce area, but it was above all the railway that stimulated inland quarries. In particular this combination of factors created a whole new village. In 1800 Kemnay scarcely deserved to be seen as a hamlet, in 1871 200 people lived there, but by 1900 986 people dwelt in the village. In 1859 the Alford Valley Railway arrived in Kemnay on the way west and made it possible to develop the potentially huge granite quarrying resources in the parish. Where once there had just been a couple of thatched cottages, twenty five sizeable new granite houses with slate roofs had been built by 1875 served by several shops.[162] The River Don was bridged at Boat of Kemnay making it easier for Chapel of Garioch people to come to the village.

Behind this success lay the enterprise of John Fyfe and the readiness of the local landowning family, the Burnetts, to allow him to push ahead with his quarrying business. From his first lease in 1858, which cost him £25 a year[163] Fyfe developed the quarries till, by the eighties, he had 250 men working for him all year and occasional help from boys taken from school from time to time.[164] He used seven steam cranes and designed ingenious lifting devices called 'blondins'. By now his lease was costing him £160 a year. He carefully obeyed the Burnett's requirements about taking precautions to avoid accidents, putting up signs and giving warning toots on horns when blasting was to take place.[165] Once prodded into life by quarrying, Kemnay then developed a service role so that by 1877 it had a baker, a blacksmith, five shoemakers, a druggist, four grocers, general merchants, and two wrights:[166] 'Where formerly there was no trace of a house beyond a shop and a farm town there are now many beautiful cottages'.[167]

Estate of Kemnay
1792 (based on plan in
Burnett of Kemnay M.S.S.)

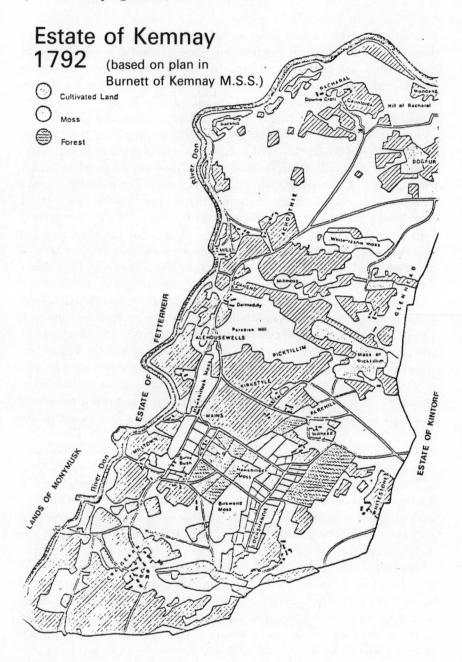

Cultivated Land

Moss

Forest

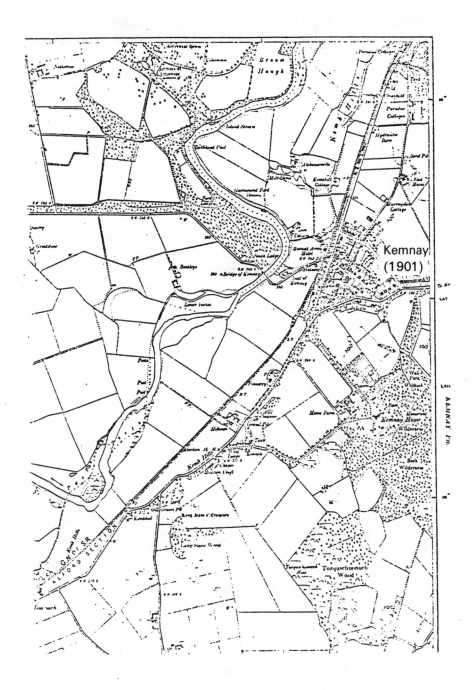

Kemnay
(1901)

Though the fortunes of many enterprises changed during the nineteenth century, small-scale local crafts and industries were by no means dead by 1900 in Aberdeenshire. Huntly possessed four little woollen factories, a sawmill, a mineral-water manufacturer, a hosiery factory and an agricultural implement maker.[168] Even a small place like Strichen with a population of around a thousand contained a corn mill, a woollen-cloth manufacturer and a mineral-water maker. In the parish of Old Deer the village itself was tiny, nevertheless the parish possessed three millers, a woollen manufacturer, a brewer, a distiller and a mineral-water maker.[169] North East Scotland was still sufficiently distinct and remote from major urban areas to contain a rich variety of activities.

As the County became more prosperous so sources of finance and places to deposit money became more necessary. For the humble saver the spread of the Savings Bank movement was helpful. By 1815 it was established in Aberdeen and thereafter it spread to a number of towns and villages. It offered a safe place of deposit for people able to find at least the £10 minimum required. In 1842 Huntly's Savings Bank contained £3,644 placed there by 318 depositors, 'tradesmen, servants and the poorer classes'.[170] Peterhead's Savings Bank had, in 1837, £2,095 deposited by 295 people.[171] The movement was partly intended to help ordinary people build up reserves that could be used in times of distress. Savings Banks worked best in towns and villages where the numbers of people made them viable though they did flourish in smaller places where well-populated surrounding farmland sustained them. Insch Savings Bank aimed to help farm labourers and was, in 1842 'in a thriving condition'.[172]

More commercially-minded banks also increased in number. Provincial banking began in the North East in 1747 and spread to several County communities in the next 30 years. Money was lent to merchants, to landowners and (to a lesser extent) to manufacturers.[173] The Town and County Bank and the North of Scotland Bank were both established by the North East's landowners and businessmen. The North of Scotland moved rapidly to establish local branches, creating them in Ellon, Peterhead and Huntly in 1836 and Turriff, Tarland, Inverurie, Insch, Old Meldrum, Strichen and Old Deer in the following year. Provincial banking declined in early Victorian times, edged out by the bigger joint stock banks. Thus the Union Bank spread by taking over the Aberdeen Bank in 1849. By 1867 most communities possessed a branch (see map) and expansion continued after that date too. Scottish banks of the period were vigorous institutions ready to respond to the demands of industry, agriculture, transport and trade.[174] Banks operated by using local

Bank Agencies in Aberdeenshire:1867

(Source: Slater's Royal National Commercial Directory and Topography of Scotland. 1867 Manchester and London)

Banks represented:

City of Glasgow................................1
Union Bank......................................13
Commercial Bank.............................2
Aberdeen Town and Country Bank..18
North of Scotland Bank.................17
Savings Bank...................................8
Bank of Scotland.............................1

Number of agencies:

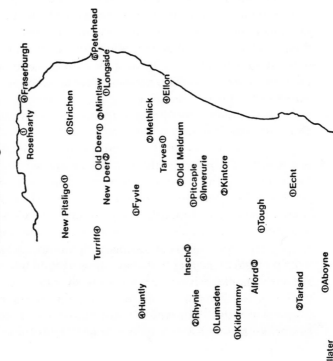

①Fraserburgh ④Peterhead

Rosehearty① ①Longside

①Strichen Old Deer① ②Mintlaw

New Pitsligo① New Deer② ②Methlick ①Ellon

Turriff① ①Fyvie Tarves①

②Old Meldrum

①Pitcaple ①Kintore
①Inverurie

①Huntly Insch① ①Tough ①Echt

②Rhynie Alford①

①Lumsden ①Tarland ①Aboyne

①Kildrummy

①Ballater

agents. In the later part of the century they increasingly employed their own full-time staff (387 worked in the County in 1901 compared to 31 in 1841) but till that time often used as agents local lawyers, farmers and factors.[175] These men used their local knowledge and contacts and were rewarded for their efforts by being paid a percentage of the business that they did. Bank agents employed clerks to chase up customers but took heavy responsibilities themselves too. The Aberdeen Banking Company instructed one of the agents 'have the money well secured in your bedroom ... have a brace of pistols in the room and lock it on the inside and have a bell to communicate with some of the rooms where the rest of the family sleep'.[176] The City of Glasgow and the Bank of Scotland merely concentrated on one of the more profitable parts of the County: each had a fishing port branch, the former in Peterhead, the latter in Fraserburgh.

The people of rural Aberdeenshire were drawn to towns and villages not only by the presence there of places where they could deposit and borrow money, but of places where they could spend it. The improved travel facilities that developed in the nineteenth century and the growing wealth of the local population helped towns and villages develop a more extensive and sophisticated range of shops. As the century progressed so shops developed that were distinctive in design and specialised in func-tion: the kind of trading that commonly went on from dwelling houses in the early nineteenth century began to shrink.[177] Equally hit were the packmen, once common in the early nineteenth century with their bundles of clothes, haberdashery goods, and even books. Near Peterhead one packman managed to operate despite being blind.[178] As the century developed so some acquired carts, some turned to shopkeeping and others simply abandoned their trade. Not all the parish ministers who noted their neighbours' increasing taste for more expensive commodities approved of the development. St Fergus's minister grumbled in 1840 that the silk gowns and cloaks of the better-off encouraged women of the servant class to spend their 'hard-won penny fee' ... to gratify a passion for outward adorning.[179]

By the 1840s specialised shops were becoming more numerous. In Turriff there were enterprises selling clothes and haberdashery goods as well as grocers and hardware dealers that showed demand for retail products was growing.[180] Writing in 1865 James Minty saw in Turriff a great number of butchers, five bakers where once two had sufficed (marking a big increase in the consumption of wheat bread) as well as more tailors and shoemakers. The shops 'had increased in size and splendour.' Minty contrasted the sixties shops with those of the early part of the century when 'there were no painted or papered walls or ceilings, no gilded cornices, mahogany counters, plate-glass windows or ashlar fronts, all was plain and unpretending'.[181] James Wilken began work in an Ellon shop in 1851 when 'everything had to be weighed and done up. There were no ready-made bags – for years after that date we had to learn to cut, paste and make all the paper bags'.[182] What these men witnessed was a retailing revolution. The second half of the nineteenth century brought specialised shop-building, advertising of a far more insistent kind, and a range of goods that included items from other parts of the world (especially tea) as well as far more fresh goods now easily moved along the railway network.[183] Demand from more affluent farmers for retail goods of reasonable quality encouraged shopkeepers to specialise, expand their stock, and seek items for sale that were made in distant parts of Britain. The resulting prosperity brought grander premises like the many recent shops seen in Old Meldrum in the 1890s with 'fine granite fronts and spacious plate-glass windows'.[184] The Directories of the period show the growing number of shops and the arrival of specialist booksellers, druggists, hairdressers and photographers as well as the tendency for 'general merchants' to become grocers, or drapers not tiny multi-purpose enterprises. It was a development with features that James Minty did not care for. He bemoaned the advertising by shopkeepers, the 'puffing paragraphs and fibbing advertisements ... goods in shop windows, bills and posters'.[185]

The directories show not only the spread of specialised shops, but the small size of Aberdeenshire villages able to support them. In 1836 in Norfolk a village needed 377 people to possess a public house, 463 for a shopkeeper and 498 for a grocer.[186] Aberdeenshire villages supported such services at a smaller size. In 1837 Kintore's 400 people were provided with a baker, a butcher, a general dealer and 2 inns:[187] Aboyne's 260 strong village had a baker and butcher, Longside (316 people) had a butcher, a baker and two grocer-drapers, and Kincardine O'Neil (population 288) owned two general dealers and a baker.[188] Between 1841 and 1901 the number of butchers in the County trebled, drapers increased from employing 64 people to a workforce of 1,271 and there were 2,192 people who were grocers compared to 374 in 1841. The increased number of horse-drawn vehicles in the County included many shopkeepers' delivery vans as enterprising men sought to expand their trade.

The shopping revolution not only ended the days of the packmen, it altered the character of – and sometimes severely diminished – the old country fairs. There were, of course, regular fairs and markets in the squares of the bigger communities. In early nineteenth century Huntly it was possible to see, at such occasions, 'Women in grey cloaks with baskets on the arm containing butter, eggs, cheese and live fowls. Mingled with these are the wives, daughters and domestic servants of the town's people purchasing the week's provisions ... (in)˝ ... the middle of the Square are cart loads of peat among which there may be a few loads of coal'.[189] Such markets prospered in Victorian times. But the County also contained a number of fairs held in the open countryside – though often quite close to one of the more sizeable settlements. These great fairs were occasions lasting several days. At them there was trade in animals, in essential items for work or household use, as well as brisk business in non-essentials. Near Ellon, on Market Hill, just such a fair flourished in the early nineteenth century. Business was done in wooden ware such as washing tubs, milking cogs and wooden buckets, spurtles, baking boards, sieves, riddles, axe-handles and hoe shafts.[190] Also on sale were items made of metal as well as gingerbread and sweets. Ellon inn-keepers gathered there and provided hot dinners (principally broth and beef) by lighting fires outside the buildings and doing the cooking there.[191]

These Ellon fairs ended abruptly when the laird shut up the access road, but other fairs declined gradually in the face of the competition provided by towns and villages. By mid century Cudgel Fair, held six miles south-west of Peterhead, was in poor shape. Once it had been the scene of busy traffic in animals drawing in 'souters hurrying in with their wallets of shoes and the sweetie wives, with other traders ... On the brae-side stood half a dozen tents with fires smoking before them while on a tripod hung a pot of broth. Over each tent hung the sign board of the publican. At a little distance ... were a couple of stands for the sale of gingerbread and other eatables'.[192] Carol Fair, in Strathbogie had once attracted many sweet-sellers, toy dealers, confectionary sellers, purveyors of pocket knives and trinkets. By the later nineteenth century it had shrunk to consist of little more than 'an old man and a small heifer'.[193] Hawkhall Fair, near Huntly, was also in decline.[194] The Head of the nearby school at Ythan Wells rejoiced. On 28th April 1874 he noted in his school logbook 'There is a market at Hawkhall ... It used to be given as a holiday. It is now, however, not so fashionable for children to attend fairs and I never gave this Market Day as a holiday.'[195] The following year he wrote with pleasure of his school's healthy attendance on the day of Hawkhall Market, 'the taste for children and women attending markets for pleasure only seems to be dying out'.[196] St Sairs Fair shrank from being a major animal market to a far less significant size[197] and even the great St Lawrence Fair at Old Rayne was in slow decline by 1865, owing to its distance from a railway station.[198] The Shiach Fair near Huntly, collapsed entirely and had to be shifted inside the town.[199]

The decline of country fairs was a consequence both of the growth of shops in towns and villages and the transformation of trade in cattle and other livestock that was brought about by the railways. It was at convenient points on the rail system that animal auctions were most handily conducted: places like Old Rayne that had suited drovers suffered if they failed to fit into the rail networks. Since rail-points were usually located at existing communities (like Inverurie or Huntly) these places were able to add animal-trading and associated functions (such as slaughtering) to their other attributes. Even when there was no community in existence, a railway site that suited the animal trade could develop into a community. Once the railway reached Maud in 1861, then animal traffic from the Buchan interior was drawn to it. By 1898 the village contained 'Mr Bell's County Auction ... Mr Findlay's Mart ... and Reith & Anderson's weekly sales'.[200] By 1903 there were four auctioneers in Maud and a village had grown up that included two butchers, a miller, a mason, three bakers and three carpenters, three grocers, two saddlers, a tailor, a slater, three bootmakers and two drapers.[201] 575 people lived in the village by 1901. Alford provides another example of a community helped by the railway to develop into a sizeable village serving the countryside, with monthly markets in grain and cattle. Yet it had been so tiny in the early part of the century that a pedestrian journeying to it had once stopped right in the middle of it and asked the way to the village.[202] By 1896 it had a post office, two banks, and several shops.[203] 634 people inhabited the village by 1901.

Many of Aberdeenshire's towns and villages became a focus for another kind of trading. The break-up of the old farming system led to a growth in the hiring of hands for agricultural and domestic work. Such events were more than occasions for the selection of a labour force. At Insch feeing fair there were 'sweeties and sweet sellers to be found' and, very often, 'numerous hordes of thimble riggers, card sharpers etc'.[204] These feeing fairs were occasions that some deplored. A County Police Committee of 1853 felt them to be 'a comparatively modern invention ... a most pernicious influence on the whole class of farm servants'.[205] Huntly's minister wrote, in 1840, that the large feeing fairs were 'unmitigated moral nuisances ... the one class being hired generally without any regard to their character as if they were mere beasts of burden'.[206] Other contemporaries deplored the way these occasions were an 'excuse for gaiety, revelry and dissipation ... within a few days of the term the whole agricultural population are in a state of great excitement'.[207] All over the County headteachers noted wearily that nearby feeing fairs were occasions when large numbers of pupils absented themselves from school. These gatherings brought people from the most inaccessible parts of the countryside into towns and villages which thus provided a social as well as an economic function.

Some communities served to entertain not only local people, but travellers from considerable distances enjoying day-outings or much longer stays. During the nineteenth century an increasing number of British people began to take holidays away from their home communities. The railway network especially encouraged a development made possible by the greater affluence of a bigger proportion of the population. Aberdeenshire possessed coastal and countryside sites that proved attractive to holidaymakers and some community growth was stimulated by the need to provide places where holidaymakers could be entertained and accommodated.

Attempts to attract people with leisure were not, however, confined to the railway age. At the beginning of the nineteenth century the place that made the most determined bid for this trade was the rather remote and bleak fishing port of Peterhead. The seaside continued to attract visitors. Collieston was, by the mid century, 'much frequented in spite of its scanty accommodation, by visitors from the interior part of the country who come for the benefits of sea-bathing'.[208] From the Forgue area of inland Aberdeenshire ordinary children regularly used the cheap fares offered by the Railway Companies to go to coastal places nearby to bathe in the sea.[209] At Cruden Bay the Great North of Scotland Railway Company made a deliberate effort to encourage tourism close by the small fishing village of Port Errol. The Company's Hotel Committee, encouraged by its success with the Palace Hotel in Aberdeen (which it took over in 1891) launched into an ambitious project to provide a luxury hotel on the coast. The Hotel opened in spring 1899, offering splendid accommodation and wide range of amenities that had cost around £22,000.[210] There, by the end of the century, 'red-coated golfers were in evidence and solitary ladies read books in the open or trifled at tennis ... picnic companies were numerous. Some had come by rail ... others had driven in farmers' carts from neighbouring parishes ... Little boats were bobbing in the bay'.[221] A few villas were built, but Cruden Bay did not really flourish. By 1909 the Hotel was running at a loss. Cruden Bay was rather remote, the Hotel depended on the well-to-do, and a community failed to develop to any great extent.

Inland places sought leisure traffic too. Huntly, by 1903 'has become a fashionable summer resort' noted a Directory of the period.[212] The most successful by far were Deeside communities and above all, the village of Ballater. It was the supposed beneficial effects of the water of nearby Pannanich Wells that led to the creation of Ballater. Encourged by

Cruden Bay Hotel. A specially developed holiday resort focussing around a great hotel failed to grow as much as the G.N.S.R. wished.

Great North of Scotland Railway Company.

Seaside and Golfing Resort.

CRUDEN BAY

(30 Miles by Rail from Aberdeen).

Splendid Beach over Two Miles long.   Sea Bathing.
Boating.   Fishing.   Healthy Climate.   Bracing Air.

*The Golf Course of 18 Holes laid out by the Railway Company is pronounced
by distinguished players to be one of the best in the Kingdom.*

A Ladies' Course of 9 Holes has also been formed close to the Hotel.

CRUDEN BAY HOTEL

OWNED BY THE

GREAT NORTH OF SCOTLAND RAILWAY COMPANY,

Occupies a charming site overlooking the Bay.

ELECTRICALLY LIGHTED.   LIFT.

Special Accommodation and Conveniences for Golfers.

BOWLING GREENS.   TENNIS COURTS.   CROQUET LAWNS.

Electric Tramway for Visitors between Railway Station and Hotel.

Same Management as the Palace Hotel, Aberdeen.

*Address enquiries to Manager, Cruden Bay Hotel,
Port-Erroll.*

W. MOFFATT, General Manager.

stories of the dramatic curing of a weak scrofula-infected old woman in 1760, people made their way to the area in numbers too numerous for local accommodation.[213] The astute local laird, the ex-Jacobite William Farquharson of Monaltrie, decided to lay out a whole new community at Ballater. In November, 1800, the Aberdeen Journal carried the announcement that 'Mr Farquharson proposes to give leases for feus ... according to a division of the same lately made'.[214] The village developed slowly, by 1841 it housed a little over 300 people. Despite the turnpike road's only reaching Aboyne, a good commutation road meant that it was, by this date, 'much frequented in summer by strangers from a distance on account of the salubrity of the air and the beauty of the scenery. Its streets or lanes cross the main street at right angles, the houses are built on a regular plan and neatly fitted up for the accommodation of summer visitors'.[215]

The building of the Deeside Line promptly accelerated Ballater's growth. No sooner had work begun on the Line than fresh feus were being offered for sale in the village.[216] The population of 366 in 1861 had jumped to 694 by 1891 and continued to climb until, by the end of the century, it had reached 1,247. Of course the community was not simply a holiday resort. Annual markets, feeing fairs, shops and services for the locality all emerged. By 1867 there were tailors, bakers, wrights, grocers and butchers in the village as well as a watchmaker, a druggist, a saddler, a cartwright, a shoemaker, a draper and a plasterer. But the opening up of the Deeside Line as far as Ballater in 1866 meant that day-outings as well as long-stay holiday-makers could come. The Line had been open but a year when the 'Aberdeen Journal' reported Ballater to be crowded on a summer Saturday in July 'a group here, another there, on every green knoll, discussing the contents of their baskets while others were tripping it on the green. They all returned by the evening train seeming in the best of spirits. There is no doubt that these excursions have a beneficial effect both on employees and employed. Monday being the annual holiday in Aberdeen, we had a large supply of Aberdonians, something over 600'.[217] By 1902 Ballater was offering 101 villas, cottages and residences for those wishing to stay for a lengthy period.[218] A number of Aberdeen families developed the habit of taking a property for two or three months. 42 of the properties advertised in 1902 were offered 'with attendance', fourteen had stabling and 69 stressed the presence of rooms for servants. There were also 89 humbler premises of one or two rooms available for rent. In addition to this large number of properties offered as temporary homes, there were several inns and hotels where visitors could stay.[219]

Not only Ballater, but other parts of Deeside teemed with summer

visitors. It was possible to spot 'tourists, sportsmen, cyclists and moun-
taineers of every grade, from the prince of royal blood who delights in
deer-stalking to the humblest city mechanic who has to content himself
with the trout-fishing or rambling of a single annual holiday'.[220]
Torphins developed from being but a house or two into a village where
over 400 people lived in 1901. Aboyne too expanded to be 561 strong by
1901, whilst nearby Tarland, once much more important, but now
without the vital rail link, saw its population fall slightly from 389 in 1891
to 367 in 1901. Even Braemar grew, despite its lack of a direct rail link.
The need to take a coach from Ballater to reach Braemar gave it a rather
exclusive character, a transformation from its early nineteenth century
condition as a small clachan of low straggling thatched homes and an inn
'more suitable for drovers and excise officers than any higher description
of travellers'.[221] Braemar's population slowly increased from 214 in 1841
to 516 by 1901.

Braemar offers an unusual instance of unsatisfactory travel being
eventually almost an asset. The towns and villages of Aberdeenshire in
1900 normally flourished when well placed to exploit road, rail, river-
crossings and – sometimes – sea travel too. All offered services – schools,
churches, shops and skilled workmen. Some provided distinctive employment – fishing and textile production for example. Thus the century
saw great variations in the growth of communities, according to the
influence on them of a number of factors.

The different communities

During the nineteenth century the County's total population expanded
from 123,082 to 304,439. A significant proportion of this growth was
caused by the expansion of Aberdeen. The City's population of 27,608 in
1801 represented a little under a quarter of the County total: by 1901 the
153,114 inhabitants of Aberdeen accounted for slightly more than half
the County growth. Aberdeen's expansion was not simply numerical, its
boundaries were extended in the late nineteenth century to absorb Old
Aberdeen, the textile village of Woodside, and the trawling community
of Torry. In 1881 over 5,000 people lived in Woodside, over a thousand
in Torry and more than 2,000 in Old Aberdeen. Areas close to the City
such as Auchmill, Bankhead and Peterculter grew rapidly too. Auchmill
expanded from 500 in 1861 to 2,231 in 1901, for example.

Away from the powerful pull of the City community fortunes varied
greatly. Not all contributors to the First and Second Statistical Accounts
attempted to provide accurate figures for villages and burghs in their
parishes, nor do the early census returns clearly itemise village size. It is,

Victorian Ballater before the collapse of the wooden bridge over the Dee in 1885. Spanning the Dee was a problem, huge rises in the water level swept down debris that wrecked constructions at Ballater – in 1789 and 1829. The present bridge replaced the wooden one.

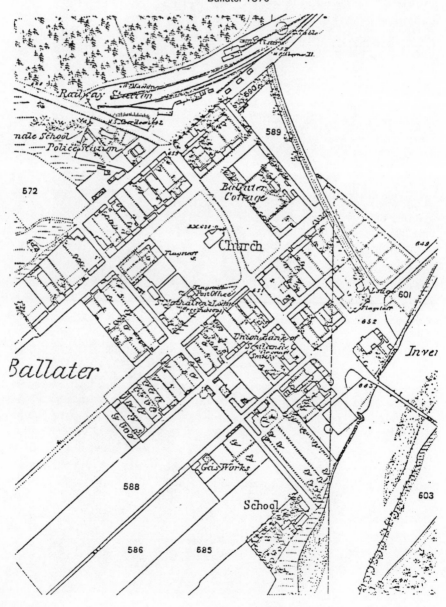

Ballater 1870

therefore, not easy to obtain a sustained and detailed picture of the fortunes of some communities.

Coastal communities

Apart from the exceptional case of Port Errol (with its massive late-nineteenth century hotel) no coastal place could equal Fraserburgh's impressive nine-fold increase over the century. The town is more fully examined in Part III, its success leaned upon very heavy expenditure on its harbour that enabled Fraserburgh to remain a flourishing fishing centre even when challenged by Aberdeen. At the end of the century as at the beginning, Peterhead remained the County's second burgh in size. It too spent heavily on harbour improvement, though not as determinedly as Fraserburgh. Most other fishing communities expanded until the last two decades; then a slow decline set in as fisherfolk were attracted away from their villages to the major centres. Rosehearty, for example, suffered from a tidal harbour and the lack of a rail link.[222] It reached its peak of 1,404 in 1881.

Expanding Inland Places

Inland places that reached their biggest population in 1901 included old-established burghs like Inverurie and Huntly and wholly new communities like Dyce, Maud and Kemnay. None of these places began life as one of the planned villages created by landowners, though Huntly especially felt the improver's hand in being re-shaped. In all cases, save one, the railway played an important role. In Inverurie's case the coming of the railway works to the town reversed what might otherwise have been a gentle decline. The railway made possible a granite-quarrying community at Kemnay and the animal-dealing village of Maud. Dyce appeared only after the coming of the railway led the laird to lay out a village. Aboyne, Ballater and Torphins all drew in holiday traffic. The sole exception was Braemar. But Braemar was well-connected to the railway by road and lay in a holiday area made fashionable by royalty. These communities tended to have a purpose additional to their role as a service centre for the immediate locality. These purposes embraced holiday business, quarrying and industrial activities and large scale agricultural business.

Declining places

Places that reached their maximum before 1901 include a number of villages that shrank to such insignificance in the last 30 years that they ceased to be worth entering as totals in census returns. Several of them – Tarland, Rhynie, Kincardine O'Neil, and Cuminestown for example –

Population changes in coastal communities.

Places	1790s	1801	1811	1821	1831	1841	1851	1861	1871	1881	1891	1901
Boddam	192					460		550	803	1117	1110	800
Broadsea	200					326		371	442	423	510	
Burnhaven						120		280	326	320		
Cairnbulg						406		427	496	459	461	569
Collieston					167	357		410	442	421	419	
Fraserburgh	1000						3093	3101	4266	6583	7360	9105
Inverallochy					450	507		652	744	741	637	656
Newburgh	170				180	393		541	570	645	654	600
Pennan						168		240	289			
Peterhead	2959	3264	3556	4783	5112	6244	7298	7541	8621	10922	12195	11794
Pitullie & Sandhaven					200	200		230	399	585	526	617
Port Errol					48	51		190	210	493	490	681
Rosehearty	213				600	750	844	908	1206	1404	1179	1185
St Combs					291	305		462	533	614	565	530

Population changes in expanding inland places.

Places	1790s	1801	1811	1821	1831	1841	1851	1861	1871	1881	1891	1901
Aboyne						260	187				341	561
Alford									482	529	535	634
Ballater						317		362	694	759	983	1247
Braemar						245		280	347	437	482	516
Ellon	190							823	811	1037	1254	1527
Dyce								45	365	561	727	863
Huntly	2000				2585	2731	3131	3448	3570	3519	3760	4136
Insch						220	316	411	533	579	567	610
Inverurie	360	450		735	994	1619	2084	2520	2524	2575	2549	3058
Kemnay									200	432	660	986
Kintore	228			312	402	464	476	568	659	661	686	789
Maud										343	377	575
Torphins											201	409

Population changes in coastal communities.

Places	1790s	1801	1811	1821	1831	1841	1851	1861	1871	1881	1891	1901
Cumminestown	404					477	477	459	572	525	428	441
Fetterangus					216	220		345	367	364	358	340
Garmond						226		230	268	220		
Kincardine O'Neil	100					288	300	190	227			
Longside					316	384		447	574	474	453	417
Lumsden					243	233		478	507	519	501	487
Mintlaw					222	240		380	446	435	402	393
New Aberdour	195				300	376		543	628	642	620	583
New Byth					302		402	454	609	491	398	351
New Deer						322		475	643	755	746	739
New Leeds					211	203		240	269			
New Pitsligo						1262	1605	1773	2094	2056	1686	1674
Old Deer								185	237			
Old Meldrum	783			1000	1004	1102	1579	1553	1535	1494	1321	1197
Pitmedden								180	249			
Rhynie						240		349	494	442	445	476
Stewartfield	200				573	614		751	647	675	557	412
Strichen						681		1030	1184	1204	1133	1025
Tarland	150					350		316	269	374	389	367
Turriff	701			922	1136	1309	1693	1843	2277	2304	2341	2273

had no railway station. No less than 16 of these places found themselves in this unfortunate situation. Nor did villages established by improving landowners seem able to sustain their growth in the later nineteenth century. New Pitsligo did best in this respect, the development of lace-making there provided a rare exception to the collapse of textiles in the planned villages. New Byth seemed to a local inhabitant of the late nineteenth century to have fallen upon sad times and it badly needed a railway connection. The population included a disproportionate number of aged, infirm and poor folk and too few tradespeople. Where once both linen and woollen industries had flourished the village had a mere two looms in 1899.[223] Older communities did not escape stagnation or decline, Tarland and Kincardine O'Neil suffered from their lack of a rail link, the former losing out to Aboyne. Old Meldrum joined the rail network later than Inverurie and suffered a sad diminution of its once important position. Neither Old Meldrum nor Turriff could match the success of Inverurie or Huntly in attracting industrial activities.

The growth of communities in the early nineteenth century shows the continued importance of major landowners. Not only did they establish new communities, they re-organised existing ones and played a part in encouraging the expansion of places like Fraserburgh and Inverurie. Landowners could attract settlers, assist bridge, road and rail developments, encourage industry, trade and fishing. When, in 1799, the Earl of Aberdeen abandoned his letting of Tarland to four tenants, to whom all the villagers were subject as tenants-at-will, the effect was dramatic. With nineteen-year leases as the Earl's direct tenants the villagers abandoned their old habits of 'dissipation, idleness and indifference'.[224] Now that they had an incentive to improve their community they began to build comfortable houses and to improve their little patches of ground. Without the positive support of the landowner a community could fail to realise its full potential. Ellon, splendidly placed at a recently bridged river crossing, close to the Ythan estuary up which small craft could travel, nevertheless failed to grow rapidly till late Victorian times. Alexander Gordon, who inherited the estate in 1845, would only allow buildings to be erected in return for a ground rent payable for 30 years, after which time the building became his property.[225] When in 1874 Ellon School Board detected a change in policy 'as the present proprietor, reversing the policy of his father, is arranging to let off a considerable number of feus' it urged the need to provide for far more school places in view of the certainty of the increase in population that would follow.[226] By 1895 Ellon was gowing rapidly, 'every hole that is fit for human habitation is occupied'.[227] Alongside the old river-side Ellon there developed the new area of Auchterellon on land bought by the

Provost from the laird. It was here that the boot and shoe factory and the Station Hotel were built. The emergence of Torphins and the stagnation of Kincardine O'Neil were due to a landowner's refusal to allow the Deeside line to take a direct westward route. But though a laird could deter development, there was a limit to what he could do to bring it about. As the century progressed and the transport revolution opened up Aberdeenshire to the many developments taking place in the rest of Britain and in the wider world, so the prosperity of communities depended more on a favourable geographical location and a vigorous outlook from banks, traders, farmers and businessmen.

The communities developed shops, housed craftsmen and provided a location for churches and schools. They served to house farmworkers, sometimes particularly womenfolk when local farmers refused to accommodate their married farmservants, compelling some married men to live in bothies. Certainly this factor applied to villages in Buchan.[228] Such a role was sufficient to sustain tiny villages, but Aberdeenshire also contained the country towns of Huntly, Inverurie, Old Meldrum and Turriff, whilst the villages of New Pitsligo and Ballater also grew to exceed the population of a thousand that has been used by historians to denote a country-town sized community.[229] In England the presence of a major regional centre has been known to have diminished the size of the nearby communities.[230] Aberdeenshire's dominant community was, of course, the City, and certainly Huntly's fortunes seem to have been helped by its distance from Aberdeen and from other competing centres. The country towns housed clergy, teachers, doctors, vets and lawyers, the professional men who found a reasonable living in the countryside. They developed amenities to occupy the leisure of local people, with lectures, libraries, reading rooms, sports organisations and various clubs and societies. Community growth brought problems as well as benefits, however, and it is these problems that are the theme of the next section.

Chapter Two

PROBLEMS OF GROWTH

The problems

The County's early nineteenth century communities were ill-equipped
to cope with sizeable increases of population. Many of them still contained small, thatched properties with tiny windows and walls and floors
that all too often were damp. Early nineteenth century Old Deer was
'like most villages, a mean unsightly place . . . many of the houses being
built with the gable to the street'.[1] On the coast the little port of
Newburgh was 'a very dirty place . . . with six or seven alehouses chiefly
frequented by sailors, smugglers and fishermen'.[2] Turriff's High Street
was full of thatched houses, gable-end on to the street[3] whilst the
numerous low thatched properties in Huntly gave the place an unimpos-
ing appearance.[4] In many of the town's but-and-ben cottages two
families lived. Few Huntly homes had proper ceilings and many had
wooden floors just at one end of the dwelling.[5] Even the main inn in
Huntly, the Gordon Arms, was but a small heather-roofed building.[6]
The textile workers operating from low damp properties[7] could, however, find numerous liquor shops and alehouses in which to forget their
travails. A considerable re-building task, as well as new building provision, lay ahead.

Between properties lay ill-surfaced streets and lanes. Small communities could cope with the disposal of waste from humans and the animals
they often kept, but as expansion took place the problem became increasingly serious. Since water supplies were generally drawn from nearby
springs, streams and wells, the dung piles that lay around were liable to
pollute drinking water by seeping down through the soil. Organized
clearing of the streets was almost unknown. In Huntly property owners
seldom troubled to fulfil their supposed obligation to clean the street
before their doors; pools and open ditches filled with foul liquids that, in
summer, were coated with thick green slime.[8] The drainage of streets
depended on open gutters and downpours of rain. In Peterhead a local
farmer might be persuaded to cart away dung in return for a sizeable
glass of gin. It was some years before the local fisher-folk realised they
commanded a commodity an improving farmer might be glad to spread

on his fields, and began to demand that it was they who should be provided with free alcohol. Even then one enterprising farmer 'gave them all a treat of ale which cost him about fourpence a head' and then sold the manure at a very sizeable profit.[9] As communities expanded, so housing began to surround service properties formerly on the fringe of settlement. In particular butchers' shambles (where animals were slaughtered, blood and offal required disposal, and offensive activities like glue making or tanning took place) became a bigger menace to health.

The inevitable consequence of community growth was an increased danger of disease. Diphtheria, cholera, typhoid and typhus all flourished at times; small pox, scarlatina, measles, T.B. and whooping cough contributed to the toll. In 1865 Scotland's death rate was the highest ever recorded[10] and the years 1865 to 1867 saw 288 cholera cases in the County of Aberdeen. It was this terrifying disease that did much to prod national authorities and local leaders into more vigorous action. Aberdeenshire remained particularly prone to diphtheria outbreaks. In the later part of the century it was the hardest hit of Scottish counties, in relation to its population size, with 986 deaths per million (1860–70) from diphtheria whilst the Scottish average was 309 and the City of Aberdeen recorded 416.[11] A vaccination programme against smallpox proved effective, but T.B. received little attention in Victorian Scotland. The health question produced a wide-ranging impact for it raised issues of housing, street cleaning, drainage, water supply, medical care and hospital provision. All were activities requiring adequate administration and finance.

Growing communities faced problems of law and order too. Disturbances among local people were difficult to deal with before the arrival of modern policing and some groups – like Turriff's shoemakers – were famous for their readiness to fight.[12] The growth of great occasions like markets and fairs, and the seasonal arrival of incomers to the fishing ports that took up the herring trade, added to the problem. In Huntly 'under the excitement of liquor, disturbances take place at markets and fairs which it is difficult to suppress with the rigour which the public tranquillity requires'.[13] The prisons of smaller communities were certainly not sufficiently secure. Huntly's was a miserable hovel with an unglazed window formerly used as a blacksmith's shop. It was so insecure that it was necessary when a prisoner was confined in it to have an officer constantly with him.[14] Resentful officers found Huntly prison-duty gave them coughs, colds and rheumatism. Inverurie's prison was so poorly-constructed one prisoner escaped by making a hole under the door.[15] Prisoners escaped from Peterhead jail with tedious frequency,[16] and

Kintore's lock-up was so open to passers-by that a prisoner put in drunk had so much more liquor passed to him from the street he 'soon got into such a state as to render his former condition in comparison, one of sobriety'.[17] Towns and villages attracted pedlars, vagrants, the wandering poor and beggars. The development of enforceable regulations became increasingly important.

National legislation

The need to respond to a range of problems that emerged as a result of population growth was not a situation unique to the North East, indeed the more heavily industrialising parts of Scotland experienced difficulties that were perhaps, more acute than those found in rural Aberdeenshire. Parliament struggled to respond to the transformation of Scotland in the nineteenth century at a time when even it was being altered by the coming of parliamentary reform. Local government had relied upon landowners and upon small self-perpetrating oligarchies that managed burgh affairs. Such a system would no longer do, and the result was a series of administrative developments that helped shape local communities and improved their ability to tackle some of the problems that confronted them.

The structure of burgh government changed in a series of reforms that began in 1833. In royal burghs, from that date, householders who paid a rateable value of £10 or more could petition for their community to become a police burgh.[18] The old town councils were by-passed and instead a group of police commissioners were empowered to use money raised from rates to light, pave and cleanse their community, attempt to prevent disease, apprehend vagrants, regulate slaughterhouses, name streets and number the properties within them. These 'policing' powers were offered, in following years, to more communities including parliamentary burghs (1847) places with a population of over 1,200 (1850) and places over 700 (1862). Thus places could become burghs that were, hitherto, neither royal burghs nor burghs of barony. In this way the recently-created village of Ballater became a burgh. In older burghs the Town Council and the Police Commissioners operated side by side until legislation in 1900 brought the two bodies together and merged them.[19]

The burgh police commissioners were given greater power through legislation designed to tackle health problems. The 1855 Nuisance Removal Act encouraged them to cleanse – or even close – insanitary houses.[20] In 1867, not long after a serious cholera outbreak, a Public Health Act gave Scottish burgh authorities a range of responsibilities including greater power to regulate common lodging houses, remove filth from the streets and houses, introduce sewage and drainage schemes and provide hospitals.[21]

This Health Act marked a big step forward for another body. The landowners who made up the Commissioners of Supply had, from their creation in 1667, built up considerable power through supervision of tax collection, land valuation and road and bridge management.[22] But for health care Parliament turned to another body, the Board of Supervision that they had created in 1845 to oversee the workings of the new Scottish Poor Law. The Parochial Boards that took charge of the problem of poverty for every parish were made up of kirk and heritor representatives and members elected by ratepayers. They found that, where burgh police commissioners' authority did not run, they were responsible for matters of health too. This situation continued until 1889 when County Councils and their district councils took charge of local government outside the burghs and the old Parochial Boards disappeared. (The Commissioners of Supply lived on, though with little to do, until 1930.) In the nineties the ability of villages to reform themselves improved greatly with the establishment of a provision allowing them to declare themselves special districts for the purpose of introducing lighting, water and drainage schemes, and scavenging activities. With money raised from a special rate applied to the district that was overhauling its amenities, it was possible for communities to improve themselves without becoming police burghs.[23] The Board of Supervision was itself replaced in 1894 by a proper government department, the Local Government Board.

The problem of poverty that had triggered this sequence of changes, in 1845, had got quite beyond the old system that depended primarily on charity, or (rarely) upon a compulsory poor assessment. It remained a sizeable problem. Even when the health legislation of 1867 added key duties to the work of the Parochial Board Inspectors, the Board of Supervision urged them not to become so concerned about health matters as to seriously hamper their poverty work.[24] One particular group who were often members of the poor had their own administrative system. A Board of Lunacy was established in 1857. The Parochial Board Inspectors were important examples of the emerging army of officials who coped with the problems of society in the nineteenth century. There were medical officers employed by the Parochial Boards, scavengers hired by police commissioners and (eventually) parish councils, and sanitary inspectors in burghs and in parishes. Improving communities needed lamplighters, too, whilst hospitals developed in Victorian times required staff. Across the country poorhouses began to be erected, run by governors, matrons and their staff. Pre-1845 Scotland had very few poorhouses, by 1895 there were 63 with accommodation for over 15,000 in them.[25] Despite the higher cost of pauper care in them, the Board of Supervision approved of poorhouses. They provided a test that helped reduce poverty, for paupers refusing admission could be thrown back upon their families for support. Just such an edifice stood in the Buchan countryside at Maud, adding considerably to the population of that tiny community.

The old poor law system had been found deficient by 1845, the old educational system staggered on until 1872. Schools provided by the Church of Scotland were joined by those constructed for other denominations and by various small private enterprises. In 1872 Schools Boards emerged, elected by localities to oversee educational provision and, as soon as possible, to make schooling compulsory. Towns and villages were the natural focal points for education, especially for the bigger schools of the latter part of the century ambitious to retain pupils beyond the minimum age and eager to evolve what was eventually to become a secondary education function.

Improvement in Aberdeenshire communities

From the pages of the New Statistical Account and from guides and directories, the many signs of improvement stand out. Street lighting proved to be one of the first changes to be adopted, with gas companies (specially established to exploit a local monopoly) springing up all over the County. Turriff obtained gas lighting in 1839, Ellon in 1827, Old Meldrum in 1845 and Ballater in 1863. A few communities moved more slowly. The village of Kemnay was still without street lights at the end of the century; the Garioch District Committee argued 'There was no congestion in the village ... There was nobody to be seen at night, not even a stray dog'.[26]

Policing (or 'watching' as it was commonly called) appeared on a regular basis once the Aberdeenshire Commissioners of Supply were allowed in 1839, to use part of their assessment to establish a permanent police force. Certainly they felt there was an urgent need, since 'not less than one thousand persons are continually wandering about in the County of Aberdeen and preying upon the inhabitants. In the town of Huntly in the week from the 19th to the 25th September (1839) the number of vagrants seen by a constable employed for the purpose was 345'.[27] A County police force was created, it consisted of mounted men and foot constables clad in uniform double-breasted blue frock coats.[28] The new police had to accustom themselves to discipline, especially over drink. In Huntly the drunken condition of the constable caused his dismissal in 1860.[29] By 1894 the force numbered 96 men, 76 of them constables.[30] Each man was, especially, to 'prevent all beggars, vagrants and other idle persons from entering his district', arrest those who were a nuisance, and discourage tinkers.[31] Their impact was so prompt there was evidence of it recorded in several of the Statistical Accounts being written at the time. In Turriff, for example, the fearsome sight of the constable in his uniform, brandishing a baton, brought a ninety per cent reduction in the number of vagrants plaguing the town.[32] Vagrants remained numerous in the County, 605 were noted in June 1894 and 341 in the December of that year,[33] but one of the first effects of the appearance of the constabulary was to tend to push them out of communities to the more remote rural fringes of the County.[34] 221 were counted, in 1853, in Aboyne district, almost double the number seen in the Huntly area. Policemen were often the target of official determination to keep down the costs of improvement and were likely to find themselves performing other duties. In 1847 Huntly's policeman also cleaned the streets[35] whilst in 1867 Kincardine O'Neil (like several other places) when required to appoint an inspector of contagious diseases, simply added this to their policeman's duties.[36]

From the pages of the minutes of parochial boards and police commissioners there emerges a gloomy picture of the mid-century condition of communities and an erratic account of the improvement in the fifties, sixties and seventies. In 1878 the village of Kincardine O'Neil was racked by diphtheria and so badly drained that sewage blocked the burn instead of flowing away.[37] It was the Parochial Board that tackled the problems with a drainage scheme that replaced the open burn with a pipe. Since the pipe fed into the lower reaches of the burn and thence into the Dee Aberdeen protested at the pollution of its water supplies. Kincardine O'Neil dismissed this complaint, arguing that a half mile stretch of burn was sufficient to allow sewage to seep into the surrounding fields rather than flow into the Dee.[38] Old Meldrum Parochial Board struggled with the problems of implementing Nuisance Removal Acts of the fifties in a sizeable community. The town contained open sewers, numerous unenclosed dunghills, pig styes and slaughter houses amid the inhabitants' dwellings. Epidemics in the sixties led to the enclosing of dunghills with walls.[39] The wells from which people drew water were clearly a health hazard but, till 1871, the hostility of the local landowner blocked the provision of proper water supply.[40] In 1889 the Garioch District Board took over the struggle with Old Meldrum's problems. Not till 1893 did the most effective administrative reform take place; Old Meldrum adopted the police acts and obtained its own police commissioners. Huntly obtained police commissioners as early as 1843 yet till 1866 the responsibility for financing effective cleaning of the town lay with the Huntly Parochial Board. Until that date the Huntly Police Commissioners were not eager to act and, when health crises faced their town, first used their policeman as a scavenger[41] then turned to recruiting elderly folk 'unable for heavy work and to whom it might be of benefit'.[42] After 1870, with the Police Commissioners in charge both financially and administratively, and with prodding from the Board of Supervision, more vigorous improvements came.

The health duties assigned to Parochial Boards began in the fifties with instructions that they check and clean their communities, and continued after 1867 with encouragement to appoint sanitary inspectors. Many places (other than large towns) sought the cheapest solution and assigned these duties to policemen, labourers or scavengers.[43] Parochial Boards appointed medical officers too but, until the 1889 Local Government Act, the appointments were likely to be part-time and casually managed. In 1883 Kincardine O'Neil had to be firmly reminded that if it expected financial help towards its medical expenses it would have to start paying its doctor the separate salary he was due as medical officer of health.[44] Improved health seemed difficult to vigorously institute in Aberdeenshire's little towns and villages. The problems of water supply, health care and cleaning may have been less dramatic than in industrial areas and the atmosphere was certainly less polluted, nevertheless the administrative machinery set up in 1845 to care for the poor struggled when it came to performing wider duties. Parochial boards were always likely to look for the cheapest solution to problems and to prefer short-term expedients.

The improvement in educational provision after 1872 did not necessarily meet with a welcome. From his home in Strathbogie, James Pirie argued that it encouraged country folk to migrate to towns, 'many of them have higher aims than the work of farms and acquire a craving to get away from the dullness of rural life'.[45] Schools were eliminated like the one in Peterhead where, in the late eighteenth century, 'filth and laziness being the only branches taught there ... many of the scholars having these special qualifications perfectly taught them at home and did not require to go there to be perfected'.[46] The expansion of old schools, the building of new ones, the reorganization of provision to create infant and senior departments in the many places where there had once been distinct male and female schools, were activities pursued all over the County.

The idea of regular attendance at school was, however, not easily accepted by either adults or children. Children provided a workforce to be drawn upon for farmwork and industrial activities when there was a pressure of business. They herded animals, helped with the harvest, did weeding and hoeing, lifted root crops, worked in quarries, served on herring boats; sometimes they stayed at home to care for infants in order to free their mothers for work. Ythan Wells' Headteacher noted in an entry (of May 1874) typical of school log books, 'Attendance considerably reduced, this is one of the busiest times with the farmers and the assistance of all who can be of any service is required'.[47] This particular teacher offered unusually full comment on the problem of obtaining regular school attendance. He found his pupils away in large numbers at feeing time, 'when any member of the family comes home for a day, all the brothers and sisters are kept to welcome him into the house where he is not treated as an hireling but where for one or two days he can feel his own master at his father's fireside. Though these things affect the attendance at school a good deal for a few days I question whether the children are not better employed than in school'.[48]

He found, as must many other village and small town teachers, that even getting children to arrive on time was not easy. 'A number of those who live in the more outlying districts of the parish maintain that there is no sort of timepiece in the house and that they have just to start for school when their parents tell them, and I believe this assertion to be perfectly true'.[49] It is not surprising that, vexed with irregular attendance and the frequent upheavals of children shifting school as their parents moved, from one job to another, a number of teachers became exasperated. As the Ythan Wells teacher wrote, 'It is rather hard to be compelled to push on the greatest dullard so as to present him when time would be better spent in advancing those that will advance, still when we think that the object of the Act is to educate the masses we take courage remembering that every pupil is an item in the mass and that we are placed here for the purpose of doing something for them.'[50]

Attempts were made in most towns and bigger villages to provide for leisure time. Even in 1837 Inverurie people read a great deal, especially newspapers and cheap periodicals.[51] Many contributors to the New Character or Genius tended most for the advancement of a man's worldly libraries grew up. St Fergus obtained a parish library in 1829, building up a book stock from gifts and the five-shilling shares of the library members. A one shilling annual fee helped sustain a stock of over 300 history, biographical, scientific and religious books; novels, political pamphlets and books of a 'controversial character' were expressly excluded.[52] Huntly's Circulating Library consisted, in 1886, of fiction, as well as religious, historical and natural history books and a separate children's list.[53] All sorts of societies flourished, particularly literary and self-improvement ones, as well as sporting clubs. The Tough Mutual

Improvement Society, voting upon the question of whether 'Cash, Character or Genius tended most for the advancement of a man's worldly interest', came down firmly in favour of cash.[54] There were lectures and concerts, cinema shows developed in the nineties, Mechanics Institutes were founded and Military Volunteers flourished. All these pursuits helped draw country folk into the bigger communities able to support them. The sporting societies' interests gave a stimulus to the development of parks and gardens that was such a feature of late Victorian Britain. Kemnay Park, for example, opened in 1897 to accommodate games but also had flower and shrub areas so that 'not only the youth but the children, the grown-up and especially the aged and infirm should have a place to resort to with feelings of pleasure, freedom and independence'.[55]

Housing and community conditions in the late nineteenth century

The County's stock of town and village housing increased yet remained inadequate, especially in its provision for poorer people. Between 1822 and 1865 at least 180 new dwellings were put up in Turriff, streets were decently surfaced and pavements with kerb-edging added to the major ones, yet even so demand exceeded supply.[56] From 1841 the County average of 6 people to a house worsened to reach 7.02 per house by 1871.[57] There was then a considerable improvement. Aberdeen County must have shared in the building boom of the later nineteenth century, for by 1901 the figure had dropped to 4.83 persons to a house.[58] The County's population were slightly better accommodated than in the country as a whole; in 1901 Aberdeen County's figure of 1.28 persons to a room was somewhat better than the Scottish average of 1.62. Although by 1901 the population was housed in such fashion as to suggest a figure of around one family per house (and a family size of just over 4.6 persons between 1861 and 1901) the housing provision in different burghs varied greatly. The fishing ports seemed to have been the worst provided: in 1871 Fraserburgh's 950 families were accommodated in only 523 houses and by 1901, 1,831 families still only had 1,024 houses. Peterhead was better equipped, 2,561 families and 2,499 houses in 1901 but Rosehearty had only 258 houses for its 312 families. Of course much depended on house size, here Fraserburgh and Peterhead were both ill-provided for. In 1901, 8,998 Fraserburgh people had to make do with 5,379 rooms and 11,763 Peterhead inhabitants crammed into 8,086 rooms. In contrast the holiday burgh of Ballater had a surplus of rooms over population – 1,435 rooms for 1,247 people. Inland burghs were a little better off, though Inverurie's 3,058 people with 2,580 rooms were noticeably less well housed than the people of Turriff or Old Meldrum. Among villages Braemar showed an impressive room surplus, 916 rooms for 516 people, a far bigger surplus than in the other holiday villages Torphins and Aboyne. In contrast the fishing villages were crowded; in Cairnbulg 569 people had to live in 255 rooms and Inverallochy, close by, had 656 people yet only 304 rooms. Inland villages were a little better stocked with housing, though Stewartfield's 530 folk had but 279 rooms.

Crowded Communities	
Place	Persons to a room
Fraserburgh	1.67
Cairnbulg	2.23
Inverallochy	2.15
Stewartfield	1.89

Thus Stewartfield was the only inland community among those where the crowding of population per room was worse than the Scottish average.

Communities with the most generous housing provision	
Place	Persons to a room
Ballater	0.86
Braemar	0.55
Insch	0.87
Longside	0.87
Port Errol	0.47
Torphins	0.76

Amidst the holiday centres (which provide a most deceptive impression of the housing of their inhabitants) two inland communities of a rural character seem oddly placed. But Insch and Longside, like Old Meldrum, Turriff and New Deer were country communities whose population tended to fall in the late nineteenth century leaving them with slightly better provision than places that continued to grow. The quality of the housing was very variable. By 1891 the County had acquired its first full-time Medical Officer of Health, Dr Watt, and from 1892 he produced a series of reports based on his own work and on the evidence of district medical officers. The target for strongest criticism was undoubtedly the accommodation provided for unmarried farm servants. This was often dreadful and offered a situation in which disease

New Maud 1873

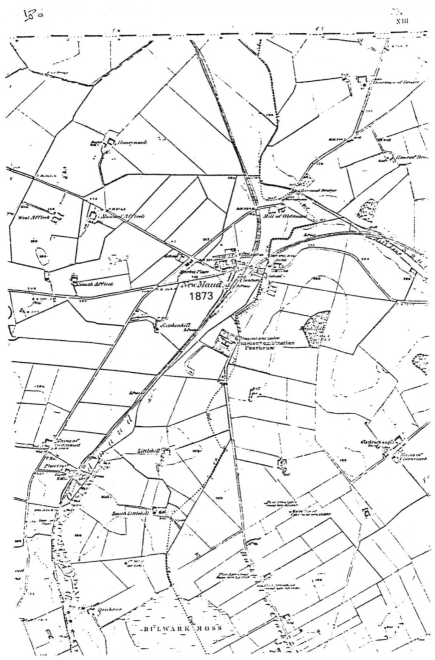

could spread speedily. Dr Watt believed that such accommodation increased the urgency with which he regarded the need for more sizeable places to be equipped with isolation hospitals. A bleak example, not untypical of many, was offered by Dr Lawson in Midmar. Accommodation there was often in stable lofts reached 'behind the heels of half a dozen horses and then up by a rickety stair or ladder. Inside the room are two or more beds according to the size of the farm, and if any space is left it is nearly all taken up with trunks, which also serve as seats. Soiled clothes, bits of harness etc. are lying about. The floor is often not very clean. There is no fireplace of any description. The place is lighted by a skylight with one or two panes broken, perhaps, and filled up with straw or a pair of trousers'.[59]

The housing in small towns and villages was less unpleasant than this. New Pitsligo homes were typical of many village properties.[60] People lived in but-and-ben dwellings, many of them thatched and some with small garrets in the roof. Even in the 1880s many of these homes had earthen floors. Inevitably the inhabitants lived a cramped and crowded life, cooking over an open fire, enduring the smoke from the fire and enjoying only the occasional good wash from the wooden washtub. Locally-made furniture – box-bed, chairs and table and dresser – filled the rooms. Dr Watt found reason to grumble about some features of working-class accommodation. Much of it was prone to be damp, especially in winter[61] with the sleeping accommodation being worst affected because ordinary people were unable to afford more than one fire in the house.[62] Most ordinary people in Kincardine O'Neil 'sleep in rooms small, badly ventilated and damp, with no fireplace. I may say this is quite common.'[63] 'Washing day must be a day of extreme discomfort' in winter, he felt, when women struggled to cope in cramped accommodation ill-equipped for washing.[64] To tackle this problem, Dr Watt urged that public baths, washhouses and drying areas should be built in the different communities. The drainage and water supplies provided to people's properties were still frequently very inadequate. In Peterculter the paper mills owned the sewer and would only connect up their own mill houses. As a result piles of refuse and dung gathered at roadsides.[65] In Tarland attempts to improve the quality of water in the Tarland Burn were hindered by dunghills alongside the Burn that drained into it.[66] Cults was entirely without a drainage scheme in 1890. In Newburgh sewer-effluent ran along the burn whilst Whinneyfold's waste of all types was simply dumped on the ground behind the lower of the village's two rows of houses.[67] Kemnay seems to have been built with no attention to sanitary requirements.[68] New Pitsligo relied for drainage upon a few open stone gutters that were highly offensive to local people

Maud 1902

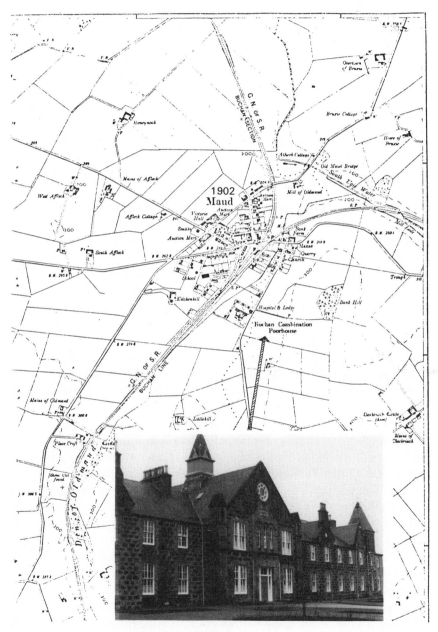

Maud

and especially to the inhabitants of one side of the High Street where houses were built at a level lower than the road. A couple of yards from their front doors lay the sewage-laden open gutter.[69]

Though Dr Watt found numerous such instances of alarmingly poor drainage he was able to chart a degree of progress in the 1890s. Becoming a police burgh, as Ellon did in 1893, could make a great difference. No sooner had police commissioners taken charge than Ellon obtained a regular system of scavenging to remove the offensive piles of dung and refuse that lay before houses and especially before the burgh's two slaughterhouses that were confined within the housing area. It was irritating to Dr Watt to see how many places lacked a proper scavenging system. Such improvement need not be expensive, as Deer demonstrated when fear of cholera in 1890 led it to institute such a system; the sale of manure to local farmers virtually covered the cost of the scavenger's wages.[70] Of course the appointment of a scavenger was not necessarily the answer, for some were incompetent. Collieston was scavenged by an aged figure paid a mere £6 a year for his trouble.[71] New Pitsligo's problems existed despite having a scavenger – indeed he left the bulk of the clearing work to the village tenants.[72] Newburgh's scavenger gathered ashpit contents only to dump them in heaps along the roadside where they lay for some time till carted off.[73] Nevertheless the opportunity that emerged in the nineties to form special districts for scavenging was taken up by a number of Aberdeenshire districts, though Dr Watt feared that all too often scavenging was less effective than it should have been since local committees were 'apt to prefer economy to efficiency'.[74]

Nor was human waste the only problem. The keeping of pigs was a common feature of late Victorian communities; in 1893 Huntly, for example, contained fifty nine piggeries.[75] The piggeries were a common source of foul smells and dung yet often lay among ordinary dwellings. Though towns and villages were still often in an insanitary state in the nineties, at least the provision of ashpits was an improvement on earlier habits of flinging refuse onto the streets.[76] Village ashpits were probably emptied less regularly than those in towns and were likely to overflow. In New Pitsligo in the 1880s 'dry closets, mostly wooden structures, stood adjacent to the midden, which was emptied once a year and the contents carried to the fields'.[77]

The success of any community improvement depended above all on an adequate supply of good water. Here, too, a defective situation in villages was being slowly tackled in the nineties, helped by the power to form special districts and thus raise rates for this purpose. It was Mintlaw's poor water supply that made it still, in 1897, a hot-bed of typhoid fever[78] that persisted through the unwillingness of the villagers

Gordon Hospital, Ellon; small hospitals, like this one, developed in most Aberdeenshire burghs in late Victorian times. Ellon's hospital began life in 1888 and was soon being expanded.

to face increased taxation. Port Errol was so short of water in the summer that in the fishing season there were water riots as fishermen strove to secure supplies at the expense of householders.[79] By the nineties the bigger burghs had well-established water schemes, though the continued growth of some places (such as Fraserburgh and Inverurie) meant that there had to be a constant search for improvement. Old Meldrum's water supply, though well established, was still irregular and even, at times, impure, in the 1890s. The lack of water affected the drainage system so that most people relied on ashpits. After extra water supplies were organized in 1896 the burgh at last began to obtain pipe drains well underground to replace the older stone drains.[80] Polluted wells and streams still supplied many villages in 1890; the problem required quite heavy expenditure and one of the arguments used for failing to light Kemnay streets was that all the money was required for a water supply scheme.

The severity of illnesses in Victorian times led to a programme of hospital building. Until the late nineteenth century many communities only established temporary hospitals when affected by an epidemic. When smallpox troubled Tarland in 1872 the cottages provided for the poor were taken over as a hospital.[81] The City's hospitals and Asylum were used by outlying areas, but the advantages of having a local provision, especially for infectious illnesses, led to a considerable effort to equip all the bigger communities. By 1901 Turriff, Ellon, Inverurie, Huntly, Peterhead and Fraserburgh all possessed hospitals. There were cottage hospitals at Crimond, Forgue, Fyvie and Tullynessie. Ellon hospital, for example, was initially a seven-bed unit built in 1888 and cared for by a labourer and his wife (who acted as matron) in return for rent-free accommodation and a shilling a day when patients were present. By 1901 there was room for thirty nine patients who, if suffering an infectious disease, were accommodated free. The removal of charges meant it was more frequently used, though still very apprehensively by suspicious patients.[82] The County's death rate of 1890 – 14.402 per 1000 was lower than the Scottish average of 20.7 and lower than the average for rural mainland Scotland – 17.3. But the bigger burghs helped drag this average down. The Ballater death rate of 16.842 perhaps reflects its popularity as a place for the aged to retire to, but Huntly's 16.675, Inverurie's 16.888 and Peterhead's 16.917 cannot be so easily explained, whilst Turriff's was a worrying 18.754 that Dr Watt was unable to account for, though he did persist – successfully by 1896 – in urging a hospital be built there.[83]

Improvement in Aberdeenshire was a slow business compounded of local determination and readiness to face costs, pressure from experts

(like doctors and Board of Supervision Inspectors) and legislative reforms that introduced the machinery necessary to make the implementing of reforms possible. One particular area demanded persistent effort
and considerable cost – the problem of poverty.

The problem of poverty

Until 1845 Aberdeenshire authorities, like those in the rest of Scotland,
struggled to contain the mounting problem of poverty according to a
system that had evolved by the late 17th century and remained thereafter, largely unchanged.[84] The country's kirk sessions used money
raised from collections, and from various charges to sustain those poor
people who were, through age, youth, or mental or bodily infirmity,
incapable of work. Although local heritors were allowed to assess themselves in order to raise a poor rate, few were ready to do this. The able-
bodied poor had no entitlement to assistance, yet upon occasion received
aid of a temporary nature when starvation and, perhaps, riot, loomed up
as real possibilities. Times of crop failure and high unemployment
produced crises. During the 1782–3 food shortage Insch Kirk Session
bought meal in order to avert local starvation.[85] In 1812 there were meal
riots in Peterhead, so impossibly high was the price of this basic commodity:[86] Peterhead's response was one to be found in other places too – the
raising of a subscription from the better-off in order to provide for the
unfortunate.

During the nineteenth century the poverty problem increased. The
decline of hand-worked textiles pushed many women, especially, into the
pauper class. George Skene Keith thought the poorer folk in early
nineteenth century Aberdeenshire were women without stocking-
knitting work trying to survive on under £4 a year.[87] Many labourers
found it hard to secure employment through the whole year; in winter-
time the need for fuel, food and warm clothes coincided with the likeli-
hood of unemployment. Illicit distilling and smuggling were stamped
out in the early nineteenth century, depriving the poor of extra income.
The re-shaping of farmland pushed many labourers into towns and villages, the provision of countryside cottage accommodation being sadly
inadequate. Insch, for example, attracted married farm servants to settle
there, many of whom were unable to find work in winter.[88] In Kintore
farm servants no longer able to work horse-teams became day-labourers
and had to move into the village.[89] Deer's Presbytery noticed that
smallholdings were declining by the 1840s and the poor, as a result,
drifted into nearby villages[90] whilst in Old Meldrum parish 'the greater
part of the poor reside in the town'.[91]

The amounts of money that were doled out to the 'ordinary' poor (ie those recognised as genuinely unable to work and, through three years residence, birth or marriage, properly the responsibility of the locality) were tiny indeed. Church collections simply did not yield sufficient income. Peterhead collections in 1815 averaged £1.15.0, Inverurie's but 2/6d.[92] Special charitable efforts and events added a little more. The young men of Strichen raised fourteen guineas in 1812 with their performance of 'Cats' and a similar effort in Turriff brought in £20.[93] Some help was paid out in meal, in coal, in clothing and in house rents: actual money payments were small – New Pitsligo's in 1793 averaged sixteen shillings for a year for each pauper.[94]

There were efforts to organise self-help so that working people saved for hard times. Friendly Societies and Savings Banks proliferated in early nineteenth century communities. In 1815 Peterhead had fourteen Friendly Societies,[95] Old Deer's Savings Bank of 1825 had, by 1840, ninety eight depositors and funds of £1,576.[96] But such organisations were no help to those on really low wages. The old Scottish Poor Law had, to some, the merit of being cheap. It had defenders who argued the system so encouraged 'the spirit of independence amongst the poorer classes that many of them had to be urged to apply for relief'.[97] Others maintained a non-compulsory system stimulated sympathy and good-will towards the poor that compulsion would demolish.[98]

The enquiry into the working of the poor law that was conducted in 1843 for Parliament turned up evidence in Aberdeenshire indicating the need for a compulsory assessment to be introduced. Kincardine O'Neil's doctor was but one of many who objected to the moral compulsion doctors were under to provide free medical care for the poor and to arrange for food to be sent to housebound sick paupers.[99] The enquiry showed the area to be in an intermediate position, not as blighted by poverty as the Highlands but worse off than many areas further south. Despite the numerous cattle in Aberdeenshire, working people could but rarely afford to eat meat: however Aberdeenshire folk were Scotland's great oatmeal consumers, received more than average quantities of milk and green vegetables, and, if near the coast, quite often ate fish. The wages paid the North East's farmworkers were very close to the average Scottish wages. The research conducted by Levitt and Smout has shown that ordinary people in small country towns with active markets fed by nearby supplies were better off than many Scots. But the impressions offered by people living at the time still suggested an unsatisfactory situation, indeed New Pitsligo's minister observed 'It is a mystery to him how they live' since homes, food and bedding were all so poor.[100] A Huntly doctor argued the poor in his care simply did not have enough clothing or food whilst their accommodation was dreadful and their bedding quite inadequate.[101] The town possessed a Dispensary that issued medicines and even wine and flannel, paid for by subscriptions, but such an organisation was not tackling the root of the problem of poverty.

In Peterhead the poor grumbled they were better off when they were allowed to beg every Friday between 9.0 and 10.0 am, and that it was very irksome being confined to their houses and prevented from begging as formerly.[102] Here, as in other towns, local people complained of the appearance of outsiders 'professing to be tradesmen out of work'.[103] Their evidence contrasted with that from Huntly where the poor licensed to beg felt degraded by the badges issued them and would not be seen wearing them.[104] So numerous were Peterhead's poor that only around fifteen shillings a year could on average be found them, a figure below the amount found for Strichen (£1.1.5) or New Deer (£1.7.0).[105] These tiny sums were meant to be supplements to the money earned by performing small tasks, or provided by relatives. As Peterhead's session clerk pointed out, for the adult children of many paupers providing help to parents would result in dragging themselves and their families down into pauperism.[106] In 1841 he attempted to total all the income a Peterhead pauper might obtain. The average earnings of the town's 259 poor came to 7d a week each, 184 of them received just over four hundredweights of coal from the charitable Coal Fund. Some benefitted from up to one and sixpence monthly from the Female Clothing Society. Yet the burden of dependents carried by some, and the house rents paid by 185 of them (and these averaged £1.9.8 a family a year) cut into the sums they received. His guess was that probably most poor had to sustain themselves on around a penny a day. As a result a good number were ill-fed, ill-clad and ill-covered when in bed. For the seventy odd paupers infirm from old age this was especially agonising.[107] One of the town's doctors, John Anderson, argued much the same case to the Poor Law Enquiry, maintaining that much illness stemmed from 'no other cause than the filth and wretchedness of the people and particularly the want of a sufficient quantity of nourishing food'.[108]

This system of caring for the poor was further weakened by the Disruption. The split in the kirk diverted funds elsewhere. Legislation finally came in 1845, introducing a system of parish by parish care administered by locally elected Parochial Boards watched over by a central Board of Supervision. Through part-time Medical Officers and Inspectors who visited and checked the poor a more regular and systematic system was evolved.[109] The raising of money by a compulsory assessment began to be widely adopted. The system gradually improved in efficiency; at first, as one Inspector recalled in later years 'Inspectors were qualified all the same – they knew nothing'.[110] The system was still designed to give relief to those unable to work, not to the able-bodied poor and, as it grew in confidence, the Board of Supervision began to issue a stream of advisory (not mandatory) points designed to produce efficiency and low cost. From 1856 it had two General Superintendents who toured Scotland, reporting their views to the Board and advising the local Parochial Boards on proper procedure. One expense the Board of Supervision did support was the construction of poorhouses. In rural Aberdeenshire one was built (at New Maud) though most communities found they had to provide much more simple poorhouses that were generally just small rows of cottages. New Pitsligo's poorhouse was one of the larger of these little buildings. It could accommodate 26 paupers. The inhabitants lived there rent-free and supplied with free peats.[111] The poor were also housed in lodgings and the Parochial Boards' Inspectors began to visit and attempt to regulate these properties. It seems to have been quite difficult to effectively regulate lodgings. In Kincardine O'Neil in 1869 the lodging house keeper was charging so much – three shillings a week for a furnished room – that the Board of Supervision rejected the Local Parochial Board's efforts to control it on the grounds that it could not be called a common lodging house.[112] In 1864 Huntly contained four lodging houses, all occasionally overcrowded, with no attempt to separate the sexes. Yet no action was taken and the Board of Supervision refused to intervene.[113] Peterhead had a lodging house by the end of the century that was really a small unauthorised poorhouse. When a 1901 Royal Commission visited it they found it 'a large comfortable pleasantly furnished private house with about thirty inmates whose maintenance cost considerably less than that of poor folk in the Buchan Poorhouse'.[114]

Aberdeenshire Parochial Boards varied widely in character. Turriff won praise for the strictness with which it observed Board of Supervision guidelines: Huntly's was attacked for being altogether too lax and generous.[115] Huntly regularly provided its paupers with a barrel of coal every winter.[116] The burdens earned by various Boards varied. Old Deer's pointed out it had to cope with the poor of three old villages whilst nearby New Deer had but one recently-created community in its charge where most of the inhabitants were quite comfortably placed.[117] At grass roots level affairs could be very informally managed: New Pitsligo promised one old lady the pair of carpet slippers she desired if she could persuade her grand-daughter to go out and work.[118] New Deer offered its paupers 2/6 each in honour of Queen Victoria's Jubilee only to find the Board of Supervision would not sanction taking the money from the rates: Board members had to dig into their own pockets.[119] Help was given in money, in house rents and repairs, in clothes, footwear, school-fees, fuel or food. Tyrie Parochial Board owned quite substantial peat stacks it had to guard against the attentions of fuel-hungry locals.[120] Help did go to able-bodied poor unable to find work, though only on a short-term temporary basis. In 1878 the Board of Supervision itself admitted 'In the case of a person really destitute the Inspector should not carry the letter of the law to an extreme ... If a person is really destitute no long period would elapse before he also became disabled from want of food'.[121]

The Buchan Combination Poorhouse

From January 26th 1869, Buchan parishes had the opportunity to place their poor in a large specially-built poorhouse. This also meant that they could thin the ranks of their poor by applying a poorhouse test – paupers refusing to go to the poorhouse could be denied outdoor relief and thrown upon the care of their relatives. The Board of Supervision was soon grumbling that several Buchan parishes were being insufficiently strict. The poorhouse was especially recommended for mothers with illegitimate children, for prisoners' wives, for widows (with families) 'who may fall into immoral habits' and for the 'idle, immoral or dis-sipated'.[122] Paupers with families able to support them ought to be offered the poorhouse, too, otherwise 'a man has only to get married and his duty to support his parents is at an end'.[123] By 1888 the effect of setting up the Buchan Combination Poorhouse could be seen in the sharp fall in the number of poor in all the parishes which had joined in the scheme save one – St Fergus. In twenty years New Deer pauper numbers fell from 130 to 55, Turriff's from 197 to 71 and Ellon's from 206 to 108.[124] The Poorhouse seemed to have succeeded in following the Board of Supervision's advice that life there should be 'more irksome than labour'.[125] One New Pitsligo old lady would certainly have agreed; she had to be punished for escaping from Maud, returning to New Pitsligo, and 'breaking into a room in the poor's lodging house and taking up residence'.[126]

The selection of Maud as a suitable site came after some debate. Peterhead pressed its own claims (and refused to join the scheme when Maud was selected) and Mintlaw had its advocates too. But Maud offered a central site where land could be obtained cheaply and which could easily be reached by rail. After meeting in Maud's Station Hotel the sixteen parishes ready to proceed authorised the construction of a very sizeable building on a four acre site. Work went slowly and the opening in January 1869 was seven months behind target.[127] For every share paid at £28 each, a bed was allocated to the parish concerned. Fraserburgh headed the list with 21, followed by Ellon with 12, Strichen, New Deer and Tyrie with 11 each, Pitsligo and Cruden with 8, Rathen and Lonmay with 7, Methlick, Old Deer, Tarves and Longside with 6, Udny 5 and Logie Buchan a mere 2. In May 1878 an extra nine and a half acres was obtained, the Poorhouse was expanded and in 1880 agreement formalised between the 16 original members and ten new parishes that had, by then, joined the scheme. Fyvie, Turriff, Crimond, King Edward, Auchterless, Foveran, Aberdour, St Fergus, Forglen and Slains became members, but Peterhead still remained outside the scheme.[128] From 1887 Peterhead was allowed to rent beds at £2.10.0 a year, along with other parishes like Macduff and Gamrie not fully members of the Buchan Union.[129]

Thus there loomed over the little village of Maud a vast new construction housing up to 143 inmates. A community already developing as an animal-market centre at a railway junction was further expanded by its new role. To the village there were some benefits in this. The Poorhouse children attended the local school, and though punished from time to time for truanting, did not feature in the Headteacher's logbook as especially naughty. Supplying the Poorhouse with food brought business to Maud bakers, Maud craftsmen were needed to help maintain the building, its farm, and its equipment, Maud tailors ran up the suits in tweed or corduroy that were eventually supplied to the inmates and a Maud carpenter constructed coffins and organized the funerals of paupers. These inmates can be separated into several categories. In the early years the Poorhouse contained a considerable number of children. The institution's Punishment Book shows them fighting, swearing, stone throwing, abusing staff and pauper adults, 'going to Mintlaw instead of going to school' and 'leaving the House by night by scaling the walls, and roaming about the village'.[130] They were dealt with by being beaten. However the Board of Supervision frowned on the placing of children in the Poorhouse and, from 1886, most of them were boarded out.[131]

Some inmates were bluntly categorised as 'lunatic' poor. The first ten of these, when visited by an Inspector, seemed to him 'of a low type both mentally and physically'.[132] They were not, by any means, mostly people mentally enfeebled by old age. Of the 191 'lunatic' poor admitted 1869–1900 fifteen were over 70 years and seventeen between 60 and 70.[133] Almost all were drawn from the labouring classes – fishworkers, servants and vagrants, though one was a schoolmaster. The cause of their troubles was most commonly recorded as not known, though for several worry about money and 'loss of property' were noted down, others were thought to have deteriorated through hard drinking, and one had supposedly ruined his wits through sexual self-abuse. The number of 'lunatic' poor climbed steadily and were generally in the fifties between 1882 and 1894. Where a patient proved really incapable or even dangerous then he was removed to Aberdeen Asylum.

The remainder were 'ordinary' paupers of whom few details have survived. Those who fell ill were located in a separate ward, after 1882, and seven years later 'dissolute women' were also separated off; 'the complete isolation of this class is very important' noted the Committee who watched over the Poorhouse.[134] Of all the different groups it was the 'lunatic' poor who were the most costly to maintain, even though the sick received extra items of diet like eggs, port wine and whisky. Whereas the authorities made do with a pauper to look after the sick, the 'lunatic' poor needed staff care on a more costly basis. In 1886, for example, each ordinary pauper cost about two shillings a week, those who were sick three shillings, but the 'lunatic' poor each cost five and fourpence.[135]

In charge of the Poorhouse was a Governor and his wife who acted as Matron. They lived on the premises with free food, accommodation, fire and light and, by 1891, were being paid £80 and £35 respectively.[136] The low pay of the staff they employed led to a rapid turnover. In 30 years forty staff came and went, though some were dismissed for disrespect, incompetence or 'too great intimacy with the opposite sex'[137] and one simply left when he found he 'could not bear the idea of living among patients'.[138] The male staff wages climbed from £16 to £32 a year, women's from £10 to £18.

The Buchan Combination Poorhouse was, at first, a bleak place. Its patients shivered in winter under inadequate coverings, lying on the hair mattresses of beds that stood on bare board floors.[139] There were no books (other than a Bible and a couple of tracts) and no pictures on the walls. Affairs were gradually managed in a more sympathetic manner, especially when a new Governor and Matron arrived in 1875. The walls were painted, linoleum and scraps of carpet covered the floors, gifts of books came from local people, the beds were improved and covered more liberally with blankets. The lack of sheets on these beds did, in 1875, arouse adverse comment from a visiting Inspector, though he did admit 'the habit of the country people seems to be to sleep in the blankets without any sheets at all'.[140] Little treats began to be introduced for the children and the 'lunatic' patients. In particular, from 1873, some sort of summer outing to the countryside took place, to Strichen woods at first, then to Pitfour, until it became a regular event. On 7th July 1900 the Governor noted 'On this date all the patients and children had their annual picnic to Aden ... each and all had a very enjoyable day with music, dancing, games etc. There was abundance of food and aerated water supplied them and home was reached at 8 pm'.[141]

Visiting inspectors were generally satisfied the poor were adequately fed and clad. The Board of Supervision offered guidelines that suggested a diet built around broth, bread, potatoes, meal and milk, with meat for those working and extra items for the ill and for infants. Local people began to send rabbits and baskets of gooseberries and every Christmas, Maud Steam Bakery supplied a large cake. At one inspection time the dinner 'consisted of broth, cold meat and bread'. The Poorhouse's food purchases show it receiving quite a variety of goods including bread, cheese, marmalade, tea, sugar, coffee, barley, peas, codfish, beef, skink, suet, rice and tobacco.[142] Clothing at first was not adequate, when shawls were supplied to the women they were too thin for winter wear.[143] Boys in the Poorhouse were, by 1894, getting suits made at 18/5d a time for the workmanship, plus 2/2d for tweed cloth and 2/- for cord.[144] The men, by then, had both Sunday suits and working clothes. In 1900 men out working the land wore 'warm underclothing, a well-fitting shirt with a knitted jersey over it, a well-cut suit of clothes and a pair of neatly buttoned leggings. Many of them also wore woollen mittens.'[145] It pleased one Inspector to note the clothing was 'devoid of features of a specially institutional character'.[146]

By this time the Poorhouse authorities were well aware that providing food and clothing that was adequate not only mattered but was a way of occupying the inmates. This problem was not properly tackled at first, especially when poor weather stopped the regular country walks organized two or three times a week. But the farmland around the Poorhouse proved the answer for most of the men. They were set to work clearing, draining, filling in an old quarry, then planting vegetables and keeping pigs and cows.[147] The farm supplied the Poorhouse with all the potatoes it needed and some of its milk. It sold pigs and calves to butchers in Maud. When blacksmith or carpentry work was needed, or crops needed threshing then Maud people were hired for the work. Meanwhile the women worked inside, sewing and knitting, cleaning and washing, so that all who were fit to labour were usually employed. Perhaps it was the success of the Governor in this area of management that helped keep the running costs of the Buchan Poorhouse so consistently below those of the average for Scottish Poorhouses.

Inveruric

High Street, Strichen, looking north

Kincardine O'Neil

Alford

Appendix 1

Aberdeenshire communities in the nineteenth century

(Sources, O.S.A., N.S.A., F. H. Groome's Ordnance Gazeteer, the Imperial Gazeteer, census schedules)

	1790s	1801	1811	1821	1831	1841	1851	1861	1871	1881	1891	1901
Aboyne						260	187				341	561
Alford									482	529	535	634
Auchmill								500	642	2,196	2,448	2,231
Ballater					317			362	694	759	983	1,247
Bankhead									393	669	699	1,110
Boddam	192					460		550	803	1,117	1,110	800
Braemar						245		280	347	437	482	516
Broadsea	200					326		371	442	423	510	
Burnhaven						120		280	326	320		
Cairnbulg						406		427	496	459	461	569
Collieston				167	357			410	442	421	419	
Culter										195	346	1,068
Cuminestown	404					477	477	459	572	525	428	441
Ellon								823	811	1,037	1,254	1,527
Fetterangus					216	220		345	367	364	358	340
Fraserburgh	1,000						3,039	3,101	4,266	6,583	7,360	9,105
Garmond						226		230	268			
Gordon Place & Dyce								45	365	561	727	863
Huntly	2,000				2,585	2,731	3,131	3,448	3,570	3,519	3,760	4,136
Insch						220	316	411	533	579	567	610
Inverallochy						507		652	744	741	637	656
Inverurie	360	450		735	994	1,619	2,084	2,520	2,524	2,575	2,549	3,058
Kemnay									200	432	660	986
Kincardine O'Neil	100					288	300	190	227	220		
Kintore	228			312	402	464	476	568	659	661	686	789
Longside					316	384		447	574	474	453	417
Lumsden					243	233		478	507	519	501	487
Maud										343	377	575
Mintlaw					222	240		380	446	435	402	393
New Aberdour					300	376		543	628	642	620	583
Newburgh	170				450	393		541	570	645	654	600
New Byth	195				302		402	454	609	491	398	351
New Deer						322		475	643	755	746	739
New Leeds						203		240	269			
New Pitsligo						1,262	1,605	1,773	2,094	2,056	1,686	1,674
Old Deer					211			185	237			
Old Meldrum	783			1,000	1,004	1,102	1,579	1,553	1,494	1,321	1,197	
Pennan					180	168		240	289			
Peterhead	2,959	3,264	3,556	4,783	5,112	6,244	7,298	7,541	8,621	10,922	12,195	11,794
Pitmedden								180	249			
Pitullie and Sandhaven					200	200		230	399	585	526	617
Port Errol					48	51		190	210	493	490	681
Rhynie						240		349	494	442	445	476
Rosehearty	213				600	750	844	908	1,206	1,404	1,179	1,185
St Combs					291	305	462	533	614	565	530	

	1790s	1801	1811	1821	1831	1841	1851	1861	1871	1881	1891	1901
Stewartfield					573	614		751	647	675	557	412
Strichen	200					681		1,030	1,184	1,204	1,133	1,025
Tarland	150					350		316	269	374	389	367
Torphins											201	409
Turriff	701			922	1,136	1,309	1,693	1,843	2,277	2,304	2,341	2,273
Woodend									486	529	677	803

Appendix 2

Changing Occupations in Aberdeen County & City 1841 & 1901

Occupation	1841				1901			
	Whole County		City		Whole County		City	
	Male	Female	Male	Female	Male	Female	Male	Female
Professions								
Clergy (and nuns)	220		63		404	52	145	52
Law	175		138		612	1	492	1
Medicine	217		114		244	3	161	18
Midwife & Nurses	1	172		179	7	625	7	407
Teaching	426	239	87			502	1,450	252
Commercial								
Merchants					26		11	
Agents, Brokers	13		13		196	1	128	1
Salesmen					4	24	3	24
Commercial Travellers	9		7		543	2	497	2
Accountants	18		13		80		75	
Auctioneers	22		6		61		42	
Clerks	426	1	373	1	1,686	1,035	1,384	909
Bank Officials	31		14		387		183	
Insurance Officials	3		3		400	4	318	3
Travel								
Railway workers					1,688	15	1,061	8
Horse vehicles	1,503	3	280	1	3,264	2	2,223	1
Trams					134		133	
Seamen & boatmen	1,001		456		1,735	5	1,492	4
Dock & harbour workers					892		873	
Warehouse porters & messengers	159		152		1,773	300	1,693	300
Agriculture								
Farmers, graziers & family helpers	6,830	210	104	1	9,742	2,015	72	14
Agric. labourers	14,980	943	617	20	12,719	369	201	19
Foresters, gardeners	573		310		1,167	27	527	18
Fishing								
Fishermen	886	75	140	1	2,329	40	976	
Netmaker		66		2				
Mines & Quarries								
Coal merchants	11		4		134	1	98	1
Stone quarrier, cutters	287		84		3,484		2,275	

Occupation	1841 Whole County		City		1901 Whole County		City	
	Male	Female	Male	Female	Male	Female	Male	Female
Metals & Machines								
Millwrights	155		73		117		52	
Iron founders	153		149		489		432	
Brass founders	82				42		38	
Blacksmiths	1,288	1	534	1	1,643	5	711	1
Fitters, turners	27		23		530		522	
Boiler makers	73	1	72	1	229		221	
Tool, saw etc. makers	4		2		62	2	61	
Mailer	20		20		1		2	
Anchor & chainmaker	40		40		2		2	
Tinsmith, tinplate goods maker	99	1	87	1	462	14	386	11
Shipmaker, boat builder	322		264		915	3	772	3
Vehicle builders & wheelwrights	172		80		627		495	
Ironmonger	41		39		245	19	179	12
Building/Plasters	101		60		403		286	1
Bricklayers & labourers					10		10	
Carpenters	1,719	1	1,111		2,802		1,464	
Masons & labourers	1,297	2	499	22	2,976		1,781	
Tilers & slaters	149		88		468		258	
Painters & decorators ⎫	248	2	203	2	853	12	722	11
Plumbers ⎭					502	2	398	2
Railway labourers					82		53	
Road labourers					530		135	
Wood & furniture								
Cabinet makers ⎫	225	2	177	2	455	1	363	1
Upholsterers ⎭					198	67	187	65
Polishers					48	78	49	73
Carvers	15		12		110	4	106	4
Dealers	19		5		37	41	37	37
Sawyers	455	1	162	1	499		325	
Turners	90		66		83	2	75	2
Boxmakers					212	7	241	
Coopers	356	1	110	1	1,076		304	
Brick & tile etc. makers	47	1	37	1	54	2	44	2
Chemical oil, soap								
Chemists	116		86		335	10	204	7
Oil millers					59	1	62	1
Candle makers					44	2	42	2
Soap makers	3		3		62	1	60	1
Manure manuf.					35	1	19	
India Rubber workers					596	267	595	267
Skin, leather, hair feathers (tanners, furriers, curriers, saddlers, brush makers)	263	1	145	1	269	28	148	28

	1841				1901			
	Whole County		City		Whole County		City	
Occupation	Male	Female	Male	Female	Male	Female	Male	Female
Paper								
Papermaker	85	88	9	14	938	1,197	222	609
Stationery manuf. & Envelope					25	244	23	244
Printer	110	1	104		560	244	482	240
Bookbinder ⎫					59	130	56	130
Bookseller ⎬	151	6	108	6	116	67	95	57
publisher ⎭								
Lithographers	4		4		141	45	127	48
Textiles								
Cotton – carding ⎫					1	26	2	26
spinning ⎪					5	236	5	240
weaving ⎬	325	1,120	274	1,088	5	44	5	44
other ⎭					29	173	29	235
Flax, linen manuf.	1,773	1,939	1,491	1,753	182	867	179	871
Wool – sorting ⎫					15	13	10	12
combing ⎪	380	425	192	205	22	13	5	5
spinning ⎬					47	145	21	100
weaving ⎭					81	408	19	323
Spinner (not specified)	4	421	2	270				
(other)	5	30	4	30	213	313	176	279
Weaver (not specified)	307	100	151	91				
Hemp & jute					96	506	94	506
Canvas & sailcloth	65		50		84	182	82	162
Hosiery manuf.	13	1,317	3	103	26	832	23	550
Carpet & mixed cloth makers	176	10	175	8	26	154	27	52
Bleachers		1	1		35	14	35	14
Printers	2	1	2		2	1	2	1
Dyers	82	3	52	2	58	20	43	20
Drapers	62	2	47		768	503	477	419
Rope maker	206	18	178	10	177	30	169	32
Dress								
Hat, bonnet, makers	134	131	112	15	36	20	34	20
Tailors, milliners	1,275	3	495	2	1,736	714	865	349
Clothiers, outfitters	80	7	55	4	151	16	120	15
Shirtmakers, seamsters	1	146	1	81	3	332	3	294
Boot & Shoemakers	1,984	49	827	40	1,191	56	519	36
Wigmakers, hairdressers	84	1	73	1	202	9	164	9
Dressmakers	3	806	2	477		3,045		1,786
Food, drink etc.								
Dairymen etc.	16	37	16	11	138	112	82	65
Provision curers	2				197	687	110	530
Butchers	250	6	170		753	10	487	7
Fish curers	46	5	10	4	303	952	285	913
Fishmongers, poulterers		3		2	192	129	196	98
Bakery dealers					165	327	146	240
Millers	367	12	31	9	424	10	90	2
Corn, seed dealers	25		11		144	7	69	6
Bakers, bread etc.	414	58	323	22	1,163	94	591	91

Occupation	1841				1901			
	Whole County		City		Whole County		City	
	Male	Female	Male	Female	Male	Female	Male	Female
Grocers	300	74	191	32	1,593	599	970	346
Greengrocers	6	3	4	2	78	127	67	114
Ginger beer & mineral water	3		3		77	80	59	71
Brewers	58		37		84	6	46	4
Distillers	36		16		66	1	32	1
Inns, eating houses (all staff)	1	130	1	107	591	915·	445	710
Gas, water etc.								
Gas works	19		16		284		255	
Waterworks					30		21	
Electricity					9		10	
Drainage					47		33	
Scavengers	6		6		126		108	
General etc.								
Animal salesmen	100		6		177	1	83	1
Drovers	17				19		16	
Chimney sweeps	16		15		27		26	
Bone & horn workers	186	35	184	35	52	55	52	55
Pawnbrokers	4		4		33	18	33	12
Pedlar, Costermongers & Street sellers	89	56	31	13	274	126	138	70
General Labourers	2,470	106	1,402	9	3,373		1,980	
Engine drivers, stokers					566		366	
Domestic								
Indoor servant } outdoor servant }	1,117	13,314	218	3,254	196 / 1,060	11,900 / 3	88 / 132	4,246
Caretakers, park keepers					112	127	82	78
Laundry & washing		220		145	10	888	11	573
Charwomen						618		496
Hospital & mstie[n] service					90	221	73	173

Source, Census returns of 1841 and 1901

Appendix 3

Aberdeenshire Carriers in 1825

(Source, Pigot & Co.'s New Commercial Directory of Scotland for 1825–6. Manchester 1826)

Place of Origin	Destination	Number of Carriers	Number of journeys
Aboyne	Aberdeen	1	once a week
Aberdour	,,	1	,, ,, ,,
Abergeldy	,,	1	,, ,, ,,
Alford	,,	2	,, ,, ,, each
Auchmacoy	,,	1	,, ,, ,,
Auchterless	,,	3	,, ,, ,, ,,
Ballater	,,	2	,, ,, ,, ,,
Banchory	,,	3	,, ,, ,, ,,
Braemar	,,	1	,, ,, ,,
Birse	,,	1	,, ,, ,,
Bremner	,,	1	,, ,, ,,
Crathie	,,	1	,, ,, fortnight
Cuminestown	,,	1	,, ,, week
Crichie	,,	1	,, ,, ,,
Cruden	,,	1	,, ,, ,,
Culsamond	,,	1	,, ,, ,,
Castle Forbes	,,	1	,, ,, ,,
Collieston	,,	1	,, ,, ,,
Daviot	,,	1	'occasionally'
Drumlithie	,,	1	once a week
Drum	,,	1	,, ,, ,,
Ellon	,,	4	3 once a week / 1 twice a week
Echt	,,	1	once a week
Fraserburgh	,,	1	,, ,, ,,
Fraserburgh	Peterhead	1	,, ,, ,,
Foggieloan	Aberdeen	4	,, ,, ,, each
Forgue	,,	1	,, ,, ,,
Fyvie	,,	1	,, ,, ,,
Glenbuchet	,,	1	,, ,, ,,
Glengairn	,,	1	,, ,, ,,
Huntly	,,	4	,, ,, ,, ,,
Huntly	Banff	1	,, ,, ,,
Inverurie	,,	2	,, ,, ,, ,,
Insch	,,	2	,, ,, ,, ,,
Kildrummy	,,	1	,, ,, ,,
Kincardine O'Neil	,,	3	,, ,, ,, ,,

Place of Origin	Destination	Number of Carriers	Number of journeys
Kintore	,,	1	,, ,, ,,
Kinmundy	,,	1	,, ,, ,,
Kemnay	,,	1	,, ,, ,,
Kennethmont	Aberdeen	1	'uncertain'
Lonmay	,,	1	once a week
Leith Hall	,,	1	,, ,, ,,
Longside	,,	1	,, ,, ,,
Leslie	,,	1	,, ,, ,,
Monymusk	,,	2	,, ,, ,, each
Methlick	,,	1	,, ,, ,,
New Deer	,,	3	,, ,, ,, ,,
New Byth	,,	1	,, ,, ,,
New Pitsligo	,,	1	,, ,, ,,
Old Meldrum	,,	2	one once a week once twice a week
Old Deer	,,	2	once a week each
Peterhead	,,	1	twice a week
Rhynie	,,	2	one once a week one 'uncertain'
Strichen	,,	1	once a week
Strichen	Peterhead	1	,, ,, ,,
Strathdon	Aberdeen	4	,, ,, ,, each
Stewartfield	,,	1	,, ,, ,,
St. Fergus	,,	1	,, ,, ,,
Tarves	,,	2	,, ,, ,, ,,
Turriff	,,	2	,, ,, ,, ,,
Tullich	,,	1	,, ,, ,,
Tarland	,,	5	,, ,, ,, ,,

Appendix 4

Housing and Population, 1901

(Source 1901 Census of Scotland pp. 31–3 and 267,8. Glasgow 1901)

Place (Burghs)	Families	Inhabited Houses	Population	Rooms with Windows	Persons to a Room
Ellon	322	322	1,527	1,388	1.10
Fraserburgh	1,831	1,024	8,998	5,379	1.67
Ballater	269	266	1,247	1,435	0.86
Huntly	975	956	4,136	3,930	1.05
Inverurie	708	551	3,058	2,580	1.18
Kintore	196	189	789	704	1.12
Peterhead	2,561	2,499	11,763	8,086	1.45
Rosehearty	321	258	1,185	815	1.45
Turriff	583	561	2,273	2,219	1.02
Old Meldrum	308	308	1,197	1,197	1.01
(Villages)					
Alford	139	130	634	572	1.10
Bankhead	245	245	1,110	721	1.53
Boddam	187	187	800	624	1.28
Braemar	122	120	516	936	0.55
Cairnbulg	126	118	569	255	2.23
Aboyne	122	122	561	617	0.90
Culter	239	239	1,068	819	1.30
Cuminestown	127	123	441	369	1.19
Dyce	193	160	863	715	1.20
Fetterangus	100	100	340	253	1.34
Insch	201	155	610	694	0.87
Inverallochy	151	138	656	304	2.15
Kemnay	220	220	986	784	1.25
Longside	115	108	417	479	0.87
Lumsden	130	115	487	439	1.10
Maud	133	115	575	507	1.13
Mintlaw	108	108	393	334	1.17
New Aberdour	158	154	583	398	
Newburgh	143	143	600	485	1.23
New Byth	109	107	351	267	1.31
New Deer	199	199	739	713	1.03
New Pitsligo	450	443	1,674	1,166	1.43
Pitullie and Sandhaven	145	103	617	462	1.33
Port Errol	147	115	681	1,425	0.47
Rhynie	108	108	476	420	1.13

Place (Burghs)	Families	Inhabited Houses	Population	Rooms with Windows	Persons to a Room
St Combs	312	258	1,185	815	1.45
Stuartfield	131	125	530	279	1.89
Strichen	301	274	1,025	896	1.14
Tarland	87	71	367	318	1.15
Torphins	94	91	409	534	0.76
Woodend	181	180	803	599	1.34

Scottish average for towns (i.e. places of 2,000 plus) 4.52 persons to a family 1.08 families to a house 4.90 persons to a house 1.26 persons to a room. (pp. XXVI).

Aberdeen County—					
Towns	39,675	37,542	177,280	126,404	
Villages	6,442	5,083	26,238	23,239	
Rural	19,685	19,369	100,921	88,923	
(p. 262)					

Thus for Aberdeen County 4.63 per family 1.04 families to a house 4.83 persons to a house 1.28 persons to a room. (p. XXVI)

Appendix 5

The Buchan Combination Poorhouse

(Source, Annual Reports of the Board of Supervision for the Relief of Poor in Scotland, Vols 1868–94 Edinburgh)

Year	Ordinary poor	'Lunatic' poor	Average weekly cost per head – for food, fuel, clothes etc. for ordinary poor	
			In Buchan	Scottish average
Jan 1896	36	11	4/4	3/0$\frac{1}{2}$
1870	31	21	2/2$\frac{3}{4}$	2/11$\frac{3}{4}$
1871	38	20	1/11	2/11
1872	31	24	2/–	3/0$\frac{3}{4}$
1873	30	26	1/11$\frac{11}{13}$	3/5
1874	50	22	2/2$\frac{1}{2}$	3/5$\frac{19}{24}$
1875	45	21	2/2	3/4$\frac{5}{6}$
1876	61	24	2/4$\frac{1}{2}$	3/5
1877	73	25	2/3$\frac{3}{4}$	3/4$\frac{3}{4}$
1878	59	28	2/8	3/4$\frac{8}{31}$
1879	54	24	2/8$\frac{1}{4}$	3/2
1880	68	32	2/5$\frac{1}{30}$	2/11$\frac{1}{4}$
1881	73	49	2/4$\frac{1}{2}$	3/0$\frac{1}{4}$
1882	71	54	3/10$\frac{1}{2}$	4/11
1883	68	54	3/9$\frac{3}{4}$	4/11$\frac{1}{2}$
1884	65	57	3/8$\frac{1}{4}$	4/11$\frac{1}{4}$
1885	67	52	3/6$\frac{1}{2}$	4/6$\frac{1}{2}$
1886	83	54	2/5$\frac{5}{8}$	3/1$\frac{3}{4}$
1887	85	51	3/2	4/2$\frac{3}{4}$
1888	80	52	2/11$\frac{1}{2}$	4/1$\frac{3}{4}$
1889	86	52	3/10	4/2
1890	91	52	3/5	4/3$\frac{1}{2}$
1891	83	52	3/3$\frac{7}{12}$	4/4$\frac{3}{4}$
1892	70	52	3/1$\frac{3}{4}$	4/5$\frac{1}{2}$
1893	58	52	4/0$\frac{1}{4}$	4/5
1894	71	52	3/1$\frac{3}{4}$	4/7$\frac{3}{4}$

Expenditure on the 'lunatic' poor, where shown, ran at higher figures e.g. 1885 Buchan 5/9$\frac{3}{4}$, Scottish average 8/6: 1894 – Buchan 6/4$\frac{1}{2}$, Scottish average 8/3$\frac{3}{4}$.

Appendix 6

The effect of the Buchan Combination Poorhouse
(Source, Banffshire Journal 10–1–1888)

Parish	Year of joining	No. of poor in May of Year preceding joining	No. of poor May 1887	Ratio to population	
				At 1st date	At 2nd date
Aberdour	1872	129	17	16.8	124.9
New Deer	1868	130	55	33.7	88.6
Logie Buchan	1868	16	12	47.6	63.9
Turriff	1872	197	71	22.0	61.1
Lonmay	1868	76	48	28.1	49.9
Slains	1873	52	26	26.0	48.3
Fyvie	1869	209	102	20.8	43.1
Methlick	1868	105	48	20.5	42.9
Rathen	1868	125	66	20.4	42.8
Fraserburgh	1868	287	182	15.7	41.7
Pitsligo	1868	96	63	19.6	41.0
Tyrie	1868	179	84	17.0	40.3
Cruden	1868	150	86	18.2	40.0
King Edward	1871	172	79	16.5	38.8
Udny	1868	55	13	30.3	38.0
Monquhitter	1868	126	78	20.3	35.8
Strichen	1868	156	66	15.7	35.5
Ellon	1868	206	108	19.0	34.2
Tarves	1868	107	77	26.3	33.2
Crimond	1869	25	25	35.7	33.2
Auchterless	1871	86	67	23.3	32.0
Foveran	1872	122	69	15.5	29.5
Forglen	1872	39	26	20.0	28.6
Old Deer	1868	334	191	15.4	26.7
St Fergus	1872	10	59	22.9	25.8
Longside	1868	222	126	13.5	25.5

All Aberdeenshire in 1887 – 1 pauper to 39.4 people.
All Scotland in 1887 – 1 pauper to 42.86 people.

The 18th century tollbooth, Inverurie.
A very old photograph, the building was demolished in 1868.

Part II

A COUNTRY COMMUNITY –
INVERURIE

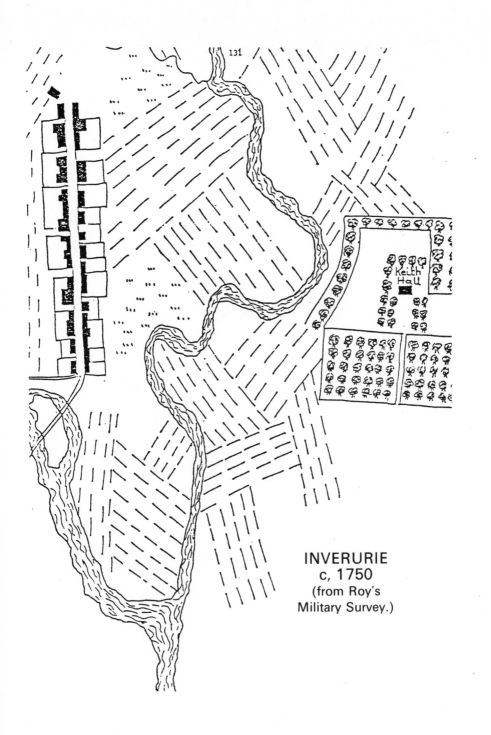

131

INVERURIE
c, 1750
(from Roy's
Military Survey.)

INVERURY 1796
(Part of 'Plan of the intended navigable
canal from the Harbour of Aberdeen
to the Bridge over the River Don at Inverury')

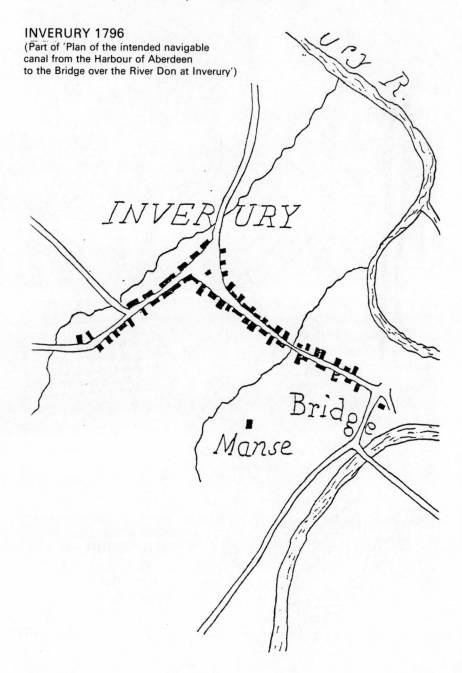

Chapter One

UNIMPROVED INVERURIE

During the eighteenth century the royal burgh of Inverurie[1] was but a small undistinguished community, a 'trifling place'[2] lying along a low peninsula of land hemmed in on two sides by the Rivers Don and Urie. In the late seventeenth century 180 people are listed in the Poll tax as burgh inhabitants, providing the immediate locality with religious, medical and educational services and craft skills in weaving, tailoring, shoe-making, smith and wright work.[3] The Poll tax was not however a com-plete count. Many under sixteens were omitted. Inverurie occupied a position whose importance could be seen in the decaying remains of the once formidable earthworks of the motte and bailey structure known as 'The Bass'. The community lay by a key river-crossing on the main Inverness–Aberdeen route and at the heart of the farming area of the Garioch.

During the eighteenth century the burgh's population rose to 450 in 1801, yet its role still seems to have been confined to serving a small locality; the rivers it guarded were unbridged till the very late end of the century in the case of the Don, and the early nineteenth century as far as the Urie was concerned. A traveller of 1792 noted 'It has no trade nor any manufactures, as the work of a few common craftsmen occupied on the immediate business of the inhabitants will not claim that title'.[4] Nor had the occupations of the inhabitants changed greatly since the late seven-teenth century. Men worked as weavers, shoemakers, tailors, cart and square wrights and blacksmiths whilst their womenfolk earned 1/6 to 2/- a week knitting stockings for Aberdeen employers.[5] A similar picture of employment could be painted for many of the larger rural townships. The burgh craftsmen owned small plots of land of between one and six acres that stretched back from their roadside dwellings and which they used for growing food. At least by 1790 Inverurie people could make their way to Aberdeen along an improved road. The traders of the early eighteenth century had used creels fastened upon the backs of ponies to shift their goods: the travellers of the 1790s were able too to use horse-drawn carts.[6] Improvements at the steepest obstacle, Tyrebagger Hill, must have been especially welcome. Another glimpse of a slowly improv-ing economy was provided by an inn[7] sufficiently respectable to attract not only the custom of travellers, but of visitors from Aberdeen who came to Inverurie to enjoy shooting and fishing.[8]

Though growth took place in eighteenth century Inverurie, it proceeded slowly, dragged back by the sluggish pace of agricultural change in the area and by the poor state of the transport network. Until the Don was finally bridged in 1791 Inverurie suffered, being cut off from Aberdeen when the fording of the river became too difficult. Even the most determined improver would have found it hard to obtain large supplies of fertilizer and to export great quantities of produce for sale. The town's fuel problems were increasingly serious, for nearby peat supplies were exhausted and coal sold in Aberdeen at 4/6 a boll cost 7/- by the time it had reached Inverurie.[9] The parish of Inverurie lacked an adequate peat moss and the inhabitants found getting peat from a distance took up their time for a great part of the summer when they might have been more profitably employed.[10] Many of the local tenants were not, however, determined improvers; the motto of most (according to one contemporary) was 'No Change of Plans'.[11] Few turnips or grasses were grown, the main crop of oats and bere (which battled for survival with wild oats) were sown on the rigs that had been churned up by the old ox-drawn heavy wooden ploughs. Many farmers paid rents in kind, and took their grain for processing to the town's meal-mill at Ardtannies. There they were liable for dues and services to the miller that included quite onerous work cleaning and repairing the mill lead.[12] The Garioch produced insufficient wealth and too small a surplus to enable Inverurie to play a big role as a service centre. The town's inhabitants were, in any case, according to James Anderson (author of the first *Agricultural Survey of Aberdeenshire*) far too interested in 'the dissipation that too much prevails about electioneering and the hopes of thus acquiring a pittance without proper exertion'.[13]

Inverurie's self-perpetuating council, composed of provost, dean of guild, three baillies and three councillors,[14] were far from prepared to lead and organise economic and social expansion, were it to come. The townspeople lived in low thatched properties, fetching their water from river, burn or well and dumping refuse outside their doors.[15] The most imposing buildings Inverurie possessed were probably the late eighteenth century kirk and the small tollbooth where council meetings took place. Were farming improvement to speed up and transport conditions to improve, Inverurie was well sited for growth, but the burgh's leadership and services required considerable improvement if such growth were to be adequately managed.

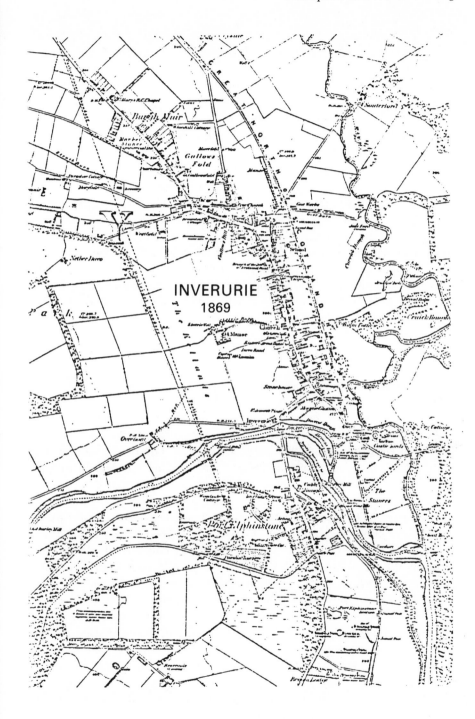

INVERURIE
1869

Chapter Two

FACTORS AFFECTING INVERURIE'S
GROWTH IN THE NINETEENTH CENTURY

Between 1801 and 1901 the population of Inverurie increased from 450 to 3,058. The pace of change was especially rapid in the earlier part of the period, rising from 360 inhabitants noted as living in the burgh in the 1790s to 1,619 by 1841. Behind this expansion lay a revolution in transport, a dramatic quickening of agricultural change in the surrounding Garioch as well as the wider factors of increased population, increased economic production and increased wealth that contributed to change in Scotland. Inverurie's role was able to expand, providing more services to a bigger locality.

The Don Bridge

One of the most important of improvements required to enable Inverurie to exploit its site was the bridging of the Don. The combined force of the Don and Urie made crossing tricky, and sometimes impossible. The solution came in 1791 at a time when bridge-building was becoming a common sight in Aberdeenshire communities. The new bridge was a very substantial structure consisting of three arches, the middle arch 65 feet wide, the other two 55 feet wide.[1] Drawings of the construction show it to have been sizeable, sturdy and elegant and thus by no means cheap to construct.[2] The Earl of Kintore took the lead in opening a subscription list to all whose economic interests would be served by a safe river crossing.[3] The Earl also pressed the bridge's cause upon Aberdeen, sending the city's Provost a letter 'respecting a plan which his Lordship had set on foot with the approbation of some other Noblemen and Gentlemen for building a bridge over Don and another over Ury near to the town of Inverury and desiring the aid of the Town of Aberdeen in the execution of the proposed plan . . . they are unanimously of opinion that both the bridges proposed to be built will be of very great public utility to this country in general and to the Town and Community of Aberdeen in particular'.[4]

Aberdeen clearly agreed that their interests would be served by spanning the Don for they dug into the fund set aside for maintaining the

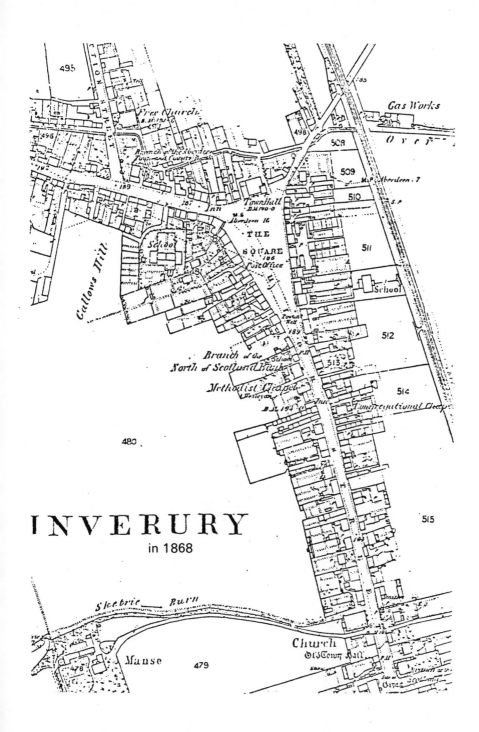

INVERURY

in 1868

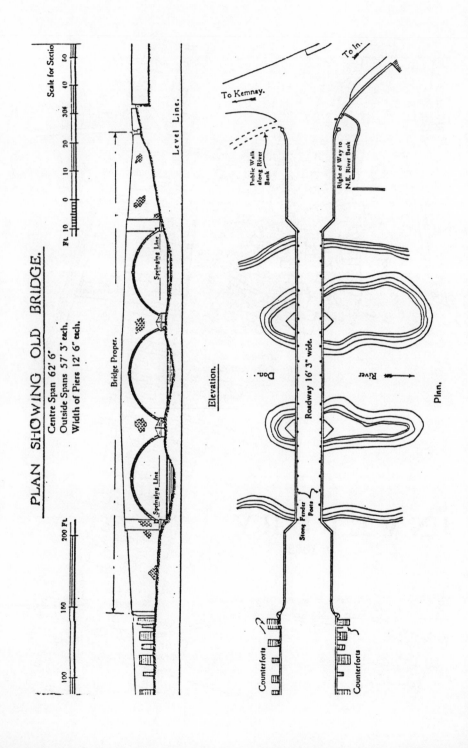

PLAN SHOWING OLD BRIDGE.

Centre Span 62' 6'
Outside Spans 57' 3" each,
Width of Piers 12' 6" each,

Scale for Section

Bridge Proper.

Springing Line

Springing Line

Level Line.

Elevation.

To Kemnay.

To In.

Public Walk along River Bank

Right of Way to N.E. River Bank

Don.

River

Roadway 16' 3" wide.

Stone Fender Posts

Counterforts

Counterforts

Plan.

old (and now increasingly inadequate) Brig of Balgownie that carried the main road north over the Don near its mouth. To the 200 guineas[5] thus added to the voluntary subscriptions was added a further sum extracted in 1789 from the Convention of Royal Burghs. Once more the Earl of Kintore pressed the case, urging that the project would immensely stimulate trade and manufactures which were being held back by the absence of bridges over the Rivers.[6] The delegates considered whether such a bridge might not have a toll system operating upon it, only to reject the idea since the grounds in the vicinity of the bridges were unenclosed and the rivers could be forded save when swelled by heavy rains and snows; thus a toll bar would be easily evaded and local people, unable or unwilling to pay these unaccustomed tolls, would be very likely to continue trying to ford the river in order to avoid payment.[7] The Convention provided a further £200 bringing the fund close to the £2,000 it was reckoned the bridge would cost.[8]

By the time this final amount was forthcoming, the Bridge Committee had already plunged into the scheme, advertising in the press for plans and estimates.[9] Would-be builders were directed to a Dr William Thom, an Aberdeen lawyer, who was responsible for providing details of the site and of quarries where stones could be found.[10] A Banff mason, James Robertson, won the contract and set to work in the summer of 1789. On June 29th, the Aberdeen Journal was able to report

> Last Saturday the foundation stone of the bridge to be built over the River Don at Inverury was laid by the Rt Hon the Earl of Kintore attended by several gentlemen of the County, a deputation from the magistrates and councils of Aberdeen, Banff, Kintore and Inverury . . . This work, of so much utility to the public is now to be carried on with the utmost exertion and a very large quantity of stones and other materials are collected upon the spot and ready to be employed in the immediate execution of the bridge.

For two years workmen laboured to complete the task; subsequent Inverurie leaders were in no doubt as to its value, however, as a great impetus to trade. Full use of the bridge depended on the adequacy of the roads leading to it. Here a major change was under way.

The turnpike road

On September 1st, 1789, seven years after the opening of the Don Bridge, a meeting was called of those interested in overhauling the Aberdeen to Inverurie road. Those attending were agreed the project was vital to the improvement of the interior of Aberdeenshire and were united in denouncing the current condition of the road.[11] Thomas Leys, the meeting's president, whose Glasgoforest estates lay along the proposed route, observed that 'from the present route of the Inverury road every agricultural improvement in that quarter must be very much retarded; while on the other hand if the Turnpike road were executed those improvements ... would proceed with a degree of rapidity hitherto unexampled in this county'.[12]

The raising of money by subscriptions produced over £6,000. The broad scatter of subscribers' residences indicated how widespread were the hopes pinned on the Inverurie turnpike. Inverurie burgh put up £50, the Earl of Kintore £300, other subscribers came either from Aberdeen, from owners of lands along the route of the proposed road or, in many cases, from people living beyond Aberdeen. Aberdeen's fourteen subscribers put up £2,000, an amount greater than that found by inhabitants along the route from the city through Woodside, over the lower slopes of Tyrebagger Hill and on to Kintore. The people dwelling in this section raised just over £1,500. But the greatest amount – £2,233 – came from people living beyond Inverurie. They were motivated both by the direct benefits of the road and by the expectation that it would be but the first stage of a network of further roads opening up the interior of the area. Thus a cluster of contributors came from the Insch area, another group from Kemnay parish, and yet more from the area between Inverurie and Huntly.

The bulk of the contributions came from landowners and farmers. Two millers raised £65, four lawyers found £375, two clergy provided £75 and six merchants raised £950. The landowners contributions ranged from sizeable sums like Thomas Leys' £500 and Robert Harvey of Braco's similar amount to modest amounts like the £20s provided by William McKnight of Nether Coullie and Benjamin Lumsden of Boghead.[13] The subscribers shared with their president the belief with which many turnpike trust contributors comforted themselves – that their venture would prove sufficiently profitable to yield tolls that would enable them to recover their subscriptions with interest.[14] The Inverurie road did indeed prove to be that rarity in Aberdeenshire, a turnpike trust that showed a profit.[15] Its financial success and the wide geographical spread of subscribers both indicate one of the attributes that enabled Inverurie to expand – it was a focal point for a wide area around it.

Once £700 had been raised work began upon creating a route agreed only after a degree of dispute as different subscribers sought to locate the road to suit their own particular interests. The contractors marked a 40 foot route upon the centre of which was to run a road surface sixteen feet wide from Aberdeen to Bucksburn, thereafter fourteen feet on as far as

Inverurie. Presumably the Trust expected an especially busy bustle of traffic in and around the City. The road itself was to have a curved surface 'fourteen inches deep in the middle tapering to twelve inches at the sides, the one half at the bottom to be broke to the size of a man's fist and the remaining half to that of an ordinary hen's egg'[16] on the first stretch of road. The Bucksburn-Inverurie section's metal depth was to be two inches shallower. At either side of the road there was to be a water ditch.[17]

By 1800 the road builders had completed the route to Inverurie and four years later had pushed on as far as Huntly. In 1839 a branch road opened extending from Inverurie eastwards to Forgue. The burgh lay conveniently placed for traffic coming from the west along turnpikes running up to Strathdon. A bridge spanned the Urie, in 1810. The traffic that began to flow upon the roads soon brought to the Trustees the worry of frequent repairs. In 1823 their engineer complained that the road through Inverurie was always in a bad state in rainy weather.[18] Road repairs were not always competently executed, drains became choked, holes appeared and there were even instances of 'a great deal of dung and black earth laid on the road near the Bridge put there by persons who ought to know better'.[19]

Road users complained of excessively high tolls. Tenants around Inverurie wishing to take produce in carts to Aberdeen, grumbled so effectively of their hardships that they were exempted from paying tolls twice on journeys to and from Aberdeen provided they returned from Aberdeen within twenty four hours after passing the toll bar at Kittybrewster.[20]

Despite all these difficulties the turnpikes seem to have greatly encouraged the economy of the area served by Inverurie. The passage of wheeled vehicles was eased so that carts could carry heavier loads and passenger vehicles could easily move at reasonable speeds. In 1819 on April 6th the Trustees received a memorial from a group of businessmen 'with the object of establishing a daily post coach for the conveyance of passengers and parcels from Aberdeen to Inverness ... The coach shall be drawn by four horses, to start at six in the morning ... to Aberdeen and on the same hour another proceeds from Inverness, both of which will reach their places of destination between eleven and twelve at night'.[21] By the time that the 1837 edition of Pigot's Directory was compiled Inverurie was being served daily by coaches including 'The Royal Mail', 'The Defiance', 'The Banks of Ury', 'The Tally Ho' and 'The Highland Lass'. Two carriers James Thompson and James Stephen travelled to Aberdeen, the former twice weekly and the latter once.[22] The regular postal services to Inverurie were marred by the tedious frequency with which letters were despatched instead to Inverary. Inverurie inns benefited from the increased custom that the coaches provided. 'The Mail' stopped so that its passengers could breakfast in the town (the New Inn on the High Street made a speciality of serving travellers)[23] and local shopkeepers, saddlers and blacksmiths all benefited from the growth of horse-drawn traffic. One of the coaching services was, however, in the hands of a rather eccentric proprietor who also drove his vehicle. With 'Geordie' Gray in charge 'The Banks of Ury' might whizz by people waiting to be picked up along the way. Appalled passengers might even observe their coachman driving with his back to the horses.[24] The undoubted benefits of turnpikes assisted the expansion of a number of communities of which Inverurie was but one; a key factor in the special success of Inverurie was the arrival of another means of transport – the canal.

The canal

Whilst the turnpike road was being built workmen were also busy with the far more onerous task of constructing a canal from Aberdeen to Inverurie. An Act allowing the Canal Company to proceed passed Parliament in the midst of the emotional canal-mania of the 1790s. The selection of Inverurie as the objective of the canal was shaped by the North East's geography as well as by the hope of opening up Garioch farmland and the quarries of the area; much of Aberdeen's western hinterland was far too hilly for canal works to be seriously contemplated in that direction. The canal engineers had to approach Inverurie by a route that differed from the one followed by the turnpike. The massive obstacle of Tyrebagger Hill was avoided by a wide arc that meant the two routes diverged until Kintore was reached.

Various difficulties attended the construction of the waterway, but eventually, in June 1805, the Aberdeen Journal was able to report the formal opening when 'The Committee of management assembled at the basin at Inverurie attended by the Provost, magistrates, minister and other inhabitants of that burgh who congratulated them on the completion of an undertaking which must lend much to the improvement of that and other parts of the County'.[25] The newspaper went on, in a later issue, to stress the canal's value in shifting bulky produce, especially coal and manure.[26] But the Turnpike Trust foresaw that, for them, the canal would produce problems. The trade that flowed upon the Canal would inevitably reduce the traffic on the turnpike and diminish the revenue from the tolls.[27] The ease with which bulky goods could be shifted down the canal meant that at last Inverurie householders, whose Kemnay peat moss was near exhaustion, could look elsewhere for fuel. For townspeople with new opportunities for profit opening up, freedom from the burden of cutting, drying and shifting peat must have been very welcome. It did not entirely root out peat fires, however. In the 1830s some townspeople were obtaining this fuel from the Moss of Fetternear which belonged to the burgh; cart loads of peats from here were being sold at one shilling and sixpence a time.[28] The canal brought not only fuel but fertilizers and house-building materials to the town and took away the produce of farmland and quarry. In 1902 Provost Jackson recalled that the canal's heyday had brought to the town 'great strings of carts from all quarters laden with grain to be exchanged at the canal head for coals, lime, manures and feeding stuffs, with generally a goodly quantity of the current coin of the realm, a portion of which would find its way to the tills of the Inverurie merchants'.[29]

In fact the canal could not reach into the heart of the town. The barrier formed by the River Don blocked its path and the terminus of the waterway thus fell short of Inverurie at a place newly-named after one of the canal's prime instigators, Robert Elphinstone, Laird of Logie. Port Elphinstone expanded from consisting of but one house in 1805 to a community where well over a hundred people lived in 1842.

Inverurie inhabitants were now offered an alternative method of transporting themselves as well as their goods to Aberdeen. From 1807 a

Articles transported on the canal (in tons)
Source N.S.A. XII p.p. 683–4

1831		1836		1840	
Coal	1731⅓	Coal	3199¾	Coal	4956½
Lime	2526	Lime	4086	Lime	3938¼
Dung	355¼	Dung	188½	Dung	379
Stones	3711	Stones	142	Stones	51¾
Slates	700	Slates	358¼	Slates	26¾
Bricks and tiles	29¾	Bricks and tiles	69¼	Bricks and tiles	94
Bark	105	Bark	106	Bark	56½
Iron	1	Iron	9	Metal	42¼
Meal	51	Meal	149½	Meal	1124¾
Wheat	2	Wheat	118½	Whisky	8¾
Flour	12	Flour	49	Flour	53
Oats and bear	1104	Oats and bear	6542¾	Oats and bear	4497½
Wood	4⅓	Wood	322¼	Wood	1098¼
Goods	21½	Goods	100	Goods	16
		Bones	498¾	Bones	1349¾
		Salt	11	Salt	54¾
		Potatoes	11¼	Potatoes	7½
				Sand	5¾
				Animals	43¼

passenger boat service operated as far as Kittybrewster (where a suc-
cession of locks carrying the canal down to the harbour made travel by
water so slow as to be pointless for passengers). The two vessels that plied
the canal were each dragged along by a single horse that trotted along
the towpath. In 1840 one of these vessels alone carried 4,765 passengers.[30] Fares of two shillings or one and six were charged for the four hour
trip but there were advantages to offset the tedium. The boat slid
smoothly along 'and being licensed for the sale of porter and ales was
frequently tenanted by parties making a day's outing who spent the
hours chiefly in playing whist'.[31] Travellers who had plodded into
Inverurie from the countryside and had endured enough of horse-drawn
transport, also favoured the 'fly' boats.

Although farming-improvement was under way before the canal was
constructed (liming of land being actively pursued on a limited scale, for
instance[32]), the compiler of the 1811 Agricultural Survey of Aberdeenshire was convinced that the new waterway was the main reason why
the Garioch countryside he observed was being so actively improved.[33]
From his vantage point in 1842 the Rev. Robert Lessel agreed with this
verdict writing that 'the main cause of the increase and prosperity of
Inverurie is without question the Aberdeen Canal which has conferred
on it many of the advantages of a sea-port'.[34] Great quantities of lime
flowed up the canal – over 4,000 tons were carried in 1836, and bones too
(1,349 tons in 1840) helped to improve the land. Nearly 5,000 tons of coal
were shifted in 1840, along with stones, slates, bricks and tiles and
timber.[35] The figures recorded in the New Statistical Account suggest a
spurt of house-improvement with slated roofs being fitted. By 1840
Foudland slates were supplying Inverurie house roofs and did not need
canal transportation. There was a switch from shifting oats from
Inverurie towards despatching the same produce in its processed form.
This latter point may well be the consequence of the enterprise of a
Crichie farmer, Thomas Tait, who opened up a grain-milling business by
the canal terminus. Tait owned his own barges and even contrived to fit
them with lights.[36] His firm was but one of several attracted to Port
Elphinstone. The Aberdeen Commercial Company established a grain
depot and bought coal and lime as return cargoes. The Aberdeen Lime
Company had a representative based at the canal terminus. Inverurie
people became used to seeing, trundling through their town, cartloads of
grain, coal, lime, bones, dung and building materials. The farm servants
driving the carts bought food and drink in Inverurie and Port
Elphinstone. By 1842 there were two saw mills at Port Elphinstone, one
steam-powered and the other water-driven, as well as wood yards and
storehouses.[37]

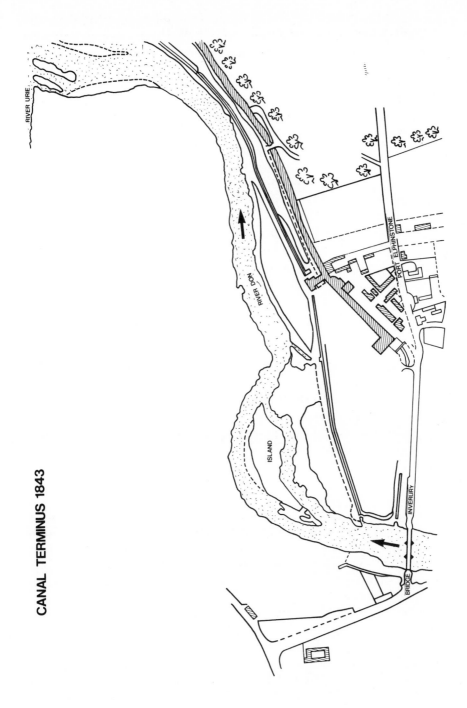

CANAL TERMINUS 1843

When the canal went out of business a number of these enterprises promptly shifted from the canal terminus into Inverurie so as to be close to the railway station. Port Elphinstone lay in Kintore parish, but Inverurie regarded its welfare with concern. When the Gordonsmill's Turnpike Trustees planned to re-route their road to the south, Inverurie's Council objected that injury would be done to the network of roads and facilities built up at Port Elphinstone 'This attempt to interfere with its prosperity is most unfair towards the traders and to the farmers frequenting the place'.[38] Between 1801 and 1841 several inland Aberdeenshire communities experienced little expansion of population; Old Meldrum, close by Inverurie even saw its population fall. Yet these communities, like Inverurie, were tied into the turnpike system. It is difficult to resist the argument that the canal brought an extra impetus to Inverurie's growth that turned it from a small insignificant place into a sizeable, thriving and bustling township.

The railway

As a direct financial venture the Aberdeenshire canal was never a flourishing success and the offer of a purchase price of £36,000 by the Great North of Scotland was readily accepted. Work on the railway began at Oyne in 1852 on the estate of the Elphinstone family who had once helped create the canal. Inverurie's Burgh Council had reacted to the establishment of the G.N.S.R. with cautious reserve and refused to be drawn into supporting its take-over bid for the canal.[39] But the merits of the railway's case and the fact that it was at last under way led to twenty shares in it being taken up by 1852.[40] Track was laid towards Inverurie very much along the line followed by the canal until Port Elphinstone was reached. Where the canal had stopped, the railway continued across the river on a viaduct of timber-piles (fitted with cast-iron bracing) that lasted till 1880.[41] It was then replaced by a sturdier structure made of Kemnay granite with wrought-iron spans. The track then continued close by and to the east of the long narrow line of Inverurie's High Street.

The flurry of activity that was an inevitable part of the construction of nineteenth century railways alarmed the council. Navvies sent formidable reputations ahead of them and when Benjamin Hall Blyth's men reached Inverurie they found the town had sworn in a number of special constables.[42] The council was able to persuade the Company to use its labour force to embank the Don and Urie so as to prevent flooding, but they failed to win their case that the proper place for Inverurie's station was in the north of the burgh by the Gas Works near the point where the principal roads met.[43] The G.N.S.R. preferred a cramped site further

The new railway station at Inverurie. The state of the platform indicates that it is barely complete.

south close to the High Street: there they erected a small and very basic timber station lit by gas.

The coming of the railway marked the decline of the coaching age and the replacement of the New Inn as the town's chief hotel by the newly-built Kintore Arms Hotel. This sizeable building was equipped with hot, cold and shower baths and even a library.[44] For a while 'The Lord Forbes' coach continued to operate until the further expansion of the railway up Donside removed the need for its services. Inverurie lay in the railway age, as in the turnpike age, close to the heart of a complex network of routes. From it a branch line to Old Meldrum opened up in 1856. At nearby Kintore another spur ran through Kemnay up to Alford. At Inveramsay Junction there branched off a line developed between 1855 and 1866 that continued through Turriff up to Banff and the Banffshire coast. To the compilers of Slater's Directory of 1867 the railway was a new stimulus to industry in the town. The railway was closely followed by the telegraph. In 1869 the line from Aberdeen to Keith was laid through Inverurie and Inverurie Post Office was connected to it with the council's blessing 'provided that no poles be placed in the Square'.[45]

By 1876 the G.N.S.R. was beginning to appreciate the need to improve Inverurie Station. The Burgh Council once more pressed the claims of the Gas Works site only to be told that the Railway Company felt that after occupying its current site for so long a move would be difficult to contemplate.[46] Not till 1902 did the G.N.S.R. admit the merits of the Council's case. By now the company had decided to shift its locomotive and rolling-stock building sheds out from a cramped site in Kittybrewster to the ample space offered to the north of Inverurie. While welcoming this development the Council commented that it wouldn't please the people of Port Elphinstone or businessmen who had established their premises by the old station.[47] The Railway Works brought an influx of new people who settled in an area (around Harlaw Road, King Street, Queen Street and Princes Street) so distinctive it was known as 'The Colony'. The century ended as it had begun with activity that stressed the importance in Inverurie's growth of an efficient transport network. Inverurie had been fortunate. The canal had given its growth a push that the railway had continued. The burgh was one of the first in the County to be linked into the railway network. In its communications advantages Inverurie enjoyed a situation superior to any other inland Aberdeenshire community.

Agricultural improvement

Although the canal and the turnpike road system contributed to the improvement of the farmland of the Garioch, around Inverurie at least the policy of the laird, the Earl of Kintore, had much to do with the changes that accelerated forward from the late 18th century. From the 1780s the Earl provided his tenants with long leases, freed them from paying multures and stimulated changes that brought formerly barren land into cultivation and encouraged the growing of grain, turnips, and grass.[48] From his Ardtannies Mill vantage point Alexander Bisset observed these changes and believed 'the appearance of the Earl of Kintore was a great blessing to the tenants in the way of improvements'.[49] The Earl and his factor offered long leases but insisted in return that improved farming methods be followed and shabby farm buildings be replaced with solid stone structures. Crop rotation, more turnip growing and improved stock raising began to spread over the countryside around Inverurie – though some local folk were suspicious of the changes that they saw. Bisset found himself faced with an indignant group of local people who had come to see the new fanner for winnowing that he had bought: a quiet demonstration of the superiority of the machine over reliance on the natural draught of the wind soon calmed their fears.

Cattle-raising grew, providing Inverurie with a valuable role to play; by 1832 the burgh's cattle markets were flourishing and well-frequented.[50] The profits to be made from this trade, especially in supplying city markets as far south as London, encouraged lairds to bring more land in cultivation. They gathered gangs of labourers who worked for small local contractors, trenching, draining and dyking new fields 'and bringing home satisfactory wages to numerous households in the country villages. The marvels of guano and bones were to the desirous imagination like the gold fields . . . improvements were trusted to bring their own compensation and all that was wanted from the lairds was barren land to cultivate and a crofter's potatoes to be added to the farm'.[51] Even the depression of the seventies did not severely damage the cattle trade. In the late eighties Inverurie was the centre of an extensive trade in dead meat sending annually to English markets around three thousand tons of beef that was sold at £80 a ton and represented nine thousand animals killed in Inverurie for export.[52]

The canal provided the Garioch with opportunities for obtaining fertilizers in a quantity that stimulated the area's farming before the railways spread bulk transport to other parts of inland Aberdeenshire. Inverurie butchers, merchants, traders, shopkeepers, craftsmen and innkeepers had good reason to feel grateful to the fortunate combination of factors that brought them increased wealth. Operating to stimulate these factors were a number of well-to-do landowners like the Earl of Kintore and Sir James Elphinstone whose enthusiasm for agricultural change encouraged them to plunge into the various transport changes possible at the time. The burgh's growth owed much to the men who inhabited the great houses dotted about the surrounding countryside.

Chapter Three

THE GROWTH OF INVERURIE

During the nineteenth century the population of Inverurie increased, at first, with rapidity from 450 in 1801 to 1,619 by 1841 and to 2,232 by 1861. By the end of the century it had crept up to reach 3,058 in 1901, a growth achieved primarily in the last few years of the century, for in 1891 the population had stood at 2,549. No doubt the G.N.S.R.s developments at Inverurie contributed to this end-of-the-century surge. The physical growth of the town that this population expansion generated was shaped by the geography of the area, the long narrow form of the eighteenth century remained the dominant feature. Housing that could not be crammed in along the High Street spread around the triangular-shaped Market Place and out along the Huntly road. The 164 houses that made up the burgh in 1821 had, by 1881, increased in number to 566.[1] Despite its loss of the canal terminus, nearby Port Elphinstone grew too. In 1851, 180 people lived there, by 1881 the number had increased to 356. The site offered an alternative house-building area to those who did not wish to settle in the area opening up to the north-west of the High Street.

Some of the land owned by the Burgh Council was developed as farmland. From the 1840s especially they compelled tenants leasing land in the Burgh Muir area and in the region to the north-east of the High Street, to drain, lime, manure and clear stones from the areas for which they were responsible.[2] But the town's expansion meant that feuing off land for housing had to be given priority. As early as 1799 they were allowing house-building on land they felt to be unprofitable for farming, selling off eleven sites – including one to an Inverurie shoemaker and another to a local mason.[3] In 1803 another dozen lots on the Burgh Muir were sold for house-building measuring 60 feet in front and 100 feet in length.[4] The bulk of properties put up at this time were stone and clay cottages of the but and ben type with earthen floors. Some were still thatched, though the nearby Foudland slate was increasingly coming to be used for roofing.[5] A number of nineteenth century properties still stand in the heart of Inverurie, indeed a few late-eighteenth century properties are still to be seen in High Street and Market Street.

Amid the modest town homes of the period stood more sizeable

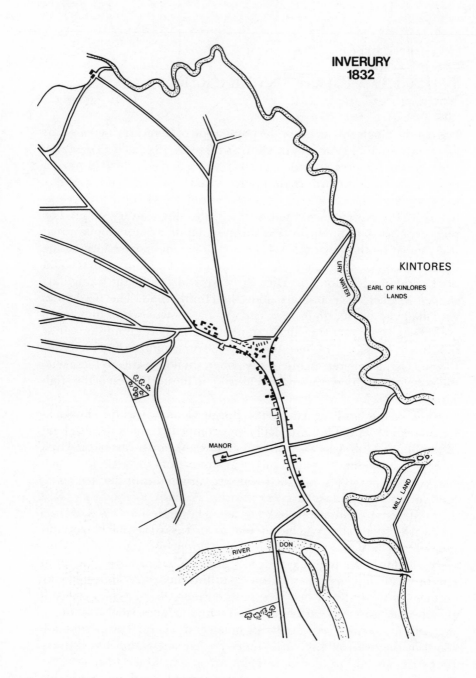

INVERURY
1832

KINTORES

EARL OF KINLORES
LANDS

URY WATER

MANOR

MILL LAND

RIVER DON

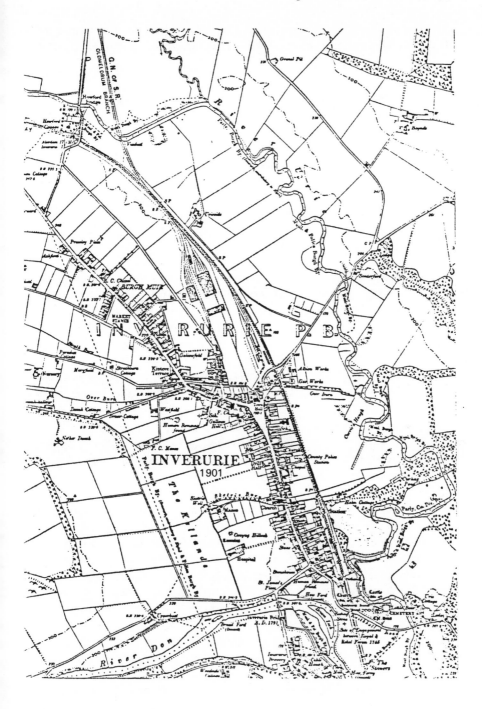

structures. The Kintore Arms of 1854, the Union Bank of 1857 and the Town House built at the top of the Market Place in 1807 were all large solid buildings. Church building added further to the stock of bigger properties; the late eighteenth century parish kirk was replaced in 1841, an Episcopal Church put up in the same year whilst the Disruption produced a Free Kirk and other sects built themselves chapels. Despite all this activity Inverurie was, at the end of the century, still very much a one-street town. It now had solidly built stone and slate properties instead of the small thatched roughly-built homes of early times, it was equipped with a range of bigger properties to serve its social, religious and educational needs. But the photographs of the period show a place without pretensions to grand architecture.

Business growth

Through the pages of nineteenth century directories it is possible to glimpse the growth of business activity in Inverurie. There have been a number of criticisms levelled at this source material. Gareth Shaw[6] has shown that the modestly produced very localised directory is likely to be far more prone to inaccuracies than those bigger-scale volumes like the ones produced by James Pigot and Isaac Slater. The entries may contain a double-counting of traders as a result of the multiplicity of business pursued by certain entrepreneurs. In Inverurie, Worrall's Directory of 1877 includes the entry for James Barron in the category of Grocer and Draper and then repeats it under the Milliner and Dressmaker label. Once more the bigger directories with their full-time professional agents were less prone to do this than local amateur efforts. Geoffrey Timmins'[7] examination of steel-makers in Sheffield has shown that the directories missed out quite a number of them from their publications yet at the same time over-recorded certain categories (showing for instance, as steel-makers, firms that were simply suppliers of steel). Inverurie entries in the directories produced by Pigot, Slater and the Lancashire firm of Worrall, do include unclear categories. Whilst various shopkeepers are clearly labelled, a vague category simply called 'Shopkeeper' also appears. However most occupations are sufficiently adequately defined to provide a broad general guide to the role the town developed in Victorian times.

'Inverurie serves as a point of concentration and a seat of miscellaneous trade for a pretty wide extent of surrounding country' noted a writer in 1885.[8] The directories bear out this comment. The pre-nineteenth century burgh had been a focus for a very small area: improved travel widened its hinterland whilst greater wealth and a full-

An Inverurie Scavenger. A key figure in burgh improvement was the scavenger, hired to sweep streets, keep drains clear, gather up manure, refuse and the contents of ashpits.

time concentration on farming increased demand for Inverurie's craft skills and services.[9] This activity attracted bank agencies. The two in operations by 1837 had increased to four thirty years later. Inverurie was a convenient site for schools, churches and the services of doctors. Insurance companies opened up agencies in the burgh; no less than twelve were to be found there in 1877.

Categorising occupations is not easy. Some retailers served also as wholesalers, others both made and sold the products in which they specialised. The occupation of auctioneer, present in 1867 and 1877 directories, is no longer entered separately by 1903. Instead a greatly increased number of cattle dealers are recorded. During Victorian times the number of people engaged in selling goods and livestock increased significantly, though falling slightly between 1877 and 1903. This fall is more than accounted for by a sharp shrinkage in the number of shop-keepers engaged in selling a very wide variety of items. In the later nineteenth century there seems to have been a slow trend towards greater specialisation in shopkeeping with fewer grocers acting also as drapers or ironmongers. Instead specialists in these trades opened up to business. The variety of shops widened as the century wore on until, by the end of Victorian times, Inverurie shoppers could visit not only grocers, drapers, butchers, chemists and ironmongers, but booksellers, cycle agents, glass and china shops and even hairdressers and photographers. The number of bakers rose, 1837–1903, from two to five. Popular preference was shifting from the consumption of the coarser home-made produce to commercially-produced bread made from wheat. By 1903 the weary visitor could not only choose from four hotels, or pause at one of the town's five spirit sellers, but, if averse to alcohol, could visit a Coffee House in the Market Square, a Temperance Hotel or newly-opened Refreshment Rooms.[10]

The burgh also housed several businesses. Here too the number engaged in making items increased over the century but, within that increase, suffered a slight fall in the last 25 years. In this latter period the small-scale enterprises of brewing and weaving closed down, though in fact the former simply moved to Port Elphinstone. Several occupations – like milling and timber cutting – depended directly on the countryside, and many others were indirectly dependent. A fall in business numbers during a time when British farming was meeting increasingly fierce foreign competition is not, therefore, surprising. It is easy to see why the leaders of Inverurie's business community were eager to welcome the Great North of Scotland's Railway Works to their town. At least Inverurie possessed a paper-making business and a mineral water manufacturer to provide some diversity of occupation.

The road leading northward out of Inverurie, lined with shops and a newly completed church.

The most numerous categories of craftsmen were tailors, boot and shoe-makers and joiners and builders. Their numbers rose but little 1837–1903, going from eighteen to twenty two. By the latter date the town's importance as a focus of animal traffic was marked by the coming of a hide factor and a sausage skin manufacturer. A cluster of occupations indicate how Inverurie provided for a growth of prosperity during the century. The number of milliners making hats and dresses rose; masons, slaters, plumbers, plasterers and paperhangers provided for the desire for a comfortable home and a cabinet maker constructed the furniture with which to fill the home. Visitors to the burgh could find craftsmen able to make and mend clothing, footwear and even watches. Inverurie shops and businesses may have lacked the variety and sophistication of Aberdeen's, yet they served the people of the surrounding farmland well enough at a time when travel by rail was too expensive for many to contemplate.

The increased business activity in and around Inverurie was observed and recorded by several of the town's inhabitants. Writing in 1842 the Rev. Robert Lessel noted how the canal terminus had attracted 'merchants, artisans and additional labourers in order to supply the wants of an industrious and thriving tenantry'.[11] But as to whether this was a desirable development, Robert Lessel was not sure. He suspected that the introduction of a manufacturing population menaced moral standards and grumbled 'the number of low public houses and of houses for harbouring vagrants is also a just subject of complaint'.[12] One of his successors, the Rev. Davidson, devoted much of the 'Recollections of Forty Years' that he produced for his parishioners as a series of leaflets, to recalling the development of different businesses in the burgh. Up until the 1870s the Inverurie people seemed to him to assume that their prosperity would steadily increase. They spent growing amounts on food, clothing and housing; several successful shopkeepers expanded into farming which some seemed to regard more as a summer recreation than a serious business.[13]

Davidson was impressed by men who grabbed the opportunities offered by economic expansion. A wood merchant, George Smith, bought up Inverurie Brewery and shifted brewing activities to Port Elphinstone. The Aberdeen Lime Company and the Aberdeen Commercial Company both emerged from the coming together of small businesses, and when the canal closed they shifted their warehousing into Inverurie and used the railway station. Gray's Bakery was set up by Alexander Gray who began in a very small way, farming land nearby and leaving his fields from time to time to see if anyone had come to his bakery to buy a loaf. He reacted to the changing eating habits of

Inverurie Market Square in Victorian times. Gas lamps are bracketed to some of the properties. The Square's surface shows the muddy and animal-dropping strewn condition of roads of the time.

Inverurie, baking loaves of white bread as well as penny and half-penny biscuits shaped by hand-cutters. In 1851 Alexander Gray's son began to make local bread deliveries in his newly-purchased horse-drawn van.[14] Some Victorian shop-keepers and craftsmen started off in very modest premises. George Pressly's shoemaking business was run from his small thatched cottage in which he had fitted a large window to better illuminate his work. Jackson's druggist business was established by its founder in one half of his father's weaving shop. George Galloway, a shoemaker, was also for part of his time a druggist much consulted by patients who did not wish to pay doctors' fees.[15] The 1803 Town House contained a smith's shop and a barber's – where books could also be purchased. Occupants of Factory Square, though mostly weavers, moved into other activities too. One of them, Willie Hogg, spent much of his time staggering along under a weight of baskets for his wife who was a travelling stoneware dealer. The shops that began informally in cottages so low that customers had to stoop to enter and were unable to keep on their hats, gradually evolved into enterprises operating from specially shaped premises. By 1902 many shops had recently been completely re-fitted.[16] By now the town also had a public slaughterhouse and a new auction market off Constitution Street. The streets on which business and homes stood had been properly named and numbered. In 1843 this had not been the case. One councillor grumbled 'that it was dis-creditable to this Royal Burgh that this had never been introduced here'.[17] Slowly streets were named and properties numbered. By 1867 the Burgh Muir had become North Street and the old Ball Green was named Market Place.

Markets

Not only private shopkeeping, but buying and selling at markets ex-panded in Inverurie in the nineteenth century. It was in May of 1798 that the Burgh Council decided that it would see if there would be a satisfactory response to the holding of weekly markets.[18] On July 3rd, 1798 the *Aberdeen Journal* carried an advertisement to indicate that Saturday markets would offer 'an ample supply of birch and hardwoods fit for husbandry implements, broad and narrow deals ... fir wood for roofing and other domestic uses'.[19] The Council urged dealers in all these items to come to Inverurie along with others, 'chapmen and tradesmen with made work are also invited, and those who bring to market Meal, Malt, Butcher Meat, Butter and Cheese will be supplied with weights and measures. Fish and Fowls will meet a ready market'.[20] The town was launching into a marketing role not long after its bridge

Inverury Markets.

1836.

.: TUESDAY, January 12.	11. TUESDAY, July 5.
:. TUESDAY, January 26.	12. THURSDAY, July 21.
:. TUESDAY, February 9.	13. THURSDAY, August 18.
.. TUESDAY, February 23.	14. TUESDAY, September 13.
. TUESDAY, March 8.	15. TUESDAY, October 18.
. TUESDAY, March 22.	16. TUESDAY, November 8.
TUESDAY, April 12.	17. TUESDAY, Nov. 15, F. M.
WEDNESDAY, April 27. .	18. TUESDAY, November 29.
. WEDNESDAY, May 18, F.M.	19. TUESDAY, December 13.
. MONDAY, June 6.	20. TUESDAY, December 27.

D. Chalmers & Co. Printers, Aberdeen.

over the Don had been built and with turnpike building underway. The opportunity was emerging to move beyond the role in which the town's craftsmen merely worked directly for the inhabitants of the burgh and the immediate neighbourhood and never bothered manufacturing articles for market.[21]

Inverurie markets were held in the winter within the confines of the Market Square, but during the spring to autumn period the wider spaces of the Burgh Muir were put to increasing use. This space was important for the town's trade in cattle, horses, sheep and grain expanded; by 1842 there were twenty fairs a year in which business was transacted in these items.[22] From the growth of market business the town revenues benefited, for traders who came from beyond Inverurie were charged customs dues for the various items they were offering for sale. At first the council's policy was to offer these dues for roup. In 1800 William Moir paid £2 for the customs of the hiring and Autumn Trysts[23] and then set about collecting in sufficient dues upon these occasions so as to leave himself with a profit. By 1826 John Annand, who had paid £20.10.0 a year for three years for the market customs had to accept an increase to £39.15.0.[24] By 1847 the amount had gone up to £56,[25] reflecting the growth of Inverurie markets. At the regular markets there were stances and, by renting these out, further revenue was raised. In 1824 the council's attempt to charge eight shillings per stance met with such resistance the price had to be dropped to five shillings,[26] but by 1852

TABLE

OF

TOLLS AND CUSTOMS

Payable from the TRYSTS and FAIRS

HOLDEN IN THE

BURGH OF INVERURY;

Fixed and adjusted by the Magistrates and Town Council.

All sorts of Wrought Timber, each Load - 6d.	Every Horse on the Market Stance, offered for Sale - - - - - - 2d.
Each Load of Candle Fir - - - 6d.	
Every Fork-Shaft, Hay-Rake, Basket-Rim, Bee-Skep, and Skulls - - - ½d.	Every Tent, or House occupied as a Tent, without a License for the same - 1s.
Harrows, each - - - - - 1½d.	Butter and Cheese, per Load - - 6d.
The largest Tubs - - - - 1d.	Every Load of Saddlery - - - 6d.
The smallest Do. - - - ½d.	Every Show drawn by Horse, each - 4s.
Turned Plates, Caps, and Trenchers, per Load - - - - - 6d.	Smaller ones, - - - - 1d.
	Every Stand of Fruit, Sweetmeats, Hardware, or Goods of any sort laid on Ground or Stand, for every Foot long 1d.
Spinning Wheels and Reels, each - - 1d.	
Wool, per Stone - - - - 6d.	
Every Cart load with Goods of any sort, for Sale - - - - - 6d.	Every Horse on the Freedom or adjacent Roads, turning, coursing, and offered for sale, if found on the Market Stance uncustomed - - - - 4d.
Earthen and Stoneware, per Load - 1s.	
Each Head of Black Cattle - - 1d.	
A Cow and Calf - - - - 1½d.	Shoes, per Pair - - - - ½d.
Every Sheep - - - - ½d.	Corn Hooks, per Dozen - - - 3d.

ALL STERLING MONEY.

The Burgesses of INVERURY are declared exempt from the foregoing Customs; but if any of them declare any Beast, Tent, or Article, to be their property, which does not belong to them, with intent to defraud the Tacksmen, the person so offending shall, on conviction, be fined Five Shillings Sterling, payable to the Tacksman.

It is enacted, that if any Article, not mentioned in the foregoing Table, shall be brought to the said Markets or Trysts, for Sale, the Custom payable therefor shall be fixed and determined by the Magistrates of the Burgh, to whom the Tacksman shall apply for that purpose.

D. CHALMERS AND CO. PRINTERS, ABERDEEN.

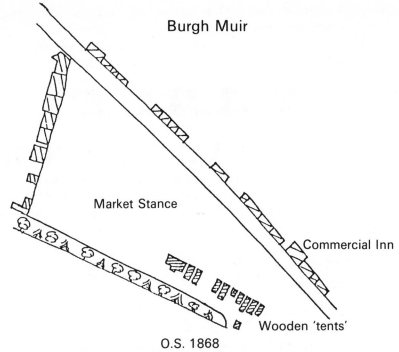

Burgh Muir

Market Stance

Commercial Inn

Wooden 'tents'

O.S. 1868

'It was resolved that the wooden buildings erected on stances in the Market
Green in North Street should all be removed'
(Burgh Minutes 8.1.1889)

fifteen shillings was being successfully demanded from those on the better
sites and by 1870 this had crept up to £1.11.0.[27]

Winter stallholders were offered more favourable terms, for a while,
than those who only set up in business at summer markets.[28] But by the
1840s the need to offer such inducements had gone, stalls and stances
were spilling out of the Market Square and their number being controlled. In 1844 the council resolved that because of 'the great confusion
and annoyance occasioned by the large number of parties frequenting
the winter markets with tents'[29] that they would not let stances to
traders who were not from Inverurie or from one of the parishes adjoining Inverurie parish. Other places began to provide markets so that by
1871 local farmers complained that Inverurie, Alford and Old Meldrum
were operating markets too frequently. The council agreed to reduce its
bigger markets to once every three weeks, holding those from October to
March in the Market Place and those from April to September on the old
Burgh Muir site by North Street. Two of these occasions – in early
summer and late autumn, were especially important, for these were the

main feeing fairs, though the late July period also included a feeing fair for hiring harvest workers.[30]

There grew up a flourishing business in animals and farm produce along with traffic in all the items needed for farm work and for much of domestic life. Local people could buy poultry, provisions and dairy produce at weekly sales held from 1846 in a wooden building behind the Town House.[31] The Burgh Minutes of 1823 list a considerable number of goods offered for sale that included cloth, gloves, shoes and stockings; there were fir candles, wooden plates, bowls and tubs, working items included harrows, carts, corn hooks and spinning wheels, whilst foods ranged from sweetmeats and fruit to butter and cheese, fresh and preserved fish.[32] The growth of shops in the later nineteenth century may perhaps have dented the trade of some market folk, but business in livestock and farm goods continued to flourish. Inverurie's growth was built solidly on its role as a place to visit for buying and selling.

The Burgh Council

The affairs of the expanding burgh were, in the early nineteenth century, watched over by a Council composed of a provost, three bailies, a dean of guild, a treasurer and three councillors.[34] Their attitude to the problems of the first three decades of the century seems to have been rather lethargic. They encouraged the development of markets in the burgh, spent a few pounds on filing up holes in the High Street and supported the turnpike road and the canal. By the early thirties, however, there was no street lighting in the town, the few footpaths were in a dreadful state, the roads were not properly named nor the houses numbered. The Council's management of the finances it controlled had been wasteful, especially in the period before 1820. Between 1807 and 1817 over £600 went on paying the Council's tavern bills, travelling expenses and newspapers. Since the travel costs were by no means all incurred on burgh business and the entertainment costs were higher than the cost of the articles supplied warranted it is not surprising that burgh management was described as 'very objectionable'[34] by those empowered by Parliament to review Scotland's Municipal Corporations. Between 1794 and 1832 the Council allowed almost £2,500 of its property to be alienated.

The town revenues were around £400 p.a. by 1875.[35] They came from its various properties that included the Moss of Fetternear, around thirty five acres on the Burgh Muir and eight acres of market stances, properties in Inverurie, market customs and the renting out of the Town House; there were also dividends drawn from shares in the local Gas

Company (which began operating in 1839) and later from shares in the Great North of Scotland Railway Company. Local businessmen dominated affairs from the early thirties, the Provosts being surgeons, a druggist, merchants, a butcher, an ironmonger and three bank agents.[36] The town's growth was not their concern alone, for the Inverurie Parochial Board (from 1846) and the School Board (from 1873) both administered important duties. The problems of growth will be separately treated, but the Council made sure of one thing at least – that they administered affairs from suitably imposing premises.

By the early nineteenth century the late seventeenth century Tollbooth on the High Street was both cramped and decayed yet had to serve as prison and occasional military store as well as a public meeting place.[37] It became a shop once the new Town House had opened, in 1807, at the north end of the Market Square. This new structure contained downstairs a prison, a Guard House and a military store. Upstairs there was a hall for meetings and a Council Room.[38] Building so grand a property (even decorating it with a clock and bell) led to the selling off of land to the value of £188 and the borrowing of £150.[39] But once complete the Town House became a source of revenue. Two shops were let on the ground floor, yielding £10 p.a. and the hall was hired out to various societies – though this did lead to damage caused by 'Dancing Masters and others, and that in consequence of Balls and other amusements being held therein the Plaister in the Shops below had been at sundry times broke'.[40]

Now the council possessed a fine Town House it could adequately receive important visitors. In 1857 the Queen's brief stop in Inverurie (on her journey to Haddo House) led to the town mustering its police, its military volunteers, a band, officials and crowds of flag-waving inhabitants. A huge triumphal arch in the centre of the burgh was decorated with loyal messages and the day rounded off with a grand Ball in the Town House.[41]

Yet by 1861 all but one member of the Council was complaining that their Town House was inadequate and dilapidated. Only one councillor argued that the expected expenditure of at least £2,000 on new premises was unnecessary extravagance. The police urged action too, hoping that from it they might obtain more spacious accommodation.[42] The foundation stone was laid in July 1862, work completed inside a year, and duly celebrated with the first of many balls.[43] The building still dominates the centre of Inverurie. It was the focus of official burgh activity that concentrated especially lavishly upon royal occasions. The marriage of Princess Louise in 1871 was the occasion for Inverurie to hold 'a banquet to consist of a service of Wine and Cake. Gentlemen's ticket one shilling.

Lady's sixpence. A Dinner to the Poor – Gratis. A service of Tea and Fruit to the Scholars attending the Schools within the Burgh and Port Elphinstone – Gratis. A Display of Fireworks. A Bonfire'.[44] Once more a ball rounded off the day (for those able to afford five shilling tickets) with dancing to the music of Milne's six-piece band. The council had made sure that the growth of Inverurie into a place of some importance should be visibly evident in a very impressive Town House. But rapid growth brought social problems too; tackling these was an important test of the competence of Inverurie's leaders and of the adequacy of the administrative machinery at their disposal.

Chapter Four

THE PROBLEMS OF GROWTH

As Inverurie expanded in extent and population, so its problems grew; what had once been acceptable methods of obtaining water, disposing of refuse and dealing with illness were no longer adequate for a community swelling from a few hundred to over two thousand inhabitants. Moreover the town's leaders were under some external pressure to adopt change. As a national system of social administration was slowly built up in bits and pieces, so Inverurie found advice, and guidance from Edinburgh became increasingly sharp, backed up by visits from outside officials. By the end of the century the burgh provision of water and health care, of street lighting, cleaning and paving, and of drainage and sewage, had all been dramatically improved. Shifting from an informal way of life in which people fetched water from wells or burns, dumped all manner of filth outside their doors and blundered along the High Street at night in unlit gloom, was expensive. By the end of the century Inverurie inhabitants had to accept the payment of rates on a regular basis and the administration of parts of their lives by a number of officials.

The Town Council

Until 1867 (when the burgh adopted the Police Act) it was the council that had to cope with some of the problems of growth. It organized itself into committees to supervise health, drainage, sewage, pavements, markets, lighting, and land matters. The burden of detailed work fell upon the Town Officer. For his many duties he received a free house and (by 1874) a salary that had edged up to £25 a year.[1] In return he was expected to call and attend official meetings, clean the Town House, act as Town Crier and go through the town calling out announcements, (and banging a drum or ringing a bell to draw attention to himself) as well as seeing the lamplighter and scavengers (when appointed) did their work properly. From 1878 he acted as Water Inspector too, visiting the springs and reservoirs, checking the street wells and the fire fighting equipment. In return an extra £5 was added to his salary and a further 25/- allowed for the hire of a bicycle.[2] When the council received complaints that rubbish was piling up in some part of the burgh, or that dung-hills fouled the streets or cesspools were choked, its normal response was to despatch the Town Officer to deal with them.[3] By mid century a problem was emerging beyond the Town Officer's capacities, for the very success of Inverurie as a focal point for the cattle trade led to the increase of slaughtering in properties scattered amongst the ordinary dwelling houses. The stench, blood, offal and dung emanating from slaughter-houses produced complaints, and proved a menace to health.

Even after Inverurie became a police burgh, the council sometimes debated matters of health. In particular it discussed the provision of organized care for illness like typhoid. Until 1872 hospital provision was an intermittent affair and involved the opening up of suitable premises as need arose. In 1872 the council purchased the Garioch Inn in North Street, turning it into a ten-bed hospital.[4] A smallpox outbreak affecting three North Street families seems to have prompted this purchase. There were further outbreaks of smallpox in 1875, 1881 and 1886; typhoid caused several deaths in 1889, diphtheria affected the town, gastric fevers swept it upon occasion and there were cholera scares as late as 1884.[5] In 1893 the council decided to join with the surrounding district to finance the building of a proper ten-bed hospital which was permanently staffed. Not till 1895 was a site obtained and work commenced to erect a hospital costing £2,250, a bill to which Inverurie contributed £506.[6]

The council also responded to the Contagious Diseases Act of 1880, organizing the inspection of dairies. Its inspector found them in a reasonably clean condition but faced grumbles that the dairymen outside the burgh were never required to regularly disinfect their premises.[7]

By 1866 the burgh seems to have been in a very filthy state;[8] its common lodging houses where tramps, vagrants and wandering workers stayed were in a squalid and unsupervised condition, its slaughterhouses were surrounded by filth. The Inverurie Parochial Board's Inspector, his duties widened in the sixties to include matters of health as well as poverty, issued a few stern warnings that persuaded a number of inhabitants 'to remove swine, offensive ashpits and privys where found near dwelling houses or on the sides of the street'.[9] One particular offensive area – Constitution Street – had a sewer laid along its surface. The improvements that were made were helped by money the Parochial Board raised with an assessment upon proprietors and tenants. Some of it was spent on hiring a man to spend several weeks cleaning the ditches, drains and cesspools.[10] This was but a very small beginning to a task of improvement that now fell primarily upon a new administrative entity.

The Police Commissioners and matters of health

In 1867 Inverurie adopted the Police Act of 1862. The Town Council began to meet (on quite separate occasions) as Police Commissioners to decide how best to deploy the revenue from rates that they raised.[11] A sixpenny rate of 1868 rose gradually and was subdivided for different purposes from 1884. In that year the total rate of 1/10 was made up of 1/3 for health matters and 7d for police work. By 1890 a sixpenny road-rate was added to the health and police rates which had not varied from the figure of 1884, and altered by only a penny to the end of the century. In 1900 the Town Councils (Scotland) Act put an end to the division of authority between Council and Police Commissioners, merging the two bodies.

The primary purpose of the Police Commission was to tackle health matters and they began promptly. The Town Officer, with an assistant, was ordered to clean the streets at least three times a week, keep drains clear, clean out cesspools and remove rubbish from lanes and pavements. The owners of slaughterhouses were ordered to wash out their premises daily, clear away dung in the early morning, make sure blood did not run into open ditches and drains and ensure the animals they dealt with were not diseased.[12] Later events were to show, however, that issuing orders was not enough. In the same year those keeping common lodging houses also received a list of instructions. They were advised that their premises would be examined and put on a register by an Inspector who would check that each lodger had at least 250 cubic feet of space. Nor was the keeper to allow persons of different sex to sleep in the same apartment unless they were married and the sole occupants of their room.[13] The lodgers in these premises had to fend for themselves, and to this end had to be able to do their own cooking and washing.[14] The Keeper had to supply bedding which had to be cleaned once in three months[15] and was obliged to sweep the rooms once every day. Human waste, collected in pails during the night, was to be regularly tipped out into ashpits. The commissioners also considered framing regulations for pawnbrokers, but the presence of but one made them decide it was not necessary. By 1877 there were two, Christina Walker in North Street and Alexander Shand in the Market Place.[16]

The issuing of regulations was not an expensive reform nor, it was hoped, would be the institution of scavenging on a regular basis. In 1868 Robert Duncan took up the duty at a wage of twelve shillings a week;[17] by the 1890s his successor was receiving eighteen shillings and was provided with a waterproof coat.[18] His duties included daily collections

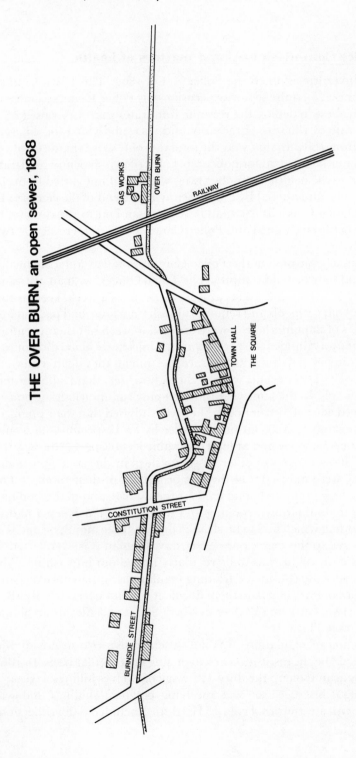

THE OVER BURN, an open sewer, 1868

of 'filth, ashes and garbage'[19] the cleaning of cesspools weekly in summer and fortnightly in winter, the keeping clear of drains and the clearing of snow from the streets in winter. But the sale of dung and sweepings to local farmers would, it was hoped, help keep down costs.

Inverurie in the sixties often smelled abominably. Open channels received filth (washed along by rains) in High Street, Mortimer Lane, Commercial Street, Gallowford Lane, Pirie's Land and Saphlock Place.[20] What was needed – underground drainage systems – would be expensive. Moreover a proper water supply had still not been provided. In 1871 the early efforts of the Police Commissioners came under the bleak scrutiny of Alexander Campbell, the Board of Supervision's Inspecting Superintendent for Northern Scotland. He arrived impressed by his initial glimpse of what seemed a well-built town with a fine new Town Hall. But closer inspection revealed defects he felt to be very serious. The inhabitants' water supply – from wells – was alarmingly unhealthy, for the light soil of the area easily absorbed material from cesspools and slaughterhouses. These buildings were scattered among private houses and thus, he concluded Inverurie needed a public slaughterhouse outside the town and with a proper water supply so that private establishments could be closed.[21] Nor had the regulations issued to the lodging houses turned them into acceptable premises. One in particular was filthy and contained rooms whose windows would not open.[22]

Campbell's visit marked the beginning of several years of tension between the Inverurie Police Commissioners and the Board of Supervision. Inverurie accepted the need to provide an underground sewage system in the main areas of the burgh, but was very reluctant to tackle the costly question of bringing in a water supply, or of shutting down the dozen or so slaughterhouses when local butchers were so hostile. Only occasionally did butchers applying to run slaughterhouses find their applications rejected. In 1868 when the Sanitary Inspector found a diseased ox carcass in one slaughterhouse, the owner struck him 'and stood in the door with a heavy stick in his hands threatening that if I dared to enter his premises he would knock my brains out'.[23] Two local police constables proved very reluctant to come to the Inspector's aid, though he did finally manage to get the offending carcass burned.

The Commissioners saw to it that work on a sewage system got under way in 1871. £1,800 was privately borrowed, at 4%, and by the summer of 1872 a sewer ran along the main street, through filter beds to the River Don, built by workmen who were paid £3 a day for their efforts.[24] Then work slowed to a sluggish pace. In 1871 people who lived near the Overburn petitioned for it to be covered in. The Overburn was an open sewer in which all manner of filth was deposited and had become a

danger to health.[25] Yet the petitioners had to wait for nine years before it
was covered in. In the later nineties several of the side streets were
provided with sewers, over twenty years from the time Campbell began
to complain that the town had contented itself with a sewer at the centre
but 'none at the extremities'.[26]

The water-supply issue was resisted by the Commissioners. In 1871,
faced with Campbell's report, they argued the project would be far too
costly and that it would be sensible to wait until the public was wholly
persuaded of the necessity of a water supply and thus prepared to find the
necessary money through the rates.[27] They hoped, in vain, that the
newly-built sewage works would satisfy the Inspector. Campbell poured
scorn on Inverurie pleas of poverty pointing out that about 6,000 cattle,
beside sheep and pigs, were annually slaughtered in the town and that
the dues on this trade would easily pay for improvements.[28] The issue of
impure water was bound up with the slaughtering trade in another way
too. As long as several butchering establishments were at work within
burgh streets, the result was filth that seeped into the soil. Campbell
stressed the point, noting the excessive filth he found outside four of them
whilst before a fifth stood 'a pool of stagnant blood in which pigs were
revelling'.[29] Campbell's superiors at the Board of Supervision followed
up their Inspector's reports with a letter to Inverurie's Police Commissioners. They advised that:

> In Towns and Villages where the whole soil is charged with animal
> matter from houses and highly manured gardens, experience has
> shown that the well-water cannot in general be restored to a state of
> purity by any improvement of sewage or abatement of surface
> nuisance.[30]

This communication produced no action. Campbell's grumbles
widened to include doubts about the competence of the Town Officer
who acted as the Sanitary Inspector ('Inverurie requires the service of a
much more intelligent and active officer than Mr Hunter').[31] His com-
ments come at a time when the Board of Supervision's efforts to persuade
all sizeable places (of 2,000 plus in population) were not meeting with
the response that had been hoped for. Some places chose as Sanitary
Inspectors, labourers or scavengers, in their search for the cheapest
solution. Inverurie seems to have followed this latter course. In 1874 Dr
Littlejohn travelled from Edinburgh to offer his opinion and took away
samples of well-water for analysis. Littlejohn was Edinburgh's Medical
Officer and had just become (in 1873) the Board of Supervision's first
part-time Medical Officer of Health. The Doctor observed of Inverurie
in general that he had reason to be satisfied with its general cleanliness.

The town was built on sandy soil that drained freely. But he was perturbed to see Inverurie people so dependant on the water of over 12 wells most of which were placed in most unsuitable situations in back-yards close to middens, dung heaps and manured garden ground, or close by the main drainage pipe.[32]

His impression that the wells of Inverurie were heavily contaminated, was confirmed by the analysis of samples from four of them (two from the south of the burgh and two in the north) carried out by Edinburgh's City Analyst. It seemed clear that 'the area supplying the water to these wells is impregnated with noxious organic matters rendering the use of these waters, especially after a continuance of wet weather, dangerous to health'.[33]

The link between the impurity of the water supply and the animal-processing centres in Inverurie led Dr Littlejohn to repeat the concern already shown by Alexander Campbell. He accepted that though for Inverurie's own needs one slaughterhouse would be sufficient, because the town was the centre of a grazing district linked by railway with Aberdeen and London, the killing of cattle for the southern market had become one of the chief trades of the place. But most of the slaughter-houses were too close to dwellings, had defective paving and were also provided with piggeries into which blood escaped and offal was thrown. Even the most recently built and best sited slaughterhouse gave off a powerful and offensive smell that affected nearby homes. Dr Littlejohn drew attention to the siting of a sausage skin manufactory (that smelled foully in warm weather) a mere fifty yards from a school and urged the need for an extension of the drainage system into the side streets to tackle the problem of cleansing refuse-strewn back courts.[34]

The response of the Commissioners to this report was to seek one of their own from a local medical man, Dr Abel. The doctor took samples from twenty wells, pronounced the water perfectly safe to drink, and enabled Inverurie's leaders to feel justified in doing nothing about the water supply question.[35] To the Board of Supervision, however, Dr Abel's techniques of analysis seemed highly unsatisfactory and they demanded that action be taken to supply unpolluted water.[36] With considerable reluctance the Police Commissioners bowed before the pressure and agreed to study ways of improving their burgh's water supply.[37]

In December 1874 Alexander Campbell reappeared. He pointed out that the burgh had revenues of £400 a year and that a rate assessment of fourpence – well below that of Huntly (ninepence) or Fraserburgh (a shilling) would suffice 'and yet the Police Commissioners of this rich Burgh of Inverurie have been so appalled by the prospect of an assess-

ment of fourpence as to condemn the inhabitants for years past to the use
of water in some parts so polluted as to be unfit to give an animal to
drink. In proof of this I may mention that a farmer up the country, on
speaking of the water of Inverurie, told me that in driving a horse and
cart through Inverurie one day he asked a woman who was pumping
water to let him have some for his horse to drink, but after smelling it he
declined to give it to his horse'.[38] He closed his report with gloomy
predictions that Inverurie would try and adopt every possible delaying
tactic to avoid spending money.

The Police Commissioners grumbled at the language of Campbell's
report[39] and protested strongly at his apparent readiness to listen to
gossip.[40] But they complained in vain to the Board of Supervision. The
Board backed Campbell, pointing out that if a Local Authority failed to
exercise their powers to carry out much-needed improvements then
sharp criticism was inevitable.[41] The Inverurie Commissioners, with
great reluctance, decided to act. A water engineer, Gordon Jackson, was
hired to study the various possible solutions to the supply of pure water.
For several months the Commissioners seriously considered simply
deepening certain wells, but by 1876 had been persuaded that though
such ideas may have been inexpensive they were of dubious value. Work
began on piping water from springs at Crimond and Isaactown, bringing
the water to a reservoir at Hillhead and then carrying it by pipe over the
Ury to Souterford Road. The project cost £3,300,[42] £2,000 of which was
borrowed from James Moir of Fyvie at 3½%. Port Elphinstone was (in
1879) slotted into the scheme[43] on condition it accepted being cut off in
times of shortage. During the later nineteenth century fresh additions of
water had to be sought to augment a supply over-stretched by
Inverurie's growth.[44]

Once the water question was settled Alexander Campbell was able to
concentrate on the slaughterhouse issue. But he complained in vain of
their poor condition, the foul heaps around them, the smells and the
especially offensive aroma around the sausage factory. He received
occasional support from local inhabitants who wrote to complain of the
smells and the menace to health posed by the slaughterhouses.[45] One lay
close by a school; so sickening were the smells from it that the windows of
the school and school-house had to be kept firmly shut in the warm
weather when the teacher most wanted them open.[46] Grumbles from
local inhabitants and complaints from visiting inspectors dragged on
into the nineties without producing any response from the Police
Commissioners. In 1895 Inverurie's own Medical Officer added his
criticisms of some of Inverurie's animal processing centres. In Gallowfold
Lane, for example, he found a piggery and slaughterhouse in a most foul

and offensive condition.[47] Intolerable smells filled the air; dirt and blood stained walls and floor. The doctor urged the closing of the slaughterhouse piggeries and reiterated Alexander Campbell's demand for just one suitably-located slaughterhouse.[48]

In 1895, following this report, action began to be taken. When slaughterhouse licences were sought they were granted only on condition the piggeries were moved. Butchers reluctant to act were threatened with prosecution.[49] Cattle dealers added their voice to those pressing for a public slaughterhouse[50] and one Inverurie inhabitant spoke darkly of legal actions he was going to take as a result of his inability to let a property situated next to a slaughterhouse.[51] Though local butchers remained hostile to change, a site was bought off North Street, £1,900 borrowed and at last work began. In vain the butchers protested that driving cattle from the station to this site would endanger people's safety; the slaughterhouse was built.[52]

In 20 years from the adopting of the Police Act the burgh had spent over £9,600 on its various health measures. Yet when, in 1892, an Aberdeen civil engineer was called to report on the cause of numerous complaints about Inverurie's poor health and unpleasant odours, he concluded that the slaughterhouses were not the only cause of trouble. Despite all that had been done numerous properties were defectively drained, most had filthy ashpits and pig-keeping was common. Many ashpits were badly constructed, in some cases they were merely holes dug in the ground, uncovered, undrained, carelessly kept and close to houses.[53] The straggling shape of Inverurie made a reform difficult, he felt; what was needed was a daily collection by cart of all refuse. In 1898 the local Medical Officer expressed his concern about the same problem. 'In several outbreaks of fever' he noted, 'the circumstances seemed to me to point to the unsanitary condition of the premises as being the source of the disease ... It is essential in my opinion that all privies should be abolished and a complete water-carriage system introduced ... Steps should be taken without further delay to arrange for a daily system of refuse removal and the substitution of water closets for privies'.[54] The century closed with Inverurie extending its system of sewers and searching for more water to make a large-scale network feasible.

These events illustrate the difficulties faced by the Board of Supervision in attempting to persuade local authorities to carry out essential health reforms that were likely to be expensive. The laying of a main sewer was fairly readily agreed to, but the bringing in of a proper water supply, a far more costly enterprise, was persistently delayed. Yet upon this reform depended not only a safe supply of drinking water but also the effective washing through of a drainage system, the installation of water-closets, and the cleaning out of slaughterhouses. Action on the slaughterhouses only came after the period of reform in local government which saw the Local Government Board replace the Board of Supervision in 1894 and steadily increase the ability of central government to insist on local reforms.

Lighting and paving

During the nineteenth century the gloomy, uneven and muddy streets of Inverurie were considerably improved. Late nineteenth century photographs show the main thoroughfares to be well-paved and illuminated by gas lights. The main street seems, in the early part of the century, to have had a footpath along its western side provided by the Turnpike Trust; such footpaths as existed were maintained by the Trust (though the Burgh provided £5 a year to help with the cost).[55] In 1834 the council decided to lay a footpath along the east side of the main street from the south end of the same to the Market Place.[56]

A joint-stock gas-light company was established in 1839.[57] The Council paid for the services of John Stephen, a shoemaker, as a part-time lamp-lighter and paid him £2.16.0 for a year's work.[58] The lamps were lit from October until April; they were ignited an hour after sunset and extinguished at ten at night on every day save Sunday (when they were put out at nine).[59] As the century progressed further lamps were erected and once the town became a police burgh the council assisted with the cost of putting up new ones. In 1867 the council decided to cease using wooden posts to support lamps, instead a metal type was adopted.[60] Each post, with its ironwork fittings, cost £2.14.6.[61] At the burgh's Coffee House Ann Gordon was allowed to put up a specially decorated lamp emblazoned with the words 'Coffee Tavern' – only to be asked to remove it seven years later.[62] From 1849 the burden of lighting and maintaining the lamps fell upon the Town Officer.[63] From 1899 a new type of incandescant lamp began to replace the older ones.[64] Gas lit the streets and various premises too, but when, in 1891, the Gas Company was asked to run supplies up the working class areas of North Street, Saphock Place and Constitution Street, it refused on the grounds that here it would find far too few private customers.[65]

The pavements and streets above which these gas lights flickered were created by ramming down smallish stones and topping them with gravel. A new piece of road laid in 1882 was made up of 'a coating of hard fresh metal six inches deep and broken so as to pass through a ring two and a half inches diameter and to be covered with a binding of good clean gravel to the depth of one inch and afterwards pressed down with a heavy

Road Roller'.[66] By the late seventies and early eighties pavements were beginning to be extended along streets other than the main thoroughfare and the Market Place pavements were being renewed.[67] To his various other complaints, Alexander Campbell added adverse comment on the poor quality of pavements in Inverurie.[68]

In 1890, as a result of local government reform, the burgh took full responsibility for the roads and bridges within its boundaries. A Road Foreman (at a wage of a pound a week) was appointed to oversee road maintenance[69] and a road scraper was purchased[70] to help keep roads clear of the mud and dung that came in quantities to this busy focus of the cattle trade and at a time of horse-drawn traffic. Work was begun on replacing the gravel-surface pavements with the 'concrete foot pavements' that Campbell had recommended.[71]

Not only horse-drawn vehicles travelled the roads of the late nineteenth century. Massive steam traction engines lumbered along and threatened to damage the Don Bridge by their juddering passage.[72] The signs of strain were sufficiently severe to lead to the closure of the bridge to these vehicles.[73]

Law and order

Local authority records do not show Inverurie to have been a place greatly troubled by lawless behaviour. In 1797 the Burgh Council dealt out a fine of ten pounds (Scots) to John Smith and Edward Goodwin for

> putting several of said inhabitants in fear with their cursing and quarreling.[74]

This is a rare entry in the period before full-time professional policing was established. Once a County Constabulary had been set up Inverurie was eager to share in its benefits but reluctant to meet the costs that this involved.[75] The burgh paid half the cost of a policeman's annual wage (£62.18.0 for 'a first class constable with boot allowance' by 1885).[76] The constable patrolled the burgh, chasing away the boys who played football in the Market Square[77] and dealing with vagrants. By 1864 he had occasional help from an inspector and another constable. Inverurie was quick to complain if its officer was removed to attend market days elsewhere or guard plantations by night.[78] On special occasions (as when the Queen visited Inverurie) or at times of special concern (as when the G.N.S.R. was laying track in the area) the constable was assisted by special constables.[79]

Chapter Five

CARING FOR THE POOR AND THE YOUNG

In both coping with the care of those unable to sustain themselves, and in the provision of education, Inverurie moved, during the nineteenth century, from inexpensive and informal approaches to more costly and systematic solutions. In these areas, as in matters of health, the burgh had to respond to legislation requiring changes from localities. The growth of Inverurie contributed to the problem of poverty by concentrating a number of poor in a small area; on the other hand growth, perhaps, helped educational provision by making a larger school feasible.

Coping with poverty before 1845

Inverurie poor in the early nineteenth century depended for help upon annual church collections. These commonly yielded around £14 but the burgh's small size meant that only about a dozen people were applying for relief.[1] The town's growth and the improvement of the roads in the area meant that as the century progressed not only did Inverurie have more of its own poor to care for, but it was a magnet drawing in poor from other parts. By 1842 there were thirty eight people requiring regular relief and about the same number receiving occasional aid. Support still came primarily from church collections (by now producing £45 a year) though at times of special need local landowners offered assistance, finding around £30–£40 and by 1842 were finding these sums regularly. The town also possessed a fund, built up from voluntary subscriptions, which was used to buy coal in winter for the very poor. By this date attempts at running Friendly Societies had collapsed but the Savings Bank established in 1837 still lived on and had attracted 692 depositors (from the town and the surrounding countryside) whose average deposit was £10.[2]

The parish minister in 1842 felt that Inverurie's growth had led to manufacturers and proprietors hiring people of a moral tone lower than that of earlier years who were not at all reluctant or ashamed to ask for aid.[3] But the evidence collected by the Poor Law Enquiry Commissioners in 1843 suggested that the life of anyone driven to seek aid was miserable to a degree.[4] A local doctor with thirty years of experience of visiting the sick in the area believed that the burgh poor were worse off than those in the rural areas. To Dr Thompson, the Kirk Session elders were too aged to pursue their charitable work efficiently and the numbers of poor in the burgh were too large for neighbourly help to be forthcoming or of much use. Certainly Inverurie's leaders felt the town was plagued with far too many poor vagrants.

The picture sketched by Dr Thompson showed the burgh poor living in the oldest and most squalid property 'very ill off for furniture, particularly for bedding and clothing' and suffering 'a great deal from want of nourishment, more so from this than from want of medicine'.[5] Their health suffered from inadequate living standards and ignorance of hygiene so that typhus fever was often prevalent.[6] Dr Thompson found he not only had to provide medicines but sometimes even felt obliged to purchase food for the desperately poor. It took very little by way of illness, accident, or lack of regular work to reduce an Inverurie family to poverty. The diet of ordinary people depended chiefly on oatmeal and potatoes, leaving little room for further economies here: the price paid for these items was only fractionally below the average prices in Scotland.[7] Cottage rents – at around £2 to £4 a year, were higher than the general level of rents in the County (in south east Aberdeenshire the average was £1.15.0). Yet the wages paid in the parish of around £10–£11 a year to farm servants, 1/8 to 2/- to day labourers in summer, were not especially high but close to the national averages.

After 1845

Dr Thompson was but one of countless medical men whose pressure for a compulsory assessment system helped towards the reform of the Poor Law in 1845 and the institution of Parochial Boards. The first volume of Parochial Board Minutes has not survived; the minutes beginning in 1859 show the usual preponderance of females on the list of those being aided, a regular level of relief commonly ranging between two and six shillings a week, with occasional provision of shoes, clothing, blankets, and funeral expenses.[8] Free vaccination was provided by the Medical Officer who received two shillings for every nearby case he treated, three shillings if the case involved a journey of over two miles.[9] The Board were, for a while, troubled by the problem of the four orphaned children of the Topp family whose father, though originally in the Free Church, had become a Catholic by the time of his death. Catholic clergy sought to place the children with families they felt to be suitable, and eventually managed this with the two younger ones. But the older boy and girl lived with Protestant relatives and slipped out of the Board's system of relief and thus beyond their power to move to suit Catholic wishes.[10]

By 1864 the Board resolved to stop providing rent payments for the poor and to construct instead Poor Houses capable of accommodating around a dozen people. With a 4% loan, the work costing £596 went rapidly ahead[11] so that by June 1865 paupers were being allotted rooms in the new building. Once the Poor Houses were open the Board brought to an end the help with rent payments that it had hitherto provided for certain paupers. These payments had commonly amounted to £2 a year. After 1865 paupers with accommodation problems were offered room in the Poor Houses instead. Those unfortunates utterly incapable of coping with life and without relatives to care for them were despatched to Aberdeen Asylum. By 1871 the Board was spending just over £515 on the regular relief of paupers, a further £14 on casual paupers and £11 on medical care.[12] The amounts received by the paupers, as shown in the Registers for 1894–8[13] had not increased very substantially; five paupers received 6/- a week, nine got 5/-, five were paid 4/-, three obtained 3/6 but the bulk – eighteen – got 3/-, three got 2/6 and twelve received 2/-.

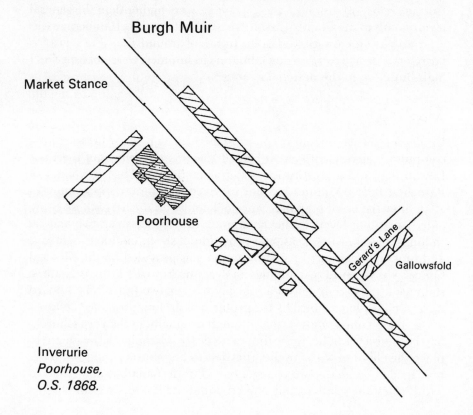

Burgh Muir

Market Stance

Poorhouse

Gerard's Lane

Gallowsfold

Inverurie
Poorhouse,
O.S. 1868.

Their numbers had fluctuated during the period 1859–95[14] between a peak of 61 in 1869 to a lower figure of 25 in 1859. Numbers rose steadily up to 1867 and remained in the upper fifties till 1872. They then fell to a figure much closer to 40, even dropping to 33 in 1881. Possibly the Board of Supervision's increasing pressure for tighter administration played its part here. Numbers then began to creep up again and 1882–95 ranged from 41 to 53 with a tendency to be closer to the latter rather than the former. This took place despite the Board of Supervision's continued efforts and may well reflect the problems of a country parish and town at a time of agricultural difficulties, though the number of paupers for whom Inverurie was responsible but who lived elsewhere makes conclusions difficult.

Of the 70 paupers listed in the Registers for 1894–98 half were able to earn a little themselves, had small savings, or were helped by family members. The kind of work they were able to perform included knitting, shoe repairing, tea-selling, taking in lodgers, washing and pedlar-work. Of these 70, 64 were women, and it was to those of these women who were struggling to support families that the higher rate of relief (6/-) was paid. Of the rest seven children, twelve mentally defective paupers and nine elderly ones were listed, the rest suffered a variety of ailments, many being those especially associated with old age.

Very occasionally the paupers were provided with treats when a great occasion seemed to warrant it. The Prince of Wales' marriage was marked by a free dinner for the poor[15] and the Queen's Jubilee by the donation to each of them of two shillings.[16] But help might also be provided to them, and to some not on the official roll of the poor, by charities too. Later nineteenth century Inverurie contained a Soup Kitchen to help sustain poor folk in the depths of winter. The Coal Fund of the early part of the century was re-constituted in 1854 and remained active for nearly thirty years.[17] The Fund was available to those who had lived in the Burgh for at least five years and who seemed to an assembly of all those who had subscribed at least 2/6 to be deserving cases. Bags of coal – usually two per pauper – were delivered once a year and, very occasionally twice. The numbers in receipt of this charity ranged from thirty seven (in January 1856) to ninety three (in January 1865) though in general around fifty five to seventy people were helped in this way. In 1860 the Coal Fund not only made three deliveries totalling 146 separate deliveries in all, but co-operated with the Soup Kitchen by buying meal as well. Fifty two paupers received deliveries of meal in what must have been a very bleak year even though the Parochial Board's Minute Books for that date show the official number on the roll to have been rather low, a mere twenty-nine.

Schooling before 1872

In the 1790s Inverurie's parish school provided education for a mere forty pupils in winter and thirty in summer.[18] The small thatched building where pupils gathered was surrounded by weeds and filth,[19] but in the early nineteenth century a more solid structure was provided. In order to save money it was constructed to but onto the Town House, the lower storey formed a schoolroom and the upper one housed the schoolmaster who reached his dwelling by an outside staircase.[20] A better building did not necessarily mean better schooling. There was no blackboard in the classroom, pupils sat on two long rows of sloping desks that faced one another whilst the master's taller desk was carefully placed close by the fireplace[21] which was fed with peats brought by pupils. In 1895 James Skinner, a former pupil at this school, looked back to recall how little teaching had actually taken place. Each pupil struggled with problems 'and when he thought he had got the answer he would go up and show his slate to the master and if it was not right, go back to his seat and sit perhaps a day or two more on the same question'.[22] From 1834 the Council endeavoured to encourage the pupils to apply themselves by offering annual prizes of books worth two guineas as a stimulus to hard work.[23]

By 1842 the school roll had edged up to ninety pupils; the master's income had risen from one hundred pounds Scots to a £30 salary with a further £32 from fees.[24] But Inverurie's expansion was starting to press hard upon school accommodation. In 1859 the Council responded to grumbles about the building voiced by the Inspectors employed by the Dick and Milne Bequests by promising to improve conditions for teachers and pupils and accommodate the growing numbers of children by building new premises.[25] The building of a new Town House in any case compelled an attack on the problem of the school building and a new site was used a few hundred yards away, off the Market Place. On it was put up a school made up of one large classroom and two smaller ones:[26] in it presided Alexander Fowlie as teacher of the boys and his daughter Margaret as teacher of the girls.[27]

The parish school was not the only educational establishment in Inverurie. Early in the century the council was aiding a female school run by Miss Anderson with £5 a year. The New Statistical Account notes the presence of five female schools in the parish, offering their pupils reading, English, knitting and sewing.[28] By 1871 there were still two schools of this type inside the burgh run by Miss Cruickshank and Miss Hay and with 27 and 14 children respectively in attendance. Reading, Writing and Arithmetic were provided, together with Music and

Sewing. Just one of these 'adventure' schools survived in 1871 in the parish outside the burgh boundaries, attended by twenty-three children.[29]

The Disruption was followed by the active intervention in education of the newly established Free Church. First a Sunday School was begun, then a day school on a site provided by Lord Kintore. Next to it an Infant School was set up by Lady Kintore, whilst in the Burgh Muir a mission school was established.[30] The Free Church School employed a certificated teacher (as the parish school did), along with an assistant. It offered a range of subjects above the three basic ones including Higher English, Maths and Latin, but not the Greek and French or German the Parish School provided. At three shillings (on average) its fees fell sixpence below those the Parish School charged. The Episcopal Church, too, set up a school. St Mary's catered for ninety three children in 1871, well below the 142 at the Free Church School and the 168 at the Parish School.[31]

In 1870 William Clark, a retired merchant living at Woodhill Cottage, Kinellar, decided to devote much of his life's savings to a school for 'the religious and moral education of poor children'. The Council provided a site off Chelsea Road for both the school bulding costing £131 and an adjoining teacher's house.[32] In September 1871 Agnes Ross opened her career in the school (having moved from North Street Mission School) by teaching thirty three pupils for £20 a year[33] and a free house. William Clark died in 1883 having appointed the Council to watch over the school's affairs. Education was provided for girls without age restriction, but for some years boys had to be under eight years if they were to attend.[34] All were to be 'children of poor but honest parents ... poor orphan or neglected children ... The Scholars shall be taught English, Reading, Spelling, Writing, Geography, Grammar and Arithmetic and the girls shall in addition be taught needlework'. Miss Ross died in 1873, her successor, Elspeth Davidson, remained at the school till its closure in 1903 and thereafter lived in retirement in the schoolhouse. The school roll rose to a peak of sixty one in 1891 and then fell steadily until it was a mere twenty four in the year of its closure.[35]

The School Board

By the time of the 1872 Education Act's passage through Parliament, eight schools were operating in the burgh. In March 1873 the Inverurie School Board held its first meeting to elect a chairman and institute a census of children of school age in the parish together with a survey of the accommodation available for them in the schools. For its second meeting the Board switched from the parish school to the Town Hall. It noted that of the parish total of 364 boys and 356 girls between the ages of five and thirteen, there were forty seven boys and fifty one girls who were not attending school.[36] The board also noted that the parish schoolmaster was earning nearly £200 a year, a quarter of it being his salary, almost half from fees, £10 for providing instruction to pupil teachers and £20 paid him to help with house rent since no school house was provided. His daughter received £70 and the two pupil teachers £20 each. One of the more curious educational functionaries was George Thompson who not only received £8 for teaching music but almost £5 more for cleaning the school. The Free Church School's master received a slightly lower salary – £150 – but did have a house provided. His assistant teacher received £60, £20 less than the male assistant Mr Fowlie had added to his school's strength by 1873.[37]

The fees being charged at the various schools ranged, by 1872, from 3/6 a quarter at the Parish School, to 3/- at the Free Church and 2/6 at the Episcopal School. At Miss Cruickshank's and Miss Hall's schools the fees could rise to as high as 15/- for pupils attempting a range of subjects that included Music and Drawing. The new fees laid down by the School Board covered the Parish and Free Church premises that they took over and to which most Inverurie children went. Four hundred children were accounted for by these two schools, the two costly private schools had but one tenth of that number, forty five were attracted by the free attendance at Clarks and eighty five went to the Episcopal School. The Board's fees ranged up in stages from 2/- a quarter in Standards I and II to 4/- in Standards V and VI. Pupils attempting 'higher' subjects like languages and mathematics paid extra and all children had still to find a shilling to pay for the heating of their schools in winter.[38]

In May 1873 Board members visited the Parish School for a day. They noted it offered Scripture, English, Reading, Writing, Arithmetic, English Grammar, Geography, Latin, Greek, French, Algebra and Geometry. Board members watched some of these subjects being taught and were able to record the methods of teaching that were used 'To the assembled classes able to read, the Bible is taught historically, the pupils being questioned as to their perception of the meaning of the statements read. These also learn the Shorter Catechism, except such as are desired by their parents or guardians not to be taught in it. In the younger classes the teacher reads the simpler Scripture narratives or gives short accounts of the biographies contained in them'.[39] Board members watched teachers giving instruction. Of those taking extra subjects twenty one studied French, eleven pupils did Latin, and ten pupils studied Greek. Algebra and Geometry each attracted five pupils.

This school – which seemed to the Board both efficient and successful – was the obvious basis for expansion. Its three staff, its several rooms, and its site with space around it, all made it a suitable focus for the effort to centralise education, towards which the Board gradually moved. In any case expansion of the Market Place parish school became increasingly necessary as a result of the closure of the burgh's private schools, the further growth of burgh population, and an increasing interest (in the last decade of the century) in the establishment of secondary education. The Board was investigating, by November 1875, what costs would be entailed on the ratepayers by the creation of an addition to Market Place School to accommodate 160 pupils and the placing of all the scholars under one teacher. By 1876 compulsory attendance had been introduced and parents were being prosecuted for failure to send their children to school. Some seemed to adapt slowly to the new requirement and promised that their children would be along eventually – when the harvest work was complete.[40] Both West High Street and Market Place Schools were overcrowded. But local ratepayers showed little enthusiasm for the phasing out of West High Street. One member of the meeting held to discuss the fusion of the two schools complained of the behaviour of Market Place children and maintained 'language was used by the bigger boys and girls it would shock one to hear'.[41] So, for several years, Inverurie made do. Minor changes were made to existing premises including the laying on of water supplies to the schools in May 1877. In 1889 the Free Church abandoned responsibility for its Infant School, handing it over to the Board for a short while but then withdrawing the property from the Board's use.[42] A gallery was put into West High Street as a way of giving more teaching space. This school's condition produced adverse reports from Inspectors and, in 1891, from a committee sent to investigate the premises. The committee found inadequate space, lack of proper divisions between classes, forms without backs, worn out desks . . . and walls and floors that were far from clean. 'The most serious defect however is the position of the offices which are within a few yards of the large windows by which the school is aired . . . The playground for the girls is much too small and there is an opening into a drain in the centre of it'.[43]

By 1895 the Board had carried out extensions at Market Place costing £1,355 that enabled it to take all the older pupils; West High Street became an infant department of the main school.[44] Three new classrooms were built each measuring twenty nine feet by twenty five feet. The amalgamation of the two schools placed two experienced male teachers – Mr Fowlie and Mr Fortune – under the same roof. The solution was to separate off and give to Mr Fowlie the newly introduced secondary department: Mr Fortune took responsibility for the standard grade work.[45] This secondary department had been established after around ten years speculation as to Inverurie's viability as a focus for such specification. The Education Department's initial enquiry was fended off by the School Board who felt that whilst their teachers were able to reach the level required, local demand would not warrant the effort.[46]

By 1888 local ratepayers were petitioning for a secondary school, complaining that at present those eager for such provision for their children had to find the cost of sending them to Aberdeen.[47] But it was five years before the Board admitted the point, having seen that around 40 children regularly went by train to Aberdeen for schooling, plus a further twenty from the nearby countryside.[48] By then it was clear that the G.N.S.R. Locomotive Works would be coming to Inverurie so that, though the Board guessed initial demand to be for around thirty children, in the longer term numbers would justify the expenses involved.[49] The rates charged by the School Board jumped up to eleven pence from the earlier levels of seven pence to eight pence. By 1890 the Board had stopped charging fees, though it did get help from the Milne Bequest with the costs of poorer pupils.

Thus one of the newly provided classrooms was set aside for the secondary department. The official opening in September 1895, was marked by local celebrations. It was planned that Mr Fowlie would teach English, Arithmetic, Modern Languages and Science plus specialist teaching in drawing and sewing.[50] But within a year there were complaints that the Secondary Department had not fulfilled expectations and many parents had withdrawn their children from it.[51] Pupils seem to have been hard to find, the Board resorted to offering prizes of a pound each to those who passed the inspection – three girls who did particularly well were given £1.10.0 After a long career teaching Inverurie children Mr Fowlie seems to have found coping with the secondary department to be too much.[52] He finally retired in 1898 after an awkward period in which the Board tried to push him into other areas of teaching.[53] James Philip took his place.

Subjects other than the basic ones were gradually added to the curricula of the various schools in the later nineteenth century. Drill and singing arrived in the seventies.[54] Drill seems to have occurred but intermittently and to have needed inspectorial prodding firstly to keep it alive and secondly to turn it into the late century fashion of musical drill (executed to the accompaniment of a piano).[55] In the mid-nineties cookery classes began[56] together with dressmaking and laundry-work. A specialist teacher, Miss Squibbs, began sewing classes in 1895 to which twenty-three girls came despite having to find one and sixpence a lesson. As for the results, 'the dresses were individually examined by several ladies from Aberdeen and pronounced to be well-made and finished in every respect'.[57]

The Board also watched over the growth in Inverurie of evening classes for adults. In 1893 sixty six adults enrolled for various classes, forty seven for arithmetic, twenty eight for writing and composition, twenty nine for shorthand and thirty for building and drawing construction. Classes seem to have been shared between Mr Fortune (who specialised in Arithmetic) and Mr Mitchell who concentrated on English, including reading from Shakespeare and other authors.[58] In 1899 came a new venture, classes in agriculture which rapidly proved to be popular, and classes in dairying.[59]

At school

Few nineteenth century log books for Inverurie schools have survived. For the main burgh school only that for the Infant Department from 1895 is available. Its entries show pupils learning songs, singing them, and carrying out drill exercises using dumb-bells. Standard I began Geography, learning 'the cardinal points and directions about the town' and classes also studied pictures of animals 'for object lesson purposes'.[61] Kindergarten work for infants, arithmetic, spelling, 'specimen writing' and knitting all put in appearances. The Inspectorate's visits provided the school with respectable reports.

The teaching was seen as skilful and vigorous and encompassed the areas of activity Inspectors wished to see. The school's success contrasted with the wretched impression made by St Mary's Episcopal School.[63] Here pupils huddled together on school furniture discarded by other establishments, in classrooms spattered with ink and graffiti. Many children used their fingers to help work out problems in arithmetic and produced writing of an appallingly low standard. Persistent criticism was beginning to make its mark, however, by the end of the century.

For teachers at both schools ensuring a regular attendance by pupils remained a major pre-occupation. Illnesses, poor weather, local occasions (like markets) and local farming needs were all likely to lead to pupils being kept from school. Indeed mere concern about 'an alarm that has got abroad about the fever'[64] was enough for children to be kept from school. In the seventies the importance of the Inverurie feeing market was recognised by the closure of the parish school; by the nineties attempts to stay open at this time were being made, but absenteeism was substantial.[65] Not only the main feeing market but others too drew pupils from school. On March 9th, 1897, the Head of the Infant School noted 'The Cottar Market is being held today. Attendance affected' and on October 6th, 'Kinkell Market is being held today and the afternoon attendance is much down'.

The feeing markets and the associated movement of many farm-workers from one employer to another brought headaches to Inverurie teachers (as to those serving any rural area) represented by log-book entries as 'The Term and flitting have interfered with the attendance'. Children departed, new pupils arrived, in considerable numbers.[66] Further distractions were provided by visiting entertainments. Inverurie in the nineties seems to have been frequently visited by travelling circuses; sometimes the Head closed his school in recognition of the likely attendance if school remained open.[67] Major entertainments in Aberdeen – like a visit from Barnum's Circus in 1899 – could also pull children away from school in Inverurie.[68]

Leisure activities

Education did not depend entirely on the school system. Inverurie inhabitants developed a number of cultural and leisure organizations and activities as the century progressed. As early as 1842 visiting lecturers were coming to the burgh; in that year for example, there were lectures on agriculture by a visiting Professor.[69] By 1858 Inverurie had a Circulating Library, an Institute and Reading Room and a Musical Association.[70] The Institute Trustees were eager to see a proper library developed and tried to prod the Council's interest by buying for this purpose 'the Pictorial History of England in ten volumes and Macaulay's Historical and Critical Essays'.[71] Courses of lectures became increasingly common. Some were regarded as important in their own right, others were also devices for raising money for a worthy cause. The Y.M.C.A. lectures of 1871 were for 'relief of cases of destitution not reached by the Parochial Board'.[72] James Skinner used fees from lectures, that included a group bravely attempting to explain the complexities of the Eastern Question, to help fund the Library and Museum he successfully sought to create.[73] By 1900 Inverurie had, too, a Bowling and Tennis Club (1884), a Curling Club, a Draughts Club that met in the Town Hall, a Cricket Club who used a part of the Market Stance that they had carefully improved, and a Football Club who proceeded, in winter, to damage the nicely levelled area prepared by the Cricket Club.[74] The town had developed to a size where it could support many varied leisure interests; in this respect at least its expansion in the nineteenth century brought benefit to its inhabitants. School improvement cost money the Council sometimes seemed to resent finding, just as it had also grumbled about expenditure on water supplies. But small towns, like large cities were pushed by the changing society of later Victorian times into increased interference in people's affairs and thus into increased expenditure. Even leisure time required that organized activities in specially-provided places be created – a marked contrast to the more informal (though more poverty stricken) days of the previous century.

Appendix 1

Subscriptions to the Inverurie Road 1799–1803
(Source, Inverurie Turnpike Trust Accounts Book)

	£	s.	d.
Sir Alexander Bannerman	100	–	–
Dr Beattie, Insch	100	–	–
Rev. Brown, Newhills	25	–	–
W. Burnett, Advocate, Aberdeen	100	–	–
John Craig, Drimmond, Lawyer	25	–	–
James Davidson, Fintray	100	–	–
R. Dalrymple, Elphinstone of Logie	248	–	–
H. Knight Erskine, Pittodrie	100	–	–
J. Staat Forbes, Aberdeen merchant	500	–	–
James Forbes, Seaton	400	–	–
Col. Erskine Fraser, Woodhill	100	–	–
Charles Fraser, Williamstone	100	–	–
The Duke of Gordon	250	–	–
Gen. Gordon, Fyvie	100	–	–
William Gordon, Rothney	50	–	–
Thomas Gray, Mains of Westhall	50	–	–
Robert Harvey, Braco	500	–	–
John Henderson, Caskieben	400	–	–
Hugh Hutcheon, Broadford	200	–	–
Andrew Jopp, Aberdeen, Advocate	50	–	–
The Earl of Kintore	300	–	–
Thomas Leys, Glasgoforest	500	–	–
Alexander Leith, Freefeld	100	–	–
W. Forbes Leith, Whitehaugh	50	–	–
Hugh Leslie, Powis	50	–	–
Archibald Lawson, Milntown of Kemnay	25	–	–
Benjamin Lumsden, Boghead	20	–	–
William McKnight, Nether Coullie	20	–	–
Roderick McKenzie, Glack	50	–	–
Rev. Dr Mitchell	50	–	–
George Mackie, Kintore, Merchant	25	–	–
John Robertson, Blackchambers	50	–	–
George Skene, Skene	200	–	–
Alexander Shand, Tanfield, Lawyer	100	–	–
James Stephen, Miln of Williamston	40	–	–
Mrs Thom, Craibstone	203	–	–
Adam Wilson, Merchant, Aberdeen	100	–	–
George Wilson, Glasgowego	200	–	–
John Stuart, Merchant, Aberdeen	125	–	–

James Harthill and others	105	5	–
Hugh Gordon and Co.	100	–	–
Robert Lamb, Merchant, Aberdeen	100	–	–
Alexander Midler, Merchant, Aberdeen	100	–	–
General Alexander Hay of Rannis	200	–	–
Inverurie Burgh	50	–	–

Appendix 2

Businesses in Inverurie
(Sources: Pigot's, Slater's and Worrall's Directories)

Occupations		1837	1867	1877	1903
Professional					
Accountants		–	–	–	1
Solicitors		–	1	–	3
Surgeons		2	4	3	2
Veterinary surgeons		–	2	1	1
	Totals	2	7	4	7
Services					
Auctioneers		–	1	2	–
Banks		2	4	5	4
Commission agent and game dealer		–	–	1	1
Insurance agents		2	9	12	6
Sewing machine agent		–	–	2	–
	Totals	4	14	22	11
Shopkeepers and dealers					
Bakers and confectioners		2	3	4	5
Beer retailer		–	–	1	–
Bookseller and stationer		–	2	3	2
Cattle dealer		–	–	1	6
Chemist and druggist		2	3	2	3
Coal and Lime merchant		2	3	4	4
Cycle agent and maker		–	–	–	3
Dairyman		–	–	–	1
Draper and clothier		–	–	–	4
Flesher		2	5	9	5
Furniture broker		–	–	1	–
Glass and china dealer		–	–	–	2
Greengrocer		–	–	1	–
Grain merchant		–	1	–	–
Grocer, draper, general merchant		6	16	26	13
Hairdresser		–	1	1	2
Horse dealer and breaker		–	–	1	1
Innkeeper and spirit dealer		9	8	11	9
Ironmonger		–	3	3	3
Photographer		–	2	1	1
Poultry and fish dealer		–	–	–	1
Shopkeeper (undefined)		–	1	4	3
Wool warehouse keeper		–	–	1	–
	Totals	23	48	74	68

Occupations

	1837	1867	1877	1903
Crafts and trades				
Agriculural engineer/millwright	–	1	–	1
Blacksmiths	3	3	3	3
Boot and shoe makers and dealers	6	9	7	8
Brazier and tinsmiths	–	1	1	1
Brewers, maltsters and distillers	2	1	1	–
Cabinet makers	2	1	1	1
Coach builder	–	1	1	1
Cooper and turner	1	2	1	–
Hide factor	–	–	1	2
Joiners, cartwrights, builders	6	6	7	7
Millers and grain merchants	1	1	3	2
Milliners and dressmakers	1	3	5	4
Mineral water manufacturer	–	–	–	1
Painters and plumbers	–	3	5	2
Papermaker	–	1	1	1
Paperhanger	–	–	1	1
Plasterers	–	–	3	2
Printers	–	1	1	2
Provision curer	–	2	–	–
Saddlers	3	2	2	2
Sausage skin maker	–	–	–	1
Slaters	–	2	3	4
Stonecutters, masons, builders	2	2	4	4
Tailors	6	6	9	7
Tanners	1	1	1	–
Watchmakers	2	2	2	3
Weavers	–	3	–	–
Woodmerchant	1	1	1	–
Wool manufacturer	–	–	–	1
Totals	37	55	64	61

Appendix 3

Numbers in receipt of poor relief in the Parish of Inverurie 1859–95 according to the half-yearly rolls of the poor
(Source, Inverurie Parochial Board Minute Books 1858–72 and 1872–95)

The list includes those residing in Aberdeen Asylum.

In June 1865, the opening of a Poorhouse led to a switch from providing help with rent payment (commonly about £2) to offering free accommodation in the Poorhouse. Entries then become numbers in Poorhouse.

Date	Total receiving aid	Male	Female	Receiving rent or accommodation in Inverurie	Residing in places other than Inverurie
2.8.1859	25	6	19	6	11
9.2.1860	29	9	20	7	12
7.8.1860	29	8	21	7	10
5.2.1861	32	8	24	8	12
6.8.1861	31	9	22	8	12
18.2.1862	33	11	22	8	12
11.8.1862	39	12	27	10	13
17.2.1862	40	11	29	10	12
17.8.1863	40	14	26	12	17
16.2.1864	41	17	24	13	13
9.8.1864	44	18	26	9	16
7.2.1865	45	16	29	14	15
1.8.1865	44	15	29	12	10
6.2.1866	45	16	29	16	2 (Asylum
7.8.1866	53	21	32	14	3 only shown)
5.2.1867	54	22	32	11	9
20.8.1867	59	19	40	5	20
4.2.1868	56	15	41	10	15
11.8.1868	58	18	40	10	21
2.2.1869	61	21	40	11	20
10.8.1869	57	21	36	14	15
1.2.1870	55	20	35	13	14
9.8.1870	57	22	35	12	18
7.2.1871	58	23	35	None entered	16
8.8.1871	53	22	31	9	14
6.2.1872	59	23	36	15	14
6.8.1872	56	20	36	No entry	15
4.2.1873	50	18	32	11	12
5.8.1873	48	16	32	11	11

Date	Total receiving aid	Male	Female	Receiving rent or accommodation in Inverurie	Reading in places other than Inverurie
3.2.1874	46	18	28	11	11
4.8.1874	41	19	22	10	12
2.2.1875	41	17	24	11	14
3.8.1875	37	14	23	12	9
2.2.1876	40	15	25	10	13
1.8.1876	41	17	24	10	11
6.2.1877	40	16	24	9	13
7.8.1877	39	15	24	11	13
5.2.1878	38	15	23	9	14
6.8.1878	41	17	24	11	13
4.2.1879	40	15	25	11	15
5.8.1879	40	14	26	9	13
3.2.1880	35	10	25	8	12
3.8.1880	34	11	23	9	10
1.2.1881	33	11	22	10	10
2.8.1881	37	12	25	10	12
7.2.1882	43	14	29	11	15
1.8.1882	52	14	38	11	20
6.2.1883	51	17	34	9	17
7.8.1883	50	16	34	8	14
5.2.1884	51	18	33	9	14
5.8.1884	44	16	28	11	13
3.2.1885	51	19	32	10	13
4.8.1885	51	17	34	8	14
2.2.1886	48	16	32	7	15
3.8.1886	49	18	31	8	16
1.2.1887	49	20	29	9	16
2.8.1887	45	18	27	10	12
7.2.1888	45	14	31	10	16
7.8.1888	44	16	28	10	14
5.2.1889	52	23	29	11	15
6.8.1889	53	23	30	10	18
4.2.1890	50	18	32	10	15
5.8.1890	53	18	35	10	20
3.2.1891	50	17	33	10	21
4.8.1891	49	17	32	9	17
2.2.1892	46	15	31	7	18
2.8.1892	47	16	31	7	20
7.2.1893	50	16	34	8	22
1.8.1893	44	13	31	8	17
6.2.1894	43	10	33	5	21
7.8.1894	41	10	31	8	18
5.2.1895	41	10	31	6	19

Royal Hotel, Fraserburgh, 1862

Part III

A FISHING TOWN – FRASERBURGH

Chapter One

FRASERBURGH BEFORE THE NINETEENTH CENTURY

In 1800 Fraserburgh was a well-established and sizeable community that had been expanding since the mid sixteenth century. The transformation of the tiny fishing hamlet of Faithlie into the town of Fraserburgh owed much to the energy of the local lairds, the Frasers. They sought to improve a site that seemed to have potential, perched as it was on the north-eastern tip of Aberdeenshire, able to tap the resources of the sea. In 1542 Alexander Fraser obtained a charter from James V allowing him to exploit the fishings opposite his lands. His tenants had to drag their tiny fishing craft up onto the beach for the community lacked any kind of man-made harbour. Queen Mary's 1546 charter established Faithlie as a burgh of barony whose burgesses were permitted to trade in goods such as wool, linen, wine and bread. Plans began to be made for building a pier.[1] In 1576 the current laird laid the first stone of what was to remain Fraserburgh's main harbour work until the nineteenth century. The pier-building and town-improving activities of the Frasers brought the family a knighthood and the right to re-name the community 'Fraserburgh'. An attempt to equip the town with a university (1592–4) produced buildings and the appointment of a Principal, but soon collapsed in failure.[2]

In 1601 a new charter established Fraserburgh as a burgh of regality and barony. The feuars, who made up the burgesses, were able to set up a market cross and hold twice-weekly markets around it as well as running two large annual fairs. The tolls from these markets, and from harbour dues, made up a revenue the town could deploy for its maintenance. But the laird remained firmly in control. He nominated the officials who managed Fraserburgh affairs and exercised criminal justice too.[3]

By the end of the seventeenth century at least three hundred people lived in Fraserburgh. Close by, to the north of the town, lay the fishing village of Broadsea inhabited by a further forty. The population included twenty-one merchants, twenty seamen, and a range of craft-workers embracing shoemaking, weaving, tailoring, smith wright and building work, coopering and hookmaking.[4] The town was laid out in a rectangular shape enclosing streets that crossed at right-angles.[5] By the

Mid eighteenth century Fraserburgh – a very general impression of the town as shown on Roy's Military survey. Its rectangular shape is clearly evident along with the main harbour-work – the small North Pier. Part of the Middle Jetty had been built by this time but does not feature.

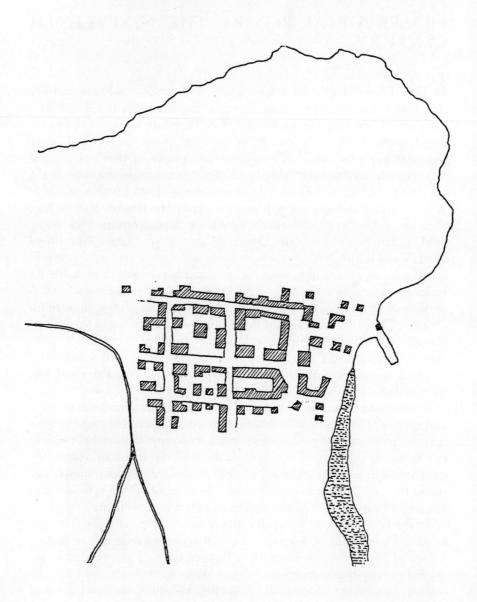

Saltoun Square, an important focus of Fraserburgh life. Gas lighting can be seen in the street.

late eighteenth century it had swelled to a population of around a thousand, with two hundred more inhabiting Broadsea.[6] Eighteenth century visitors stressed the value of the harbour in the town's growth and the primary concern of its inhabitants with fishing.[7] A wide-range of fish, including cod, ling, skate, turbot, whiting, haddock, mackerel, lobsters were caught close to the shore from the small open boats of the fishermen.[8] The Frasers, who had tried to stimulate this activity, also tried to control it through a tacksman. Those who dared 'sell fish to a Contractor without leave from the Proprietor of the Town should be turned out of the Town and not allowed to settle in it again'.[9]

The improvement of agriculture in the area around Fraserburgh was also slowly under way. Greater efficiency and productivity were likely to benefit the town's food supplies and perhaps aid its trade by providing a surplus for export. Tree-planting, turnip and clover growing, the drainage of land and the regular use of fallowing were all being implemented in a few places by the late eighteenth century. But most tenants stuck resolutely to the infield and outfield they knew well, and were slow to accept modern techniques of crop rotation. A little flax was grown and some of the town's women busied themselves producing yarn.[10]

The Fraser family was well aware of the need to work upon townspeople's attitudes and encourage a range of improvements. An estate notebook of the 1780s kept by Lord Saltoun (or possibly by his factor) includes the view 'When there is a thriving village on an estate it is very much the Interest of the Proprietor to encourage it, when it is a good Sea Port and situated so that the finest advantage is to be gained to the Proprietor by his lands surrounding the Town, then it is unquestionably the cheapest and surest Improvement he can attempt upon his Estate. . . . the more the Town increases in Population the higher will the neighbouring lands rise in value therefore everything that will contribute to increase their number is most worthy of the Proprietor's attention'.[11]

The aspects in need of most urgent attention seemed, to the author, to include improving the streets and buildings, (in order not to deter incomers with the sight of properties in such a shabby state as to suggest Fraserburgh was a very poverty-stricken place) encouraging manufacturers and making sure the town's school was in a satisfactory state. The fuel shortage that plagued Fraserburgh might be eased if a Coal House were put up from which the poor could be supplied with small quantities at a time. Peat was costly to purchase and expensive in time to gather. But most importantly the author discussed harbour improvements. Shipbuilding should be encouraged (in fact a firm had opened up

before the century ended),[12] the porters properly licensed, issued with
badges, and organized and the harbour works further extended. By the
late eighteenth century it was clear that the ten-to-eleven foot depth of
water in the harbour at high tide, its virtual drying up at low tide, and its
exposure to east and north-easterly gales were all serious handicaps.[13]
The Town Council itself felt the harbour had become dangerously
decayed,[14] whilst the expert advice it sought from John Rennie included
the observation that when winds blew from the east 'the water is so
agitated (the boats) are nearly in as great danger as if they were in the
open bay'.[15] At least the town now had a lighthouse. In 1787 the
Commissioners of Northern Lights added it to the top of the four-storey
castle-remains at Kinnaird Head.[16] Such changes were significant for a
community that saw the sea as a main source of income both for fishing
and for the general trade in food, fertilizers, building materials and other
bulky necessities.

The town itself was in need of improvement too. It had no proper
water supply for the thousand people packed into its confines.[17] A
number of properties were substantial stone buildings with tiled or slated
roofs[18] but grass grew in streets which lacked both pavements and water
channels.[19] Dunghills and peatstacks littered the by-ways and pigs
wandered loose among the houses.[20] The roads to Fraserburgh were in a
poor condition with statute labour proving unequal to their adequate
maintenance.[21] Yet the revenue from the harbour and market dues
produced little more than £60 in a year for the town council.[22] In 1802,
for example, the dues were leased to William Couper for £65.[23] In an
attempt to improve town revenues Lord Saltoun allowed the town
certain properties in 1787. Rent from the Links (where a few cattle were
tended by a herd), from various parks and properties brought in a little
over £20.[24] Nor could the town boast an impressive array of commercial
or service buildings. A small tollbooth housed a jail beneath it; a bank
operated – but only from the upper room of the Oak Tree Inn, whilst the
proprietor of the Post Office sold sugar, tea, ale and clothes to customers
over a locked half-door that kept them firmly in the streets.[25]

Though well placed to exploit the fisheries and to serve the nearby
countryside, Fraserburgh was far from certain of being able either to
cope with a flurry of increased economic activity or to provide adequately for the people such economic activity would pull into the town.

Chapter Two

THE IMPROVED ECONOMY

Fishing

Eighteenth century Fraserburgh was one of many communities that were partly sustained by harvesting the rich shoals of fish that swam close to the coast of north-east Aberdeenshire. But more efficient than local people at hauling in sizeable catches (especially of herring) were Dutch seamen who sometimes pushed so aggressively into coastal waters as to edge out local people from their own accustomed fishing grounds.[1] Though the seas swarmed with all kinds of white fish and herring shoals passed nearby[2] Fraserburg fishermen made but small inroads into this vast potential resource. The area lacked a large and thoroughly secure harbour. The small open boats used for fishing ventured no more than ten miles from the coast and, upon return, had to be dragged onto the beach. In vessels without either cooking or sleeping facilities the crews sailed off on their expeditions for part of the day only.[3] In the 1790s the fisher-town of Broadsea supported a mere seven boats[4] crewed by men hired by a tacksman and bound to hand over a sixth of their catch to him and a further portion to the minister.[5] Not until 1828 were Broadsea men allowed to own their own boats. This change removed a long-standing source of resentment and helped encourage a more vigorous pursuit of fishing that improved the prospects of Broadsea. The Reverend Simpson, the parish minister in the 1790s, urged the creation of a better harbour as the proper solution to Fraserburgh's limited success as a fishing centre;[6] certainly the improvement of the habour was to be a key factor in helping both fisheries and the town of Fraserburgh to expand in the nineteenth century.

Other factors also played a part. Dutch dominance of herring fishing was attacked by the Government in the mid eighteenth century through a subsidy to those fitting out vessels for this work. Even more effective was the introduction of a bounty of two shillings a barrel in 1786 paid on herring cured to conform with regulations laid down by the Fishery Board.[7] By 1815 this bounty had been raised to four shillings, and though it fell away after 1826 until finally abolished in 1830, it had served its purpose well.[8] As early as 1805 large catches were being taken off

Fraserburgh: in 1810 four thousand barrels at least were crammed with cured herring.[9] In 1814, the 'Aberdeen Journal' noted an especially successful fishing season that could have been even more productive had local people been better prepared with supplies of salt and barrels. Five vessels were loaded up with barrels of fish to take from the town. It is not surprising that Lord Saltoun urged fishermen to come to Fraserburgh and share in what was looked on as an expanding opportunity, especially since an improved harbour was at last taking shape.[10] With government bounties, sales in Britain and Ireland, and exports to the continent too, the herring business drew in men tempted by the chance of prospering amid its erratic fortunes.

At the same time white fishing continued to be pursued. Whereas herring fishing attracted outsiders, white fishing was prosecuted through much of the year by local people. The building of a railway to Fraser-burgh in 1865 helped considerably by offering speedy access to British markets. The local railway network enabled fishwives to visit nearby places (like Strichen and New Deer) in a day selling their catches or exchanging them for eggs, butter and cheese. It was possible to visit several places when, before the railway age, a journey to one inland village alone meant a very long weary day's trudging.[11] For a time, in the fifties and sixties Fraserburgh was one of the centres from which Green-land whaling and sealing was pursued. In 1857 five whalers sailed from town, in 1859 there were six. But then decline rapidly set in.[12]

It was herring fishing that attracted the largest numbers. Boat design improved and the twenty-foot vessels of the early part of the century had been replaced, by its end, with sixty-foot decked boats able to sail far out into the North Sea.[13] The replacement of heavy hemp nets by cotton ones in the 1860s increased boats' catching capacities even further. A Fraserburgh boat of 1875 was carrying around fifty five nets, fifteen years earlier it would probably have carried a mere thirty.[14] The numbers of boats increased. Boats owned for fishing in the Fraserburgh district (which embraced Rosehearty, Pitullie and Pennan) rose from under a hundred in the early years of the century to 227 in 1863, 626 in 1872[15] and 688 by 1882.[16] Since the average boat employed a crew of six there was plenty of work not only for local people, but also for many incomers who came to Fraserburgh for the herring season. Boats and their gear were becoming more costly, a process much aggravated by the introduc-tion of steam power in the area at the end of the century, but Fraserburgh fishermen managed still to keep a grip on sailing boats at least, through shared ownership of their craft.[17]

The great growth of fishing in the nineteenth century had several important results for Fraserburgh. It encouraged continued investment in harbour improvement, built up a range of trades directly dependent on fishing, and helped other businesses indirectly. At times the town seemed dominated by fish. In streets and lanes gutting and packing proceeded; on the roofs of fisher-cottages gutted split and salted fish were spread out to dry; endless shoals of dead fish stretched out on the rocky shore, drying, and watched over by children charged with the task of keeping seagulls at bay. But fishing brought problems too. It provided a living that fluctuated very considerably, whilst the flood of folk who poured into Fraserburgh for the herring season created problems of health, housing and law and order.

Farming

The presence of a large community not chiefly concerned with agriculture may well have stimulated nearby farmers to seek to produce a surplus for sale. Certainly the proximity of a port helped those interested in exporting their bulky produce. By the late eighteenth century improved agricultural techniques were making their impact on Fraserburgh's hinterland. Not only the traditional crops of oats and barley were being raised, but also yields of turnips, potatoes, peas, cabbage, beans and clover. To the south and west for a mile and a half enclosure had made a considerable impact, though in the bulk of the parish, despite pressure from landowners, tenants clung to their open areas of infield and outfield. Still, a sizeable surplus for sale was being produced.[18]

By 1837 considerable quantities of grain, potatoes and butter were being shipped out of Fraserburgh, as well as several cargoes of locally reared cattle, bound for the London market.[19] Infield and outfield soon vanished, instead individual farms of between fifty and three hundred acres dotted the landscape. The pace of agricultural change seems to have quickened very rapidly in the late thirties and early forties. To one local inhabitant 'it was not gradual, but sudden, like lightning'.[20] Gangs of men ploughed and drained, burned whins and built dykes. Untouched land was leased to crofters to break in. Productivity was helped by the ready availability of materials that improved the soil including shell-sand, sea-weed, bone manure, and fish refuse that was especially plentiful in the herring season.[21]

The men who farmed the area in Victorian times did so with the security of nineteen year leases. Their prosperity was marked by a re-building of farm houses and steadings including 'some extravagantly large dwelling houses for the ordinary class of farmers'.[22] The productive hinterland of Fraserburgh helped feed the town's sizeable population, furnished produce for sale at its markets, supported increasingly wealthy

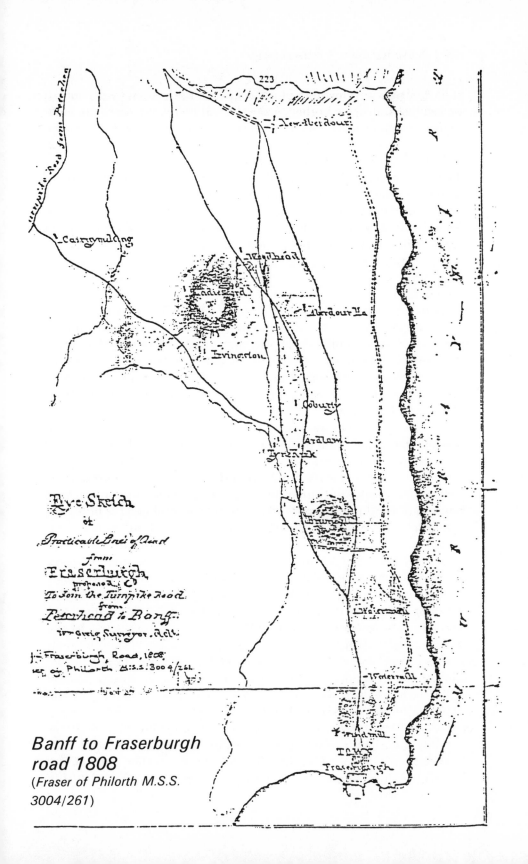

Banff to Fraserburgh road 1808
(*Fraser of Philorth M.S.S.*
3004/261)

farm folk who patronised the local shops, and generated surpluses that flowed from the port to the benefit of local merchants and seamen.

Travel

The roads of the Fraserburgh area, though more energetically repaired in the late eighteenth century than in earlier years, were not up to coping with a sizeable volume of wheeled traffic.[23] The harbour, however, provided facilities for trading and travelling. Fraserburgh in the 1790s supported seven vessels of 50 to 100 tons engaged in coasting and foreign trade.[24] As the town and the harbour expanded, so did the ease with which goods and people could be moved by sea. By 1837 there were regular sailing services to London (every ten days) and on a Peterhead-Aberdeen-Leith run (fortnightly).[25] At the end of the century three steamers, the 'Active', the 'Susan' and the 'Sweet Home' were bustling regularly in and out of the port providing regular services to Peterhead, Aberdeen and Leith. In addition a very considerable number of vessels put in to Fraserburgh from other parts of Britain and from abroad, to pick up local produce and bring in a wide range of goods especially timber, coal and salt.[26]

Fraserburgh had to wait until the early nineteenth century before it was linked to a well-built main road south to Aberdeen. In 1795 several Buchan proprietors joined with men from the Aberdeen-Ellon area with a view to constructing a turnpike road from the northern outskirts of Aberdeen at Bridge of Don to Ellon, and onwards to link up with both Peterhead and Fraserburgh.[27] The initial subscription of a little over £5,000 proved insufficient to finance even the stretch to Ellon and the more northerly heritors had to agree to their money being devoted to the first stretch of road.[28] Not until July 1802 did the Trust begin to advertise for contractors to build the road beyond Ellon. The route ran along a thirty foot wide track, the central twelve feet of which were metalled to a depth of one foot in the centre, tapering to ten inches at the sides, 'the Metal to be broke the one half at the Bottom to the size of a man's fist and the upper half to that of a Hen's Egg'.[29]

The Trust plunged deeper into debt, borrowing on the strength of tolls coming in and yet to come.[30] By 1808 the point at which Fraserburgh and Peterhead roads went separate ways had been reached.[31] By this time the Buchan proprietors had begun to attend the Trust's meetings regularly. More than mere attendance was required however. Shortage of funds compelled the local proprietors to find yet more money, both Lord Saltoun and John Gordon of Cairnbulg being called upon, before the road could be completed.[32] With a fresh injection of funds William

The Turnpike into Fraserburgh
(Fraser of Philorth M.S.S. 30910)

Kelman was able to report to his employer, Lord Saltoun, in March, 1809, 'the road is going on very fast, it is already past Philorth and will be finished at the end of the summer'.[33] The following year Kelman carefully noted that the road 'was well and truly made' and urged the Trust to block up all the side roads down which travellers eager to avoid toll-paying could dodge.[34] This final stretch from six miles north of Ellon to Fraserburgh had cost around £10,000, though it was built to a slightly more generous fourteen foot width and was finished off with a two-inch skim of gravel.[35]

On the southern outskirts of Fraserburgh a toll house and bar were put up. In the first few months of operation (from October 1810 to May 1811) just over £22 was collected in tolls. These are listed in Appendix 1.[36] Thereafter the tolls were offered for roup to bidders who then had a strong inducement to collect revenue efficiently in order to end up with an adequate profit. Only in 1826 was this policy not pursued. In that year the Trust paid William Adam five shillings a week to collect the tolls and Adam gathered in a total of just over £81. The sums raised from the roup of the Fraserburgh tolls do give some idea of the value of traffic on the new turnpike. The place was never as attractive to bidders as the tolls on the stretch of road from Aberdeen to Ellon where the Bridge of Don tollhouse normally fetched by far the biggest sum, frequently at least double the amount Fraserburgh earned. Nor did Fraserburgh seem quite as profitable as Peterhead, whose tolls generally produced slightly higher offers. Only the tolls between Ellon and Fraserburgh produced smaller revenues. The picture that emerges does suggest that a considerable part of traffic going south from Fraserburgh was bound for other parts of Buchan, the tolls at the next site south of the town being consistently considerably less than those at the first toll house. Over the period 1812–65 the yield from Fraserburgh tolls rose quite considerably from a figure around £60 to (after 1845) sums over £100 for the rest of the turnpike era. In 1860, at £170, Fraserburgh tolls fetched more, for once, than the £162 Peterhead yielded. When the toll-collecting system finally ended the tollhouse was bought by Lord Saltoun for £15.8.0. Since the railway did not reach Fraserburgh until 1865 it is not possible to see the impact it had on road traffic. The figures suggest a growth in traffic at the time of more vigorous agricultural improvement and the expansion of Fraserburgh itself. But once the big surge in farming change was over (by 1850) the traffic on the turnpike did not greatly increase in profitability. Nor did Fraserburgh itself grow as rapidly in this later period (increasing by around a thousand people 1851–65) as it had in the period from the late eighteenth century to 1851 – when its population trebled.

VICTORIA STREET, FRASERBURGH. 12609. G.W.W.

In 1874 only one private house, and a manse fronted the recently laid-out line of Victoria Street. By 1901 these neat granite villas housed middle class people including (at No. 29) John Cranna the Harbour Treasurer and author of a substantial history of the town.

In the next few years turnpikes linked Fraserburgh to Banff and Strichen. The Banff road's first ten miles, costing £2,825, were paid for by the four heritors (including Lord Saltoun)[37] through whose lands it ran. Up and down this network trundled a variety of wheeled traffic. A Mail Coach was soon providing a daily service, travelling via Mintlaw to Aberdeen whilst the 'Lord Saltoun' coach carried passengers to Peterhead on three days of the week.[38] Carriers offered a network of services that included, in the pre-railway days, journeys to Aberdeen on three days of the week.[39] The railway seems to have demolished this service just as it demolished the stage-coach services too, but shorter runs remained in operation. In 1877, for example, two carriers went daily to Rosehearty and horse-drawn bus services operated daily to Aberdour whilst Rosehearty was served by two bus operators each running three buses every day.[40] By the end of the century not only did William Hendry's Aberdour bus meet the 2.50 train daily and Rosehearty services flourish, there were buses every Tuesday market day from Strichen, Tyrie and New Pitsligo, daily buses to Inverallochy and weekly services to Lonmay.[41]

Although the Great North of Scotland Railway had plans to build track up into Buchan as soon as its first line to Huntly was open, lack of funds prevented work beginning and in the event Fraserburgh had to wait nineteen years later than Huntly before it was linked up to the railway system.[42] When a plan was produced in 1854 it showed the G.N.S.R. thinking of laying a line only into central Buchan and Fraserburgh. People were thus encouraged to look favourably upon the plans of another organisation. However, the Aberdeen, Peterhead and Fraserburgh Railway's plans to build track through Ellon and Mintlaw to Fraserburgh failed to win the necessary approval of Parliament. Instead, in 1858, a G.N.S.R. subsidiary, the Formartine and Buchan Railway, was given approval for its new scheme that virtually duplicated that of its rival. By 1861 the line had been laid to Ellon and on to Mintlaw. Financial uncertainty then brought work to a halt. Only the provision of a guarantee for £6,000, should it be needed, brought into being the final stretch into Fraserburgh. In April 1865 the line at last opened to a station in Fraserburgh – and past a small private one at Philorth that Lord Saltoun had insisted be constructed.[43]

The railway provided a regular and fairly speedy service for people and goods, though it did attract frequent grumbles that its tariffs were excessively high.[44] The markets opened up to fresh fish from Fraserburgh were much extended. By the nineties a further stretch of line was being considered – a light railway to link the town to the fishing villages of Inverallochy and St Combs. Though Lord Saltoun felt the project mistaken since it would encourage Fraserburgh to swallow up the villages, it did in fact go ahead at the beginning of the Edwardian era.[45] It was approved by an act of 1894, built to a 4′ 8½″ guage and finished four miles away at St Combs.[46] It no doubt reflected the necessity for the village fishermen to work the bigger boats of the time from Fraserburgh harbour rather than from their own open shore. The evidence of a contemporary involved in fishing does suggest that life in fishing villages several miles from Fraserburgh's harbour, markets and businessmen was much more of a struggle than for the people of Fraserburgh and Broadsea.[47]

Fraserburgh's harbour meant that it was bound to be better placed for travel facilities than inland communities in Aberdeenshire. But the building of roads and railways did help the town play a fuller role in the local economy and, eventually, in the national one. The growth of a wide range of shops and businesses in the nineteenth century demonstrates the valuable role Fraserburgh played in serving people in the area able to reach it without over-much hardship. During the century the town moved from the age of 'the running post' to mail coaches, the telegraph and finally in 1898 to trunk telephone connections.[48] This, too, must have greatly eased the business transactions of Fraserburgh's wealth-producing inhabitants.

Chapter Three

THE IMPROVED TOWN

Business growth

During the nineteenth century the town of Fraserburgh was transformed. The original tight rectangle of land occupied by urban properties expanded outwards, especially to the north, and swallowed up the hitherto distinct and separate village of Broadsea. Shops, warehouses, yards, mills and other business enterprises multiplied in number and, in some cases, in size too. The wealth generated by this activity helped pay for new housing and for the partial replacement of older housing by grander and more substantial properties. Enterprises stimulated by Fraserburgh's port facilities lay, inevitably, at the centre of this expansion. Above all, the herring fisheries stimulated the expansion of the town's business activities, contributing considerably to swelling the population of the parish from 2,215 in 1791 to 3,615 in 1841, 7,596 in 1881 and 9,715 by 1901.[1] The bulk of this population lived in the burgh – 3,093 in 1851, 4,266 in 1871, 6,583 in 1881 and 7,360 in 1891.

Even at the beginning of the nineteenth century Fraserburgh burgesses were not excluding outsiders keen to trade at the harbour or do business in the markets. They did, however, place upon them various dues and customs that both reduced their ability to compete, and furnished revenue for the town.[2] Herring fishing grew in the nineteenth century injecting an eight-week burst of furious bustle into the longer term areas of activity like white-fishing, kelping, linen spinning, trading and shipbuilding. As the century wore on linen spinning declined and kelping shrank from an activity that had once produced £150 a year to the town from the letting of sea-shore rights, to a yield of a mere £5.[3] Bigger profits were to be made from herring fishing than from those other activities and the whole business community was, directly or indirectly, affected.

The harbour was steadily improved during the nineteenth century and furnished Fraserburgh with business other than that of fishing. An analysis of directory evidence on business forms Appendix 2. The timber required for fish packing as well as for house building helped stimulate the setting up of saw milling and timber yards to process the imported wood. By mid-Victorian times steam power was being used to operate sawing machinery, driving up to forty-five vertical saws at one time.[4] Shipbuilding and repairing went steadily along till the last quarter of the century. Then it became less secure. Four vessels were launched 1875–8, but none 1879–81.[5] The increasing complexity of ship design seems to have operated against Fraserburgh builders who were happier with small and fairly simple craft. Nevertheless four boatbuilders were at work by the end of Victorian times (a similar number to that of 1837) whilst two blockmakers and two rope and sailmakers were in operation too. Grain, lime, salt, cattle, coal, potatoes and household goods passed in and out of the early-nineteenth century port, as well as timber.[6] By the latter years of the century these items were still of importance in trading, as well as iron, hides, bark, barrels, paraffin and kerb and paving stones for the town's improved thoroughfares.[7]

Before the opening of the railway the harbour played a major part in focussing agricultural business on Fraserburgh. The improved farmland of early Victorian Buchan fed the town shops and markets with produce but also poured in grain and cattle for export to other parts of Britain. The cattle trade encouraged the concentration of a considerable number of butchers in the town: by late Victorian years there were fourteen[8] of them operating where sixty years earlier there had been but three. Moreover they now had a public slaughterhouse to use.[9] The town's increased affluence provided business for at least eight dairymen by the end of the century. Milk was usually sold from their homes which contained 'a press or small compartment below stairs for keeping any quantity that may not be sold'.[10]

Attempts to profit commercially from Fraserburgh's coastal situation even included a venture more comendable for its courage than for its business acumen. Despite the bleak climate, the sharp winds and the bitter chill of the North Sea, early nineteenth century Fraserburgh made a bid to become a health resort. Since the scheme long preceded the coming of the railway it is hard to see how sufficient custom could have come in to make a profit from the centre-piece of this enterprise – a group of baths. There were two cold baths hacked from the rock and fed by the tide: their hardy users were charged sixpence per visit. Four warm baths and a shower at bigger fees were also provided as well as a bathing machine that could be hired for a shilling.[11] A considerable number of local people fitted up their houses in order to let them out as lodgings.[12] The whole enterprise, aimed at promoting the prosperity of Fraserburgh was a failure and the baths fell into decay. But the idea lived on in the occasional wistful thoughts of local leaders who wondered whether even the all-pervading smell and activity of the herring season might not become a tourist attraction.

Fishing and trading made possible the existence in the town of rope and sailmakers, block-makers, timber merchants and coopers.[13] The herring season brought numerous shopkeepers profits that helped Fraserburgh obtain a wide range of well-stocked premises. Older and more casual enterprises were hit by the rise of professional services. In Victorian times Fraserburgh moved from possessing but one hotel to containing eleven (including a number of late nineteenth century temperance establishments). This damaged the business of the cluster of houses in Shore Street where once as many as twenty-seven women sold spirits.[14] The expansion of shops also turned the once-flourishing twice-yearly fairs on the Links into insignificant gatherings made up of a few stalls selling sweets and gingerbread.[15] Late Victorian Fraserburgh contained twenty-one bakers and confectioners, twice as many as it had possessed in mid Victorian times. No doubt local people were turning increasingly away from their home-made oat-cakes to commercially-made wheaten bread. Boot and shoemakers too grew in number from fourteen in 1867 to twenty-two thirty-five years later. The decline of home-made clothing may well have followed from the emergence of seventeen drapers in 1903, for in 1837 there had only been five. Milliners and dressmakers and a dozen tailors were well-established in the town in the later nineteenth century. Fraserburgh's solitary ironmonger and only druggist of 1837 had both been services run in conjunction with general grocery businesses. By 1903 there were six full-time ironmongers and four chemists. The town also contained five greengrocers and five hairdressers (at least one of whom also offered his customers hot and cold baths)[16] and even a full-time 'fitter of artificial teeth'. Grocers and general shopkeepers numbered at least fifty by 1903, more than double the figure of 1807. Cycle agents, a toy dealer, photographers and several tobacconists all set up business in late Victorian times. The expansion and improvement of housing provided work for a gas fitter-plumber, three other plumbers, a plasterer, builders and masons. Well-made furniture came from the six cabinet-makers of 1903 – in 1837 there had been none. Five enterprises dealing in glass, china and earthenware offered their wares to local householders. There was even an enterprise selling people fried fish, as well as one or two eating houses.

In and around the Victorian town could be found a brewery, saw-mills, a bone mill, rope works and seven coal-dealers. Blacksmiths, however, declined in numbers from six to three (1877–1903). Perhaps some had branched out as cycle agents or even ventured into the new career of 'engineer'. There was only one saddler left in the town by the

The use of steam-powered machinery in work on the Balaclava Breakwater.

end of the century whereas in 1837 there had been four. But legal business grew. Ten firms were functioning in 1903, double the number of twenty-five years earlier. Two building societies were, by then, competing with the older savings bank for the town's spare cash.

The big rise in the number of carters in Fraserburgh – there were seventeen by 1903 – was no doubt helped by the herring trade. Although this growth suggests the attraction of the profits to be made, the carters were not without their grumbles. They complained[17] that the curers who hired them were ready to pay more to coopers and even labourers than to carters who had to find £20 for the horse, harness, cart, food etc of the herring season. Farm sent carts to shift the herring and curers built bothies and stables to accommodate the men and their horses. Coopers, like curers, were very dependent on the fluctuating fortunes of the herring season. When working steadily, a cooper could turn out around twenty four barrels a week[19] but he needed a satisfactory volume of fish to keep going. White-fish curing involved only a minority of Fraserburgh yards (seven out of forty-two in 1841 for instance)[20] not only because of the lower volume of catch but also because of the continuation of curing in creeks and villages. The coming of the railway affected this business for soon three-quarters of the white-fish catch was being sent off fresh.[21]

At least fourteen curers were at work in early nineteenth century Fraserburgh. Their yards were scattered about the town, though quite a number operated in the Links area and others simply used the streets. In the later years of the century more of them shifted to the north of the town as the railway station and yards made inroads into one part of the Links and concern was shown to preserve the rest for recreation. A few still operated from there. The last thirty years of the century saw the building of new roads in an area formerly used for net-drying.[22] Around Denmark Street and Barrasgate as well as the older Castle Street and the Balaclava harbour a large number of curing businesses gathered. To the west, in Cross Street, yet more were active. The herring season's impact must have been inescapably dominant throughout the town.

The curers' fortunes were inevitably tied to fluctuations in the catch and the availability of markets. The quantity sent abroad increased from 40% in 1841 to 84% in 1871.[23] The type of contract the curers agreed with the fishermen also affected their profits. Until the early eighties curers offered terms to a group of boats that they then had to honour regardless of the actual market value of the fish caught. There were years when an unexpectedly large volume of fish brought fishermen considerable rewards yet ruined the curers unable to cover their costs in a market where the price had fallen. In the early eighties many a fisher-cottage was re-built in solid granite whilst curers' fortunes crashed.[24]

The late 19th century harbour packed with sail-powered fishing craft. The funnel of a solitary steamer can be seen. Despite its expansive size the harbour was none too big for all the craft seeking to use it during the summer herring season.

Then a system of daily auctions was adopted and this problem at least disappeared.[25]

Between the occupation of curer and cooper there was considerable overlap. Some curers continued to be coopers, others felt they had moved on out of the cooper class in a fashion described by an editorial in the 'Fraserburgh Herald'.

'If he happens to be in luck he will make a few hundred pounds, take a fine house, dress his family in purple and fine linen, fare sumptuously every day ... drawing the line in the social scale between himself and the coopers that he was "hail fellow well met" with six months before, squeezing himself edgeways into the "set" that is treating him very much as he is treating the coopers, talking contemptuously of the "infernal greed" of fishermen, turning Tory in politics ... and putting on airs generally.'[26]

The fortunes of a man such as this were far from secure. In 1839 there were sixty curing firms at work – twice the number of two years earlier.[27] By 1860 their number had dropped to thirty-six[28] and seven years later plummeted yet further to eighteen.[29] Yet in a further three years they had risen to forty-one[30] and by the end of the century there were sixty-nine.[31] Many firms, then, did not enjoy a long life. In 1880 only three of the Fraserburgh curing firms had been in existence for more than thirty years,[32] whilst between 1883 and 1889 twenty-nine of the town's sixty-one firms were forced out of business.[33] When a curer like the one described by the 'Herald' fell into debt to those who had financed his fishing season 'he drops back into the cooperage and is forgotten unless by the banker that gives him the advance, the coopers and fishermen who could not get their wages, the merchants who supplied staves and hoops and a few tradesmen that kept him in food supplies and clothing'.[34] When George Davidson's business collapsed it left him with debts of nearly £4,000, nearly eight times the value of his assets.[35] George Flett, who had moved on from building boats in Findochty to opening a shop in Fraserburgh with fifty pounds from which to sell groceries to fishermen, joined with a local cooper to cure the catches of four herring boats. The venture failed leaving the unfortunate Flet with debts of over £1,500.[36]

The late nineteenth century editions of the local paper are full of advertisements from firms in Scottish and English cities seeking Fraserburgh catches in return for daily cash payments. Linked to this, the occupation of fish salesmen expanded to furnish nine people with jobs in 1903.[37] At least, by then, the activity could be conducted in the new fish market instead of on and around the open piers. The market opened in March 1899 amid a flurry of reminiscences of the unimproved and unhealthy state of the town 30 years before.[38]

Not only did business fluctuate from year to year in a town so alarmingly dependent on a single item, within each year Fraserburgh experienced times of very contrasting commercial activity. In late spring and early summer the place was considerably emptied by the departure of local people for herring fishing further west and north. At times the town was left so quiet the local press was hard put to it to find sufficient news to print. On occasion during the 1880s steamers called in to collect as many as five or six hundred people at a time. The passengers included curers, herring buyers, ship brokers and coopers, but above all, herring gutters. Bus loads came in from nearby Banff and Buchan to join the departing throng.[39] The period of quiet that followed must have made all the more impressive the two-month bustle that began in early July with Fraserburgh's own fishing season. In early Victorian times at least 1,200 outsiders poured in, many of them[40] Highlanders who, till the railway was built, often trudged along the roads with bundles on their backs.[41] Each of them was marked by 'the aroma of his native peat reek that clings to him like a brother'.[42] This virtual doubling of the town's population continued; in late Victorian times about five thousand outsiders, carters, dealers, preachers and vagrants as well as fishermen came in for the season. The activity of the herring season brought excitement as well as wealth to its traders and inhabitants. During the herring season, it was possible to hear in Fraserburgh not only the Buchan dialect but Gaelic, the accents of Fife, Shetland and numerous other places.[43] It even upset the schooling of older boys who joined boat crews, despite the best efforts of the School Board to prevent skippers from taking on lads of under fourteen who had yet to pass the Fourth Standard.[44] Other children hung around the harbour, sometimes tempted to grab fish off boats and carts in return for little gifts from enterprising entrepreneurs 'loitering on the quays for the purpose of buying herring from Boys, thus encouraging Boys to steal'.[45]

Loads of herring were trundled by carters to the curing yards; there the women set to work to gut, salt and pack the fish. Herring barrels piled up in such numbers that yards could not contain them. They spilled out into the streets where they were stacked in rows that steadily narrowed the way through. Since the little space remaining was often blocked by horse and cart traffic visiting the yards the local authority had to try and stop the practice. But fines of twenty shillings do not seem to have ended the habit.[46] No doubt too many town leaders were caught up in the profits of the herring trade to press hard upon those who pursued it and brought so much change and development to the town.

Managing the town

The older inhabitants of Victorian Fraserburgh were very aware of the alteration of their town from a small square-shaped settlement clustered close by the harbour into a far more substantial and extensive community. The physical improvement of the town was facilitated by the nearby quarry at Broadsea and the ease with which bulky items like timber and slates could be brought in by sea. The site of the settlement was sufficiently level and dry to enable expansion to take place in several directions and in a planned fashion that retained the very regular shape already established in the eighteenth century.

Steady expansion in the early nineteenth century produced, especially, tenement building.[47] New streets were laid out, North Street (1845)[48] and Saltoun Place, Commerce Street and Victoria Street were all well established by 1865.[49] Several older properties survived the nineteenth century building boom, though large numbers were pulled down. Shore Street, one of Fraserburgh's older centres, contained low houses five to six feet high with clay, mud and straw roofs and hollowed-out floors.[50] A number of these were demolished in the later nineteenth century. Even so many crowded, confined and ill-ventilated buildings survived, like the Braehead property with its 13 foot gable to the lane, its walls built of stone and clay and its tiled roof in a decayed, mis-shapen and sunken state.[51] Some of the worst older housing was in Broadsea where old, low cramped cottages provided by the fishermen for themselves were, in 1868, in very poor shape.[52] Lord Saltoun forced many of the tenants to overhaul or replace their houses in return for the greater security of a thirty-seven year lease.[53] The irregular and unnumbered properties of Broadsea even bemused Victorian postmen trying to make proper deliveries.[54]

In the second half of the nineteenth century there was a vigorous surge of new and re-building activity. The 'Fraserburgh Herald' estimated the area covered by buildings had virtually doubled during this period.[55] More new streets were laid out, the net-drying ground in the north east being built over as feus were let off the new network of roads like Denmark Street (1875).[56] The town expanded both east and south too, with a mixture of housing, schools, churches, and places of work. North-western growth pushed out to merge with the once distinct village of Broadsea. In 1872 it was absorbed into Fraserburgh's administrative boundaries.

Within the expanding town large new properties were put up. The 1803 parish church was overhauled and a new West Parish Church erected in 1867. The Disruption produced South, East and West Free

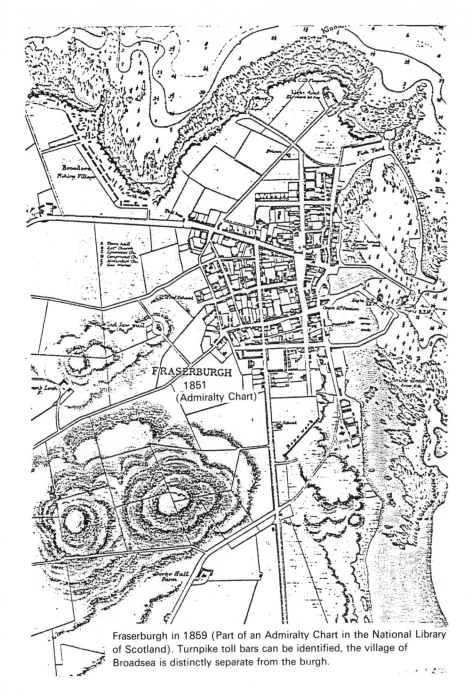

Fraserburgh in 1859 (Part of an Admiralty Chart in the National Library
of Scotland). Turnpike toll bars can be identified, the village of
Broadsea is distinctly separate from the burgh.

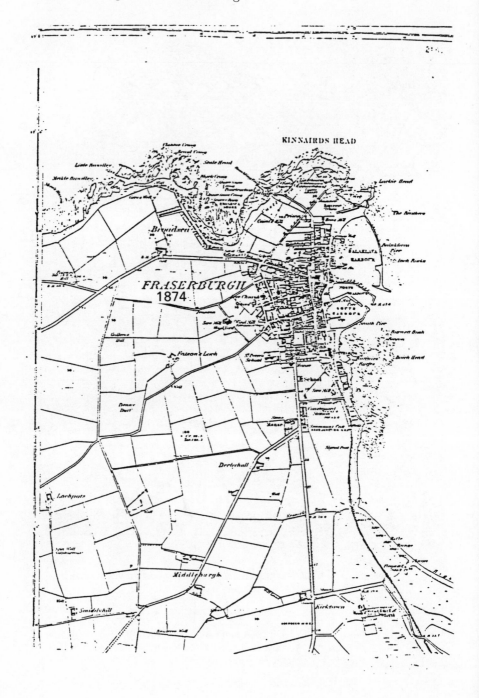

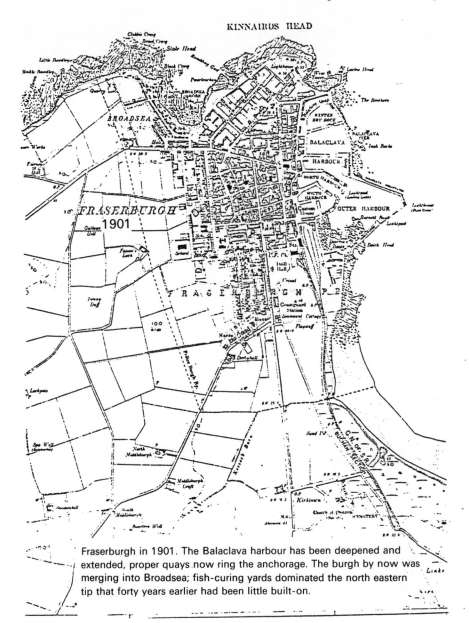

Fraserburgh in 1901. The Balaclava harbour has been deepened and extended, proper quays now ring the anchorage. The burgh by now was merging into Broadsea; fish-curing yards dominated the north eastern tip that forty years earlier had been little built-on.

churches as well as a Free Church Mission to the Highlanders who came for the fishing season.[57] Congregational and Baptist chapels, Episcopal and Roman Catholic churches added to the very considerable array of costly structures housing Christianity's many sects. In 1856 the old Town House was pulled down and replaced by a much grander property with market stalls on the ground floor and a meeting room above.[58] Further building was generated by the railway (1865), the expansion of banking, a new Academy (1870), a new public school (1882) and a fish market (1899). The housing put up for the better-off is visibly evident in old photographs and on the ground today. Some tradesmen were assisted by the Building Society the Rev. McLaren helped to found.[59] Working people were less fortunate. Some complained of excessive rents – one 'Herald' subscriber felt £10 for his but and ben was twice what most property owners of the North East charged.[60] When improved working class housing was put up – like the block erected in 1898 – two rooms including water laid on and a lavatory, was offered for between £8 and £15 a year.[61]

The improved town reflected not only increased wealth but better management. Early nineteenth century affairs were supervised by a town council appointed by Fraserburgh's perpetual provost, Lord Saltoun.[62] The income from various lands and properties and from petty customs and dues exacted at the harbour and at markets swelled with the community's increased prosperity.[63] Proclamations were conveyed to citizens by the Town Drummer who went through the town every morning at 5.0 o'clock (except Sunday) with his drum, 'to be paid fourpence to sixpence for each cry according to the trouble he may have'.[64] In 1840 Fraserburgh adopted the Police Act in order to cope with the problems posed by urban growth. At first the new Police Commissioners concerned themselves with lighting and 'watching': in 1850 they took on the tasks of tackling water-supply, housing and health. Twelve of the fifteen commissioners were elected by the occupiers of property worth £10 or more. Only three were chosen by the Town Council.[65]

The old Town Council lingered on until 1892. To the end it was nominated by Lord Saltoun but its activities were confined to controlling the Town's property. This 'Common Good' consisted of invested funds, parks, the Links (used for net-drying, fish curing, cattle grazing and recreation) various properties and the petty customs.[66] When the Council disappeared the Police Commissioners became first Burgh Commissioners then (1900) the Town Council. But the Common Good was still managed by another body representing the feuars making Fraserburgh one of the few Scottish towns where this fund is not controlled by the

Council.[67] The Town's managing bodies were – not surprisingly – dominated by fishcurers and merchants. When the meeting to first settle upon creating Police Commissioners met more than half of those there came from these two groups.[68]

As private individuals Fraserburgh's leaders profited from the herring season: as official figures, however, they found it brought them problems. The influx of five thousand or more outsiders during Victorian times threatened the good order of the town. The fishing season pulled in Highlanders – who formed a distinct group not necessarily on good terms with Buchan people – as well as vagrants and beggars from other Parishes[69] and even 'a great number of the Roughs from all parts of the country'.[70] The majority of offences facing the local Police Court in the later nineteenth century were committed in the fishing season in the July to September period. Many of the offenders came from other parts of Scotland. The bulk of them were labourers, though fishermen and the vaguely defined 'vagrants and pedlars' also furnished many of the guilty. Apart from seamen and carters and coopers no other groups show up significantly.[71] Thus the local police were kept very busy by the influx of folk during the summer and enjoyed a relatively peaceful autumn and winter apart from the January disturbances connected with New Year celebrations.

Until 1866 Fraserburgh controlled its own police constables, there-after it became a part of the county force.[72] The town's two constables had to be reinforced for the fishing season by three or four more men: by the end of the century a sergeant and inspector were to be found in the town. The fishing season regularly brought to the Police Commissioners fearful apprehensions of 'riot and disturbance'.[73] The extra constables they hired patrolled 'chiefly on Saturday nights from 3.0 p.m. to 10.0 or until the streets shall be quiet and clear of disorderly people . . . and that their attention be directed to tippling houses'.[74] The huge riot feared by the authorities happened at least twice, in 1848 and 1874. In the former, food riots persuaded the authorities to call in troops. Angry fisher folk waving sticks and hurling stones rapidly reverted to orderly behaviour when confronted by the army.[75] In the latter at eleven one evening the police arrested a drunk Highlander. A furious crowd composed of several hundred Highlanders demanded his release and though the police gave way, were further inflamed by the sound of a despairing howling from the cells. There, a man arrested earlier, was locked up. His cries led the crowd to conclude they had been cheated and the freed fisherman they had been promised was still in jail. They marched to the Town House and Police Office, knocked out doors and windows from both, gutted the Police Office and carried off looted items. One policeman was knocked

The plans for Denmark Street as entered in the Police Commissioners' Minutes. The construction of this street in 1875 was part of the expansion and re-location of fish-curing premises.

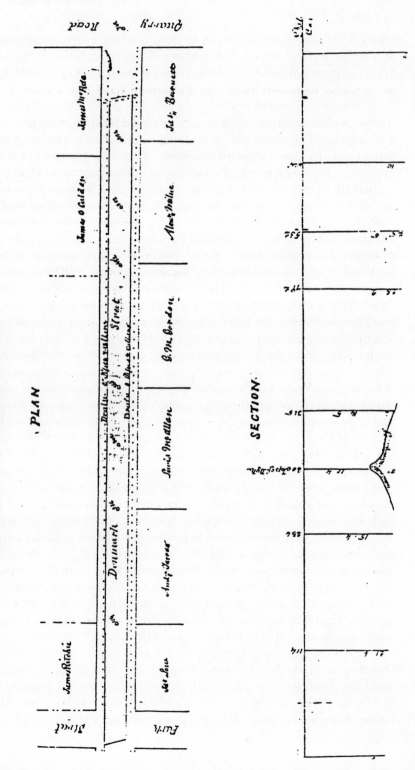

PLAN

SECTION.

down and badly hurt, the rest were powerless to act despite the presence in Fraserburgh of the Chief Constable himself. The release of the second man calmed the crowd but the authorities fearing what would happen now '3,000 turbulent Highland Fishermen have got a taste of their power' called in the troops.[76]

Duties during the rest of the year must have seemed pleasantly dull in comparison. The police were frequently called upon to clear away large gangs of men gathered at street corners.[77] They had to attempt to deter boys from knocking at doors, shops and windows and ringing door bells at night[78] as well as window breaking. Dealing with vagrants and with drunks on a Saturday was a regular chore, though on at least one occasion the police constables themselves were found to be the worse for drink.[79] The prison they used ceased to be adequate, and rather than repair a decayed property it was decided to despatch prisoners to Peterhead or Aberdeen despite the fact this cost eight and fifteen shillings respectively.[80]

The Police Commissioners' very first obligation was, in fact, to provide the town with adequate light. Their desire to do this led a joint stock Gas Company to set up in business sometime in 1840–41.[81] As a first step seventy lamps were put up in the early forties, forty of them of the cheaper £2 type bracketed to buildings, the rest of the more costly £3.5.0 type erected on square posts and protected by globular glass containers.[82] The contractors, Blaikie and Company of Aberdeen, thwarted the Commissioners ambition to copy the lamps in Aberdeen's Union Street which were of a striking square design: Blaikie's failed to fulfil this obligation.[83]

Once the lamps were installed the Commissioners engaged two men to light them. The work took four or five hours each day during the late autumn and winter season, each lamplighter having to be paid eight shillings a week.[84] The lamps were lit by clambering up a ladder and using an oil lamp. Not till 1885 was a more efficient method adopted. Then rods and matches wielded by the two town scavengers brought down expenses to an extra three shillings a week for each man.[85] The gas itself was rather costly. At 15/6d a lamp for a season Fraserburgh fared badly compared to Peterhead (9/6d) or Stonehaven (10/-).[86] By 1856 the cost had fallen to 14/6d and by 1863 to 10/-.[87] But not until 1911 did the Council itself take over the Gas Company.[88]

The nineteenth century thus saw both an expansion of the town and an expansion of the authority of bodies managing the town. Rules and regulations embodied in local by-laws proliferated to be enforced by a squad of professional police.

Improving the harbour

Fraserburgh's position, close by seas swarming with fish and convenient for trading vessels going north and into the Moray Firth, was no guarantee of success. A harbour adequate to the needs of shipping was essential and by the beginning of the nineteenth century it was clear that Fraserburgh's was by no means satisfactory. The late-sixteenth century harbour-works left the town with a small anchorage emptied at low tide and very exposed to the fury of gales from the north and north-east. To develop Fraserburgh into a port of some consequence[89] would require building and deepening work that was bound to be costly, and lack of adequate finance delayed the construction work until the early nineteenth century.[90]

Lord Saltoun was very conscious of the importance to Fraserburgh's prosperity of a safer and enlarged harbour.[91] He played the prime part in providing funds when, in 1804, local people began to put together money in a subscription list for harbour alterations. By January 1805 almost £2,000 had been raised including £800 from Lord Saltoun, £100 from a local merchant and another £100 from a nearby heritor. The rest of the subscriptions were generally for small sums of under £40.[92] The money was to be used to put into effect the plan drawn up by John Rennie for pier-building that would create both proper shelter and a low-water depth of around eight feet.[93] But when estimates came in, the lowest (from Patrick Scott, an Aberdeen mason) came to over £9,000. The Town Council accepted Rennie's advice that they appoint William Stewart to oversee the work and to hire workmen in a piecemeal fashion.[94]

Stewart had won a reputation for lock-building on the Crinan Canal. He accepted Fraserburgh's offer of a £200 a year salary (later raised to £230) and came up to Buchan to begin work in 1807.[95] The Council pressed him to look first for local men when seeking masons, carters, quarrymen and labourers. With the help of two horse and cart conveyances, stone was trundled down to the harbour from Memsie and Broadsea Quarries. By 1809 William Kelman was able to report to Lord Saltoun that building was proceeding with vigour.[96] However the costs – especially of the men's wages – were high and when Stewart left Fraserburgh in August 1811 only a North pier had been built and this had cost over £11,000.[97] The sea still crashed into the harbour where it 'produced an agitation to the vessels against which no mooring could afford proper security'.[98]

The advice of Robert Stevenson was sought. He recommended the building of a South Pier and, in 1818, this was begun.[99] The Act of

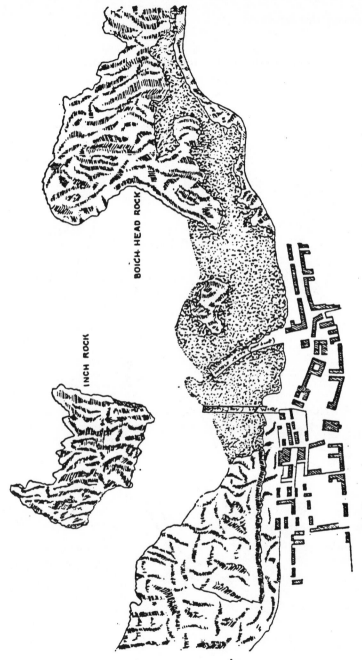

FRASERBURGH HARBOUR IN 1746. — ONLY PIER THEN BUILT WAS UPPER HALF OF NORTH PIER AND NUCLEUS OF MIDDLE JETTY.

BOICH HEAD ROCK

INCH ROCK

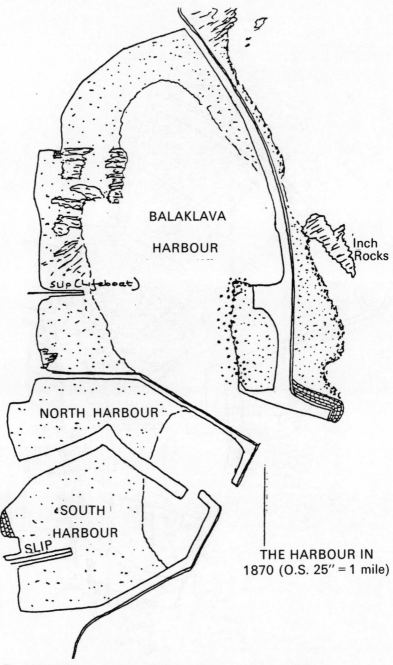

FRASERBURGH

BALAKLAVA

HARBOUR

SUP (Lifeboat)

Inch
Rocks

NORTH HARBOUR

SOUTH

HARBOUR

SLIP

THE HARBOUR IN
1870 (O.S. 25″ = 1 mile)

The 1870 harbour includes the Balaclava harbour works in their basic
form of a long arm embracing sheltered water.

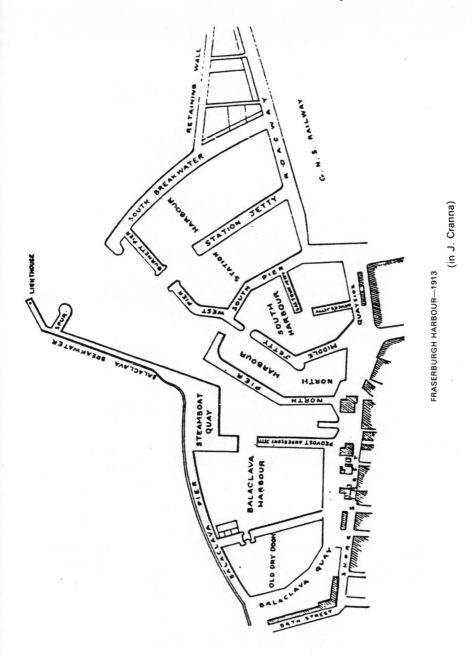

FRASERBURGH HARBOUR—1913

(in J. Cranna)

Fraserburgh herring girls, accompanied by a group of coopers, waiting to start work.

Fish wives with creels for their loads, wait at the quayside.

Parliament permitting the works also created a distinct body – the Harbour Commissioners – to take charge of port affairs. Until 1878 they were as undemocratic a group as the Town Council, thereafter (after the passage of the Harbour Act, 1878) they were elected by harbour ratepayers and by heritors.[100] Their first charge – the provision of a South Pier – was completed in three years by William Minto for a little over £6,000. Local people celebrated with a dinner and ball till six in the morning.[101] The addition of a middle pier in 1830 completed a range of works that had cost around £30,000 when bills for further deepening parts of the harbour around the piers and jetties were added. Fraserburgh now had a far more secure anchorage and a low water depth at the pier heads of around six feet.[102] The success of these works was demonstrated by the upward climb of harbour revenues from around £1,000 in the eighteen twenties and early thirties to around £2,000 by the early forties.[103] Local subscriptions and loans provided the money.

A driving force behind these early works was Baillie Chalmers and no sooner were they complete than he began agitating for a considerable extension in harbour size by the building of a brand new pier and breakwater farther north.[104] The North harbour (three and a half acres) and South harbour (five acres) would be dwarfed by the projected fourteen acre extension.[105] The contractor, John Brebner from Aberdeen, began work in 1850. Violent storms wrecked his construction, and he abandoned it: work resumed in 1856–7 under Stevenson's guidance and when complete was named the 'Balaclava Breakwater' in honour of the Crimean conflict of the time.[106] Yet by the mid 1870s the harbours were again insufficient to adequately shelter and service the large fleet of fishing boats and cope with other vessels.[107] At least by then money was easier to come by. The Fishery Board switched, in 1860, from scattering aid among numerous centres to concentrating on a few large ones. Loans could be obtained from the Public Works Commissioners and here Fraserburgh's earlier expenditure brought benefits. The Commissioners' loans were provided against the security of revenue from dues and in order to offer such security it was necessary to already possess a harbour.[108]

Armed with a £60,000 loan the Harbour Commissioners were able, in 1875, to develop an extension to the Balaclava harbour.[109] A breakwater, sheltering vessels entering the harbour and reducing the heavy swell at the harbour entrance edged out along a ridge of rocks. The pier was enlarged, with a thirteen foot wall being put up to reduce the frequency with which seas swept over the breakwater.[110] By 1882 it was complete, but its concrete construction (novel at the time for sea-works) was by no means sound and further bills for patching and repairing kept trickling in.[111] Further deepening work added yet more to the never-ending cost of the harbour. But its benefits were clear. On 11th April 1882, 'The Scotsman' attributed the huge growth in Fraserburgh's harbour revenues (over £10,000 p.a. by now, plus money from letting curing yards) 'to the skill and perseverance with which the harbour has been enlarged, deepened, and improved ... where fishermen are supplied with a good harbour they are willing to pay adequate dues for the shelter and safety which it enables them to command'.[112]

By the end of the century Fraserburgh was equipped with a very large harbour in which up to a thousand fishing boats could safely shelter.[113] The series of harbour-deepening activities meant that steamers calling to load up with herring could dock easily, though the ever-increasing size of fishing vessels meant that deepening work had to still continue. In 1898 a new South Breakwater costing £80,000 had been completed and a dry dock formed at the head of the Balaclava harbour.[114] Harbour works undertaken since 1745 had, by 1902, piled up costs totalling £308,375.[115] Yet without this kind of expenditure Fraserburgh would not have been able to win the powerful position in herring fishing that it had achieved by the end of the nineteenth century.

Chapter Four

IMPROVED HEALTH

Urban expansion in Fraserburgh produced all the problems commonly found in the nineteenth century British towns. Authorities with inadequate experience, revenue or staff, struggled to react to a situation in which health risks increased as more and more people crammed together in a cramped environment. The provision of fresh water, adequate sewage systems, and properly cleaned streets were services that had to be undertaken once it became clear that the alternative was the acceptance of outbreaks of savage diseases. The treatment of those who were ill could not be wholly avoided when their numbers were sometimes so considerable. But Victorian Fraserburgh also experienced additional difficulties. For two months of the year five or six thousand extra people crowded into the town. The diseases they brought, the ease with which illnesses spread amongst them, the accommodation crisis they regularly created and the unpleasant problem of human waste that they generated were all factors adding to the routine worries of the local authorities.

Coping with illness

Severe illness was a common experience to nineteenth century people, yet even so an outbreak of cholera readily spread panic amongst them. Just such a panic hit the expanding town of Fraserburg in 1832.[1] The disease afflicted the fisherpeople of Broadsea particularly badly. Their damp cramped houses, without a nearby plentiful fresh-water supply, and without any kind of drainage or sewage systems made vulnerable inhabitants already weakened by frequent poverty. In 1848 Broadsea[2] was again visited by a cholera outbreak that killed at least sixteen of the fisher people. By then the Parochial Board had been established and seems to have made some effort to begin to tackle the problem. The village school was fitted up as a temporary hospital to receive the sick. Drainage channels were cut to collect the refuse from houses, and the inhabitants were provided with soap and lime as well as food, fuel, clothing and bedding for those deprived by the disaster of their normal living. Heaps of dung scattered among the houses were cleared away, but the parish medical officer felt little optimism about such actions being more than a temporary measure. The personal cleanliness of the fisher-people seemed to him too defective to hold out much hope for the future.[3]

In 1849 an outbreak of typhus added to Broadsea's miseries.[4] The Parochial Board's doctors toured the village advising people 'to keep their premises free from all noxious or offensive matter and, during suitable weather, to expose their bedding and whole moveable effects to the open air and to get their bedding and furniture thoroughly cleaned and the walls of their houses washed with quicklime'.[5] The town of Fraserburgh watched apprehensively. When the schooner 'Pilot' entered the harbour having put off its captain in Yarmouth with cholera, the Parochial Board insisted the vessel be visited by a doctor, the captain's cabin thoroughly fumigated and his clothes soaked in the harbour.[6] Only then were crew members allowed ashore. Cholera appeared in the nearby village of Cairnbulg but Fraserburgh kept it at bay. Townspeople were forbidden to entertain Cairnbulg friends and the local constable was stationed on the approach road to make sure Fraserburgh was not visited by people from the infected village.[7] An old school house was rented to serve as a hospital,[8] lodging house space obtained lest anyone be made homeless by cholera, and chloride of lime was distributed to the poor for cleansing their properties.[9]

In 1866 Fraserburgh was visited by a severe outbreak of cholera. The disease exposed numerous deficiencies in the burgh and was followed by efforts to tackle them. There was insufficient pure water; burgh streets – and some houses – were frequently in a foul state, polluted by the waste of man and beast. The very short-term approach to hospital care – renting a site when a crisis occurred then abandoning it afterwards – began to look highly unsatisfactory. Out of the dreadful experience of 1866 some improvements came.

Once cholera appeared in 1866 a hospital was sought. This time the authorities rented a Rope Works on the Links that had ceased operation in the previous year after sixty-two years of activity.[10] After handing over £5 rent the Police Commissioners did in fact buy the site – paying nearly fourteen pounds for it.[11] It does not seem to have been suitable for long-term care. A pig-stye and a byre leaned against its southern wall[12] and its general condition was so dilapidated as to fill the medical officers with despair.[13] It was fitted up at first with just two beds and with bedding borrowed from the poorhouse.[14] To nurse the sick the Commissioners engaged Elizabeth McLeod,[15] paying her sixteen shillings a week for her work. She proved to be decidedly unsatisfactory and was dismissed because of her absences from her duties. This reduced the poor woman to poverty and to appealing to the Commissioners that she had no money and nowhere to go.[16] They took enough notice of her argument that she was denied employment due to her having been a cholera nurse to grant her five shillings. Lord Saltoun believed that what was needed was a 'strong-minded Bible woman possessing tact and free from religious hypochondria'.[17] Whoever was appointed would be considerably harrassed as more patients squeezed into the hospital and families from homes afflicted by cholera were found accommodation there too.[18]

In the town the Police Commissioners had tar-barrels set burning in an attempt to purify the air, infected houses thoroughly disinfected and white-washed, and chloride of lime tipped into drains. An extra doctor was called in to help the two already at work.[19] Above all it forced the Commissioners to look very carefully at the cleaning of the burgh, and to insist, for the moment, on a much higher standard. Lord Saltoun noted that the 1866 cholera outbreak had killed forty five people and had cost the town £400 directly though the real bill was far higher since the season's fishing had been badly hit.[20] Some of his own Broadsea tenants fell behind with rent payments as a result of the cholera affliction.[21] So sensitive were other ports to Fraserburgh's cholera that the Fraserburgh fleet were denied entry to Peterhead harbour when driven there to seek shelter from storms.

Not only cholera outbreaks, but frequent cases of typhoid fever[22] and severe onsets of diarrhoea every summer, made the authorities tackle the problems of water supply and cleaning. This left, they felt, too little money to take up the matter of proper hospital provision.[23] They concentrated on trying to keep cholera at bay, paying especial attention to vessels from stricken ports which were carefully checked by a doctor before they were permitted to berth.[24] Yet the hospital was clearly quite inadequate. A patient with a severe case of measles when taken there in 1875 found it so crowded that the matron was packing in patients two to a bed and had an official bedding supply to cover but one bed.[25] The matron ran the hospital with an allocation of seven shillings and six pence a week to pay for the board, washing, fire and light for each patient; she herself received a weekly nursing fee of twelve and six.[26]

The much-needed hospital was built in 1878. The funds – £3,000 – came from a local fishcurer, Thomas Walker, and the ground from Lord Saltoun. Till 1891 Buchan parishes nearby joined with Fraserburgh in this venture. To the Police Commissioners this was a dubious benefit, for they feared the infection of the town at the height of the fishing season by disease brought into it from another parish. This potential source of danger[27] was reduced by an agreement that, between July and September, the hospital would not admit non-Fraserburgh people with infectious diseases unless such diseases were already prevalent in the Burgh.[28]

Patients admitted to the new hospital had to pay for their stay themselves, or have their bills met by an outside body like the Parochial Board. Poorly-paid workers in need of care yet unable to attract the charity of either their employers or the Parochial Board went untreated.[29] Before long the hospital was extended with a wing to cope with cases of the dreadful (and still all too common) illness of diphtheria.[30]

The hospital sometimes found itself swamped with patients. Though serious cholera outbreaks were avoided for the rest of the century, other diseases spread very easily in the crowded premises inhabited by those coming to Fraserburgh for the fishing season. In 1887, for example, measles killed several herring-girls once it had got into the house into which they were packed nine to a room.[31] Improved health required authorities to do more than employ medical officers and sustain the hospital.

Water supplies

At the beginning of the nineteenth century Fraserburgh people obtained the water that they needed from a limited number of increasingly polluted wells. The revenue brought in from the property Lord Saltoun allowed the town in 1787 meant improvement could now be contemplated. In 1804 a scheme was completed that ran water from the farm of Pitblae, conveying it through wooden pipes to a reservoir on the West Links.[32] For thirty years this seemed adequate[33] before the town's growth and the particular need of the fishing industry created a crisis. In 1845 the Town Council completed its second project, a supply from Smiddyhill Farm, before handing over responsibility in 1850 to the Police Commissioners.[34] The Commissioners' power to raise money from the rates gave them the chance to consider ambitious schemes, yet it was twenty years before they made a really significant addition to the water supply.

In 1851 the Commissioners had a new reservoir constructed on the town's eastern margin. Clay pipes were used to carry the water but proved liable to burst and had to be replaced with four-inch cast-iron ones.[35] A little extra water came in 1865 when the Railway Company found the supply it had created for itself provided a surplus that it was prepared to sell to the town, running it off in two-inch pipes to the town reservoir.[36]

The cholera crisis of 1866 jolted the authorities into the recognition that it was no longer enough to tinker with the existing supply, turning it off during the fishing season for long periods, and grumbling that local people wasted water by leaving open taps on the public wells.[37] Lord

Saltoun pointed out very firmly in 1867 that Fraserburgh's supply of $9\frac{1}{2}$ gallons a head compared badly with Aberdeen's 30 gallons, and that Fraserburgh's inactivity contrasted with newly completed water schemes in Huntly and Peterhead.[38] The cholera outbreak showed the need for pure drinking water and for plentiful supplies if a better cleaning and sewage system were to be contemplated. For the moment the Commissioners paid up £7 to dam a stream at Glenbughty and hire a carter whose waggon was fitted with a huge timber water cask, bound with iron straps. The carter trundled down into Fraserburgh, selling water for $\frac{1}{2}$d a bucket.[39]

By the seventies the new Glashiemyre supply was flowing, yet total supplies were still insufficient. More was channelled at a cost of £6,000, in from Tyrie Burn,[40] and still local businessmen and householders grumbled.[41] The tenpenny water rate was swelled by money levied from local shopkeepers (grocers paid an extra pound a year, for example, and bakers ten shillings) and from the fishcurers who were asked for 2/6d for every boat they had contracted to them.[42] Not only was the supply insufficient, the Commissioners had also (from 1872) the extra responsibility of Broadsea. The fisher people here were particularly badly served – a visiting doctor noted in 1872 'I saw the inhabitants coming to the nearest well in Fraserburgh for water at great personal inconvenience'.[43] An Aberdeen engineer, Gordon Jenkins, whose advice the Commissioners sought observed that during the fishing season the higher parts of the Town were often without water for several days and commonly had no water at night.[44] Water was still being cut off from local businesses at night, whilst a request from traders that a water-cart dampen the dust in the streets in dry weather was abruptly rejected as wholly unrealistic.[45]

In 1883 supplies from Ardlaw and Tyrie Mains flowed into Fraserburgh and considerably eased the situation.[46] Yet still more water was needed and a new scheme was under way when the century closed.[47] The authorities had to proceed slowly in urging the fitting of water-closets in houses when water supplies were still not completely satisfactory.[48] It was, above all, yet another example of the difficulties facing the town during the fishing season. In 1893, despite the Ardlaw scheme, the supply dropped to $18\frac{1}{3}$ gallons a head during the fishing season and the town's higher districts were still inadequately served[49] with insufficient to enable upstairs water-closets to function. Lack of water thus played an important part in explaining the inadequate sanitation of some Fraserburgh housing.

Housing

Those who prospered in nineteenth century Fraserburgh had built for themselves very substantial properties that were, before the century was over, decently fitted with water, sewage and gas connections. Many working-class properties were far less satisfactory, whilst lodging houses and the various premises inhabited by people who came for the fishing season (and could not find the opportunity or afford the cost of squeezing into the homes of local people) posed a grim health hazard that remained through the century. The arrival of five or six thousand more people than Fraserburgh usually housed virtually doubled the population and provided the Police Commissioners with endless worry.

The properties near the harbour and in Broadsea were especially unsatisfactory permanent homes. Until the seventies the Broadsea fishermen had no security of tenure. They paid one or two pounds rent for houses that were crowded together and sited on badly made streets so that 'the whole place had a look of disrepair about it'.[50] Many of the fishermen were recorded on their rental list by nicknames – 'Gunner', 'Donkey', 'Brickie' and 'Bobbin'. When they signed a document it was often with the mark of an illiterate.[51] Their homes were clearly a health hazard. Not only were they small, they did not usually possess a piece of ground to accommodate a privy. Piles of filth thus lay around the dwellings.[52] When the Police Commissioners assumed responsibility for Broadsea in 1872 Lord Saltoun pressed his tenants to repair or replace their houses. To homes in good order, in line with the street he was prepared to offer the security of a 37 year lease. To tenants of really sound properties a 99 year lease was offered.[53] But six years after 1872 twenty-two families were still on one year leases and eleven had no proper lease at all. Given the poverty of Broadsea it is surprising forty-eight families were able to obtain 37 year leases. Only two buildings were let on 99 year leases and one of these was the school.[54] But by the end of the century the village had been much reshaped. Old cottages worth around a mere £3[55] had been pulled down and the road levelled so that it no longer 'vied with the house tops in reaching for the moon'.[56] Nor were there any longer cases of inability to pay rent such as that of 1868 when Alexander Noble got into difficulties because of his age and because he had a wife and cholera-stricken son-in-law to support as well as the funeral costs of 2 grandchildren tragically killed by the disease.[57]

The rest of Fraserburgh contained crowded and unhealthy properties too, indeed Lord Saltoun declared in 1867 that Shore Street alone was full of houses that were a health hazard.[58] There were properties in Braehead in the nineties that were of an old type, thirteen feet high, gable-end on to the street with walls of stone and clay surmounted by a tiled roof sunk with age.[59] In April 1874 the Sanitary Inspector found a house in Love Street whose twenty four rooms were crammed full of fishing families yet had no privies in its tiny yard, just a small ashpit in a foul state. Not only was the site crowded and badly drained, a stable stood in the small yard whose horses added to the general filth.[60] A High Street house of 1879 had, in October (and well outside the herring season) fourteen families in it yet no water supply and no drain laid on. The tenants emptied all their waste, however foul, into the street.[61] A house in North Street so horrified a visiting plumber that he declared he would not sleep in it one night, even rent-free. This house had a water closet, but the house occupants could not (or would not) flush it so that its contents spilled out and spread over the floors.[62]

Through Fraserburgh streets wandered hens and ducks, rooting in the dung-hills and – in times of cholera – considered a health hazard by the Medical Officer.[63] Probably even more offensive were the numerous piggeries that were scattered in the gardens and yards of many houses. In 1892 there were forty-one such piggeries containing in all 105 animals. Most of them were housed in dilapidated conditions in boxes and barrels, situated on sites without drainage. The smell from them was, in summer, highly offensive, piles of dung lay around them whilst foul liquid soaked the ground and gathered in pools.[64]

In June, 1868, the Police Commissioners urged upon Fraserburgh lodging-house keepers the need to avoid overcrowding their houses during the fishing season.[65] It was a hopelessly optimistic request. For two months the herring fishing created living conditions in parts of the town that were abominable. There were but three or four lodging houses in Fraserburgh, situated in poorer streets and generally sufficient for the vagrants who might normally come to the town. By 1882 the one in Kirkbrae was in poor shape, 'a mass of confusion, filth, and disorder. The smell is dreadful. The timbers of roofing and flooring are very much decayed and in places giving way and the whole, or part, may at any time fall down on the inmates'.[66] The Commissioners had drawn up a list of regulations for lodging houses the year before the Kirkbrae premises were inspected.[67] They urged that rooms be washed out weekly, bed-sheets monthly, and blankets several times a year. They demanded that the rooms be not overcrowded, the occupants supplied with straw or chaff-filled mattresses, and a decent supply of clean water had to be available. But, under the pressure of the arrival of five or six thousand people, rules and regulations do not seem to have been observed.

Some of the incomers stayed with local families during the fishing; others found rented rooms. There was a temptation to pack in people in order to profit from the fishing season: when the Sanitary Inspector closed a house in Frith Street where typhoid kept recurring and conditions were filthy the owner demanded £30, as compensation for the rent of the rooms for the fishing season.[68] Girls who came to process the herring were packed in as many as nine to a room in apartments often entirely without washing and sanitary amenities.[69] It was in such circumstances that illnesses could spread so speedily, claiming life and causing misery and poverty. Even worse was the accommodation that consisted of empty barrel stores built without any provision for sanitation; rooms measuring fourteen feet by twelve were commonly occupied by twelve or more women.[70] Even in the 1890s herring girls were living in smoky, dirty, draughty rooms without cupboards or shelves and with only one bedstead to every three girls.[71] In tiny spaces they had to live, sleep, cook and wash. Some of the worst accommodation was found among the houses of Shore Street, Castle and Hunter's Lane and the curing yards of Denmark Street and Barrasgate. Women in one of these properties told a Church of Scotland Deputy that they were decent people yet, in Fraserburgh, they were 'treated like Beasts, although they came out of comfortable homes they had to put up with any sort of treatment and pay high rents too'. 'These high-rented rooms' the Deputy noted, 'tend to overcrowding. Widows with married sons and daughters and lodgers all living and sleeping in one room, sometimes as many as twelve'. The problem of adequate accommodation during the fishing season remained one never solved in the nineteenth century.

Cleansing

At the beginning of the nineteenth century the waste and rubbish produced by Fraserburgh's inhabitants and the animals they kept, gathered in heaps in the streets. A number of open channels carried off the waste from time to time, according to the weather. Broadsea village did not even have open gutters. The Town Council made sporadic efforts to clean the streets, hiring men to clear away grass and farmers to cart away dung.[72] Although the streets were at their most offensive in summer, the council were attracted by the idea of tackling street-cleaning in winter when there was considerable unemployment and labourers could be hired more cheaply than when work was plentiful.[73] In the 1820s the Council edged towards a more organized system of cleaning hiring a scavenger at tenpence a day to 'work constantly every day thereon and to keep all the sewers perfectly clean by raking and sweeping with a broom and taking away the stuff immediately'.[74] The piles of dung the scavenger gathered by clearing out the open sewers

RULES & REGULATIONS

RESPECTING

COMMON LODGING HOUSES,

FOR THE

BURGH OF FRASERBURGH,

1881.

The COMMISSIONERS OF POLICE of the Burgh of Fraserburgh, as Local Authority under the Public Health (Scotland) Act 1867, do hereby, in virtue of the said Act, and at a Meeting held this Thirteenth day of June, One Thousand Eight Hundred and Eighty-one, make the following RULES and REGULATIONS respecting COMMON LODGING HOUSES, as defined by the said Act, within the Police limits of the said Burgh :

1. The number of Lodgers which may be received in any room of any Common Lodging House shall not be greater than in the proportion of one person of the age of eight years or upwards for every three hundred cubic feet of space contained therein (exclusive of Lobbies, Closets, and Presses, and of recesses not extending four feet in depth and not having a separate window therein, and not perfectly clear from floor to ceiling, and from wall to wall, and exclusive also of recesses in which there is any fixture whatever).

2. In estimating the number of Lodgers authorised to be received in any room, two children under the age of eight years respectively shall be reckoned as one person only.

3. The Local Authority will furnish to the Keeper of a Common Lodging House, when registered, a ticket for each room in each house in which Lodgers may be received, assigning a number to each such room, and specifying the number of Lodgers which may be received therein ; and such Ticket may be in the following form:—

. "Room, number (state number) this Room is registered to accommodate not more than (state number) persons."

4. The Keeper of a Common Lodging House shall at all times keep the Ticket applicable to any room in such house hung up in some conspicuous place in such room.

5. Such Keepers shall not deface any Ticket, nor permit the same to be defaced.

6. Such Keeper shall also at all times keep conspicuously placed both on the outside and inside of the door of each room, the number of each such room assigned to it in the Ticket applicable thereto.

7. The Keeper of a Common Lodging House shall not receive or accommodate, or permit to be received or accommodated, in any room in any such house at any one time, a greater number of Lodgers or other persons than shall be specified in the Ticket applicable to such room.

8. Such Keepers shall not permit persons of both sexes, above the age of eight years respectively, to occupy the same sleeping apartment, except in the case of husband and wife.

9. The Keeper of a Common Lodging House shall keep the windows of each sleeping room in such house continuously open, to the extent of at least one-third of the superficial areas of such windows respectively, from Ten to Eleven o'clock in the forenoon, and from Two to Three o'clock in the afternoon, of each day, unless prevented by tempestuous weather, or by the illness of any inmate of such room.

10. Such Keeper shall well and sufficiently wash the floor of each room, passage, and stair, in such house on Saturday in each week before Twelve o'clock noon.

11. Such Keeper shall wash and clean the bed sheets used in such house at least once in each calendar month, or oftener if found necessary by the Sanitary Inspector.

12. Such Keeper shall thoroughly cleanse and scour the blankets, rugs, bed-clothes, and covers, used in such house in each of the months of January, April, July, and October in every year.

13. Such Keeper shall, on the occurrence of any fever, or any infectious or contagious disease within such house, cause all blankets, rugs, bedclothes, covers, and other articles which may have been used in such house by the person affected by any such fever or disease, to be thoroughly cleansed and disinfected, immediately after the death or removal of the person so affected, unless, in pursuance of the statutory provision in that behalf, the Local Authority shall direct the destruction of such clothes, bedding, and other articles.

14. Such Keeper shall thoroughly cleanse all the rooms, passages, stairs, windows, doors, walls, ceilings, privies, ashpits, cesspools, and drains of such house to the satisfaction of the Sanitary Inspector, and so often as he shall require such keeper to do so.

15. Such Keeper shall use straw, or chaff, or some other suitable material in the beds and mattresses in such house.

16. Such Keeper shall not receive any lodger into any room in such house unless there be sufficient bedsteads and bedding in such room in a clean and proper state to accommodate them.

17. Such Keeper shall provide a chamber-pot for each bed in such house, and one or more slop-pails in each room thereof.

18. Such Keeper shall not permit any filth to remain in such house after seven o'clock in the morning, from the first day of April to the last day of September inclusive, and after eight o'clock in the morning from the first day of October to the last day of March inclusive.

19. Such Keeper shall have at all times in such house a proper supply of pure water for lodgers therein.

20. Such Keeper shall maintain and enforce good order, sobriety and decorum within such house, and shall prevent persons occupying or resorting to such house for immoral purposes.

21. Every Keeper of a Common Lodging House offending against any of the foregoing Rules and Regulations shall be liable to a penalty not exceeding the sum of Five Pounds for each offence ; and in the case of a continuing offence, to a further penalty not exceeding the sum of Forty Shillings for each day after written notice of the offence from the Local Authority.

22. The expression " Keeper of a Common Lodging House," used in the foregoing Rules and Regulations, includes any person having or acting in the care and management of a Common Lodging House, as defined by the said Act.

JOHN PARK, *Chairman.*

were, from time to time, shifted by a carter and sold to local farmers. The development of herring fishing affected street-cleaning, too, as the century progressed. The growing number of people coming for the fishing season generated waste to be cleared: so too did the activities of the fish-curers whose buckets of brine and fish-offal added to the Council's worries. Their usual response was to hire a second scavenger for a limited period and to insist that special attention be paid to Shore Street and the harbour area. Whereas in winter a weekly clean of this heavily-populated spot was sufficient, in summer it had to be done daily.[75]

But the Council never seems to have put great energy into cleansing the town. The setting up of the Parochial Board and the Police Commissioners provided Fraserburgh with more effective authorities with power to raise money from the rates. What prodded them into greater activity was fear of cholera outbreaks. The appearance of cholera in Broadsea in 1848 brought action from the Parochial Board – but only after the Board of Supervision had firmly pointed out the duty of the local Board to see that areas for which it was responsible were clean. The village ways were cleared of their customary collections of dung and waste.[76] The Board held joint meetings with the Police Commissioners and the Harbour Commission to concert action on Fraserburgh.[77] Extra men were hired to clear out the drains and sewers, sweep the streets, and cut drains in Broadsea.[78] At seven every morning a cart proceeded round the area collecting dung. The ditches at the sides of the main roads were cleaned out by the Turnpike Trust.[79]

But after 1849 efforts to keep Fraserburgh clean were relaxed. Once more the town became filthy, stagnant pools of foul water and heaps of manure and refuse lay about the streets. Waste from pigs and cows added to the dreadful smell that hung over the houses. An outbreak of cholera in Newcastle caused sufficient alarm in Fraserburgh for a new burst of cleansing to occur in 1853.[80] The authorities grumbled that 'it has been the practice for some of the inhabitants of Fraserburgh to throw down or empty their night soil on the pavement, street and gutter courses, and for some of them to allow their children to commit nuisances on the public street'.[81] The Town Drummer was despatched to march around the streets proclaiming official displeasure at such misdeeds. A cart was sent daily to clear away the ashes and filth from the houses.[82]

The increasing burden of cleansing the town during the fishing season was not easily solved. The Police Commissioners (who dealt with the problem from 1850) were not eager to pay decent wages to find extra scavengers for the summer. The twelve-shillings a week they offered was not very attractive at a time when men readily found employment.[83] Yet piles of filth developed so speedily that something had to be done. A grudging extra shilling a week (for a ten-hour day of labour) was added to the scavenger's regular wages. Carters were hired to shift the dung and refuse (collected in heaps by the scavengers) to a dung depot on the Links south of the Rope Works.[84] At times the local police constables were pulled in to help the work of cleaning.[85] The dung was sold off to farmers for a few pounds a month.[86] But for the rest of the year the town continued to manage with but one man to clean and clear the streets.

The 1866 cholera outbreak was sufficiently severe to jolt the rather casual ways of earlier years. Lord Saltoun argued that the disease was very considerably due to the poor state of the town's badly-built sewers. He drew unfavourable comparison between Fraserburgh and Greenock: the latter was far freer of piles and pools of filth in the streets.[87] The Police Commissioners instituted as an emergency measure the daily collection of all dung, offal, and rubbish that was gathered by householders in boxes to await the carter.[88] Dr McRae, who came from Aberdeen to help during the emergency, was allowed to divide the town into three districts for each of which a scavenger was responsible. Yet even his reforms left accumulations of filth lying about the streets.[89]

As the cholera crisis faded the town once more began to deteriorate. Only two scavengers were at work, the dung-collecting cart dropped to three collections a week,[90] and there were to be found (for instance on Castle Street) sights like 'a stinking gutter full of the refuse of a curing yard, blood, and other offensive matter'.[91] The very poor drainage system meant that waste from houses and works on higher ground ran down into their neighbours' drains or into communal drains too small to convey a quantity of water and refuse.[92] The inhabitants of Shore Street dumped filth on the street and on the beach; people in Duke Street had such poor drains they threw their slops, water, etc. over the wall in front of the houses into the street. Around some houses the ground was saturated with sewage.[93] However the cholera does seem to have led to long-term changes, helped by prodding from central government. A visit to Fraserburgh by the General Superintendent of the Poor was followed by complaints from him about the state of the town, its lack of sewers, and the very poor state of Shore Street in particular.[94] His views were pressed upon Lord Saltoun who clearly wished action to follow, though his local agent, Alexander Anderson, did argue Fraserburgh was no worse than most places and was healthier than Banff, Buckie, Huntly and Keith. Even the Commissioners began to accept the inadequacy of a cleansing service in which, for years, a key figure was the carter William Simpson who was incompetent and whose cart was pulled by a horse too old to move at a fair pace and too weak to pull a fully laden cart.[95] They raised their scavenger's wages to twenty shillings a week and increased the payment made to carters too.[96]

In 1870 the Commissioners began to consider adopting a proper scheme of underground drainage and sewage.[97] Plans were drawn up by an Aberdeen engineer, Gordon Jenkins; a successful bid put in by Murray Urquhart of Aberdeen, an overseer hired for thirty shillings a week, and four thousand pounds borrowed from the Public Works Commissioners.[98] In 1876 work got under way digging trenches and laying pipes; by 1877 it was largely complete, running to an outfall into deep water north of the Baths.[99] The town also began to press for full control over its own streets. The condition of the streets had much to do with the general cleanliness of the burgh. A programme of laying solid Caithness-flag pavements began in the mid century.[100] But the streets themselves were covered in mud and animal droppings. This surface coating was occasionally scraped into heaps but these heaps then generally lay around for days or found their way into gutters and sewers which they helped to clog.[101] Only with full control of the roads would efficient cleaning and drain-building be possible. Not till 1890 did this come about for the Road Trustees kept control until the whole County agreed to let burghs of populations of 2,000 or more manage their own areas.[102]

Amid the bustle of improvement Broadsea was neglected. When brought into the Police Commissioner's boundaries it was promised a vastly improved cleansing service.[103] In fact, upon inspecting the village, the Commissioners concluded it was beyond ordinary cleaning. They put two scavengers into it for a week, helped by the carter for a couple of days, but this did not provide a permanent solution.[104] The authorities argued that Broadsea's main road was so dreadful they could do nothing till it was put in order.[105] Yet the fishermen were too poor to do this themselves, especially at a time when Lord Saltoun was demanding they repair or rebuild their houses. After being within the police boundaries nine years the fishers complained that their roads were at least a foot deep in mud whilst pools of sewage lay throughout the village.[106] The open drain between the houses was easily blocked and sewage discharge mingled with a fish midden far from the beach. Two years after this complaint, and with nothing still having been done, the fishermen sent a letter to the Board of Supervision. 'We will be left to wallow among filth', they wrote in despair, 'until cholera or some other epidemic overtake us and carry off a third or perhaps even more of the population'.[107] The Police Commissioners were moved to spend £300 on trying to improve Broadsea.[108]

Even after the completion of the drainage scheme all was far from well in Fraserburgh. Some pipe connections were so poor that sewage

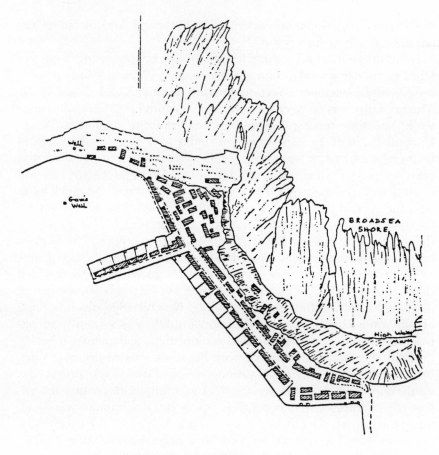

Well

Gow's
Well

BROADSEA
SHORE

High Water
Mark

Broadsea 1870
(O.S. 25″ = 1 mile)

Broadsea in 1870. The poorer properties lay in jumbled fashion close
to the sea-shore. Those a little way inland had the best chance of
overhaul and survival.

seeped out under house floors.[109] There were still cesspools in the town and (in 1896) 155 properties – excluding Broadsea and the fishing season accommodation – that did not have any water closets.[110] Householders put out waste for collection in most unsuitable containers, favouring old coal scuttles and herring baskets in particular.[111] Stables and piggeries still contributed to fouling the town. But the fishing season posed the biggest problem of all. Not only did the numbers of people produce insanitary housing, the lack of privies at their workplaces meant the beach and outskirts of the town were in a disgusting condition.[112] Enough had been done to keep cholera at bay and improve living conditions for the bulk of the town's regular population: the fishing season in this, as in other areas, produced problems that were not solved in the nineteenth century.

These efforts at improvement pushed the Police Commissioners into raising rates that began at a shilling in the pound, rose to two and five pence in the eighties, and settled at two shillings in the nineties. (See Appendix 4.) This total figure embracing at first just lighting costs, had 'watching and preserving public peace'[113] added in 1846 and cleansing and water-supply provision in 1850. The balance between these respective burdens varied: the water-supply works of the eighties, for instance, raised that element in the rates to one shilling and twopence from a figure as low as sixpence in 1876.[114] To these burdens have to be added the cost of coping with poverty and the school rate raised from 1874, duties that fell not upon the Police Commissioners but the members of two further bodies concerned with the improvement of Fraserburgh.

Chapter Five

POVERTY

Before 1846

At the beginning of the nineteenth century Fraserburgh dealt with the problem of supporting the desperately poor by the distribution of money raised in the fashion commonly found in Scottish communities of the period. The church collected in around £50 in a year and a little more came from a fund built up from the bequests of well-to-do former local inhabitants. It meant that there was sufficient to provide small donations to the eighty odd poor for whom the parish felt itself responsible:[1] but it did not furnish enough for extraordinary circumstances. Fraserburgh attracted wandering poor from other areas who annoyed those administering poor relief by attempting to settle in the town.[2] Despite attempts to discourage vagrants, this problem remained, possibly because the beggars were attracted by the other forms of poor relief provided by the town.[3] Fraserburgh itself produced very few who sought to survive through begging and these few were issued with special badges.[4]

The repeated occurrence of serious mid-winter poverty when work was not easy to find and provisions were expensive meant the town organized extra forms of relief. A 1782 crop failure, for example, led local gentry to put together subscriptions that were used to import flour that was sold cheaply.[5] Lord Saltoun urged the desirability of building up a stock of coal that the poor could buy in small quantities.[6] A sharp rise in meal prices in December 1800 moved the better-off to organize a fresh subscription list with which to buy bread. £88 was collected, £31 of it coming from Lord Saltoun, much of the rest made up of a long list of gifts of around ten shillings.[7] In this fashion Fraserburgh survived, providing for its eighty odd poor with weekly or quarterly handouts of up to 2/6d for the wholly destitute and 1/- for those with some little means of their own.[8] The system was operated by the elders of the kirk who divided the town into four districts with an elder responsible for each area. The fisher-folk especially disliked it being known when they were driven to seek help. Orphans who were destitute were placed in suitable homes and watched over by one of the elders.[9]

This minimal system contained no provision for the medical treatment of paupers, yet their cold, unhygienic homes, their straw or chaff-pallets on the ground, their inadequate coarse woollen bedding and their poor diet all made ill-health very probable.[10] Local doctors were sometimes so moved by the poverty, the lack of clothing and foods and ill-health of local people that they personally paid for medicines.[11] The fund that was built up by subscriptions and managed by Lord Saltoun continued to dole out meal and coals, and a clothing society was formed.[12] The poor were encouraged to save a little and by 1843, after thirteen years of existence, this savings bank contained £522, a little of which came from the elderly and from fishing people.[13] By the forties a soup kitchen was being operated in the worst winter months to provide soup and four ounces of bread at very low cost.[14]

The system was far from satisfactory. The Disruption hit the funds the kirk commanded, cutting them by one third.[15] There were children too ill-clad to be sent to school and many who went barefoot through the whole year.[16] There were labourers struggling to support large families whom one observer felt to be even worse off than the recognised paupers.[17] Certainly a common wage of a shilling a day for labourers cannot have been enough to allow significant savings for times of winter hardship. By March many families were well through their meagre stores of herring and potatoes and sometimes reduced to meals made up simply of tiny portions of potato alone.

The Parochial Board

In late 1845 the Fraserburgh Parochial Board met, selected an Inspector at an annual wage of £12.10.0d and checked the list of the poor. There were thirty three people who were receiving between a shilling and two and six a week and another thirty three who were paid monthly at sums ranging from two to (very rarely) ten shillings.[18] They found it necessary to at once apply a legal assessment of a shilling in the pound on local landowners and tenants:[19] the scale of poverty and the inadequacy of voluntary payments left them no alternative. The Board was able to at once make up one of the deficiencies of the old system for it began paying for medicines and for footwear for those it accepted as sufficiently deserving.[20]

People from a vast range of occupations sought help, but the largest single group were made up of the aged, especially women, many of whom were troubled by various illnesses of old age.[21] In 1876, for instance, one half of the total of 112 poor were over the age of sixty.[22] Their ailments, as identified in the 1850s (Appendix 5) included blindness, rheumatism, deafness, being lame or crippled, asthma, various degrees of mental incapacity and a complaint vaguely categorised as 'weakness'. The occupations of the poor in the 1850s and 90s are listed in Appendix 5 and Appendix 6. In the 1850s the biggest single group are simply identified as 'able bodied', a category that was officially not entitled to assistance. For the rest the occupations included outdoor workers like cattle herds, sailors, labourers, masons and fishermen, and skilled craftsmen like shoemakers, wrights, coopers, blacksmiths, weavers and even a book-binder. By the 1890s the pauper lists were dominated by labourers; they formed a category three times as numerous as the next – fishworkers. Connections with the fishing industry feature in the numbers of fisher-men, fishmongers, fish sellers and coopers on the list. Pedlars, hawkers, farm workers are unsurprising paupers, but the lists also include tailors, shoemakers, tinsmiths, blacksmiths, masons, bakers and even a doctor. Not all applicants were, of course, successful. Some found the Board opposed to their drinking habits,[23] others (the Inspector discovered) had able-bodied relatives well able to provide support.[24] One lady claiming to be in dire straits, unable to support her family, was turned down on the grounds that she had already been paid a monthly advance on her husband's wages (as a seaman on the 'Alibur', bound for Greenland) and would soon receive more.[25] The Board had frequently to help around ten or more able-bodied people without work as well as women who were neither elderly nor ill but had been left with a large number of small children to support.[26] The Inspector was required to check the circum-stances of those on the roll making occasional journeys to see the condition of those for whom Fraserburgh was responsible but who lived elsewhere. This threw up the occasional case like the woman found in 1852 in Aberdeen who 'went for the most part idle'[27] and was brought back to Fraserburgh to work for her parents. Sometimes temporary relief was given to people in particular difficulty. These included seamen (landed from ships) injured or unwell,[28] and a soldier shipped home from India because of ill-health[29] and in temporary difficulties over his pension.

Quite a number of poor earned a little themselves from time to time.[30] A widower with eleven children to support (the youngest of whom was a baby) 'earns a little by selling sticks'.[31] Stocking knitting was the most common mid-century employment of poor on the roll, though there were a wide range of other means of earning a little. Some sold bread or fish, or eggs; others took in washing. Some laboured in the fields or spun hemp, engaged in knitting, weaving, sewing or dressmaking, and yet more mended nets, went to the fishing, made shoes or toys (see Appendix 6). Not everyone regarded as deserving by the Inspector was ready to admit their need. Alexander Fraser, despite being of a delicate constitution, preferred to sleep in boats on the shore. The fires he lit there led to the police intervening, yet he still refused to accept official aid.[32] Fraserburgh also found itself faced with a number of men whose wanderings had lasted much of their lifetime until age or misfortune put a stop to them. There was, for example, William Sutherland who had been tramping for thirteen years and never settled in any parish[33] and John Campbell who had worked all over the country for forty years on railways and public works.[34] The occasional pauper was in an appalling state. In 1859 William Innes 'was in such a state of filth that no person would receive him into a house . . . he would require a pair of drawers, a pair of stockings, a shirt, a pair of moleskin trousers, a moleskin Jacket and Vest . . . his present wearing apparel was crawling with vermin and would require to be burnt'.[35]

Amounts paid to the poor went up very slowly during the century and rose by a mere shilling for most cases. The mid-century weekly payment of one shilling and sixpence, up to two and six by the nineties, was thought by the Inspector of that time to be as large as was necessary or desirable.[36] Certain cases of special need (particularly those involving large families) did win higher amounts of around five to seven shillings. But the Board provided other forms of aid. From the 1860s it began to pay school fees for the children of destitute parents.[37] Most children cared for by the Board were orphans or had been deserted by their parents: a few were simply beyond the capacity of their family to support. For the most part they were boarded out with working-class families (fish-workers, tailors, shoemakers, coopers and crofters being amongst those prepared to undertake this duty). The Board paid for clothes, boots, and school books as well as furnishing a small weekly payment – usually one and sixpence. Henry Lee, for example, remained on the poor-roll eight years when his father could no longer support him. He boarded with Mrs Simpson till fourteen (the age at which children were struck off the roll) then joined a local druggist as an apprentice. During his eight years he was provided with four pairs of boots and one of shoes (at around three and six a pair), twelve items of clothing and one set of schoolbooks. Boys were commonly apprenticed, at fourteen, to local farmers, shopkeepers and craftsmen. One – George Thomson, rose to become a coal-mine overseer: another joined the G.N.S.R. as a ticket clerk.[38] Shoes, blankets, coal, meal and house repairs were all provided to particular cases from time to time. In 1859, for instance, ten paupers were receiving shoes and clothes and fifteen were receiving meal. The Medical officers who worked for the Board from 1848 were allowed an amount to cover the costs of medicines for the poor.[39] The first man appointed, Dr Grieve, who cheerfully accepted a £15 annual payment

for his work found at the end of a year that he had made nearly five
hundred visits, spent £12 on medicines, and successfully pleaded for his
salary to be raised to £27.[40] He had not been at his post long before he
was plunged into helping tackle a cholera outbreak in Broadsea. Here, he
observed, 'most of the Broadsea fishermen and families were destitute of
food, clothing and fuel and he had found it necessary ... to afford supplies
of meal, blankets and coals to invalids and supplies of sugar, tea and
coffee'.[41] His work soon included vaccinating the poor against smallpox
for which payments of one and six a case were made for nearby visits, two
and six for those living more than two miles away.[42] The Board was
occasionally prepared to meet funeral costs; in 1848 it hired a local
undertaker who charged five shillings for each interment.[43]

Raising sufficient money to meet these many burdens was not easy.
Until August of 1854 there was no proper valuation of Fraserburgh
available and the Board found that no sooner had it fixed an amount
upon proprietor or tenant than it was promptly challenged.[44] The one
shilling in the pound figure of 1846 was soon shown to be insufficient.
1847 proved a particularly burdensome year for the potato crop failed,
large quantities of meal had to be bought in February and help had to be
given to destitute able-bodied people.[45] By March, several inhabitants
had successfully sought help with their rent until the beginning of the
herring fishing season.[46] The uneven pattern of earnings in Fraserburgh
led the Board to drift into accepting a system that lasted till 1899 when
the Local Government Board denounced Fraserburgh's practice of
letting a large number of the rate-payers defer payment of their assessment until the herring fishing season.[47] A successful herring season was
vital; it enabled the repayment of the advances made to fishers by
tradespeople and helped Fraserburgh people set aside a store to support
themselves in winter.[48] The results of a poor season were felt by the Board
in the following winter. The burdens of 1847 meant an assessment
increase to one and sixpence: by 1860 it had reached two shillings.[49] This
brought a check on Fraserburgh by an Inspector from Edinburgh. He
felt the two shilling figure to be too high, noted the Board's steadily
growing debt at the bank, and complained very strongly that the local
Inspector was not at his post. Instead work was being done by an
inexperienced and ill-informed boy.[50] Yet by 1863 Fraserburgh's assessment was up to two and six, the debt with the bank had passed the
thousand pound mark, and money was owed to other parishes who were
caring for poor who were Fraserburgh's financial responsibility.[51]

Some of the blame for this situation was laid upon the current
Inspector. He resigned to be replaced by a former bank official, Thomas
Lawrence.[52] Very slowly the assessment began to fall. By 1871 it was

down to two shillings and continued to fall until it had dropped back to its one shilling figure by 1878, thereafter for the rest of the century it remained at a figure just under a shilling.[53] But the unfortunate Inspector who was pushed into resignation could also have argued that the high assessments of the early sixties did come at a time when the number of poor were exceptionally large. Until this period the roll of paupers rarely exceeded one hundred but the period 1862–64 saw a huge rise up to the figure of two hundred and thirty-eight.[54] Thereafter it fell once more until the mid-eighties when unfortunate economic conditions (especially during a bad winter of 1885–6) led to a rise to two hundred and eleven people obtaining parochial relief. The local newspaper noted that the severe weather had seriously hurt outdoor workers who lived a hand-to-mouth existence at the best of times. Coopers and artisans were without work: a man who visited the Fraserburgh poor during a midwinter blizzard found 'in forty houses there was not a spark of fire'.[55]

Accommodating the poor

The Parochial Board preferred to see the poor for whom it was responsible accommodated in their own homes or with relatives. If need be it helped with rent and repairs. In 1859, for example, 45 paupers were receiving help with their rent payments. The quite hopelessly ill or mentally handicapped were transferred to Aberdeen at first, though eventually the setting up of the Thomas Walker Hospital in Fraserburgh helped absorb some of the sick. But there remained a need to provide accommodation for those in temporary difficulty with no relatives who would take them in. By 1852 the Board was beginning to cast around for premises. Its first would-be site was a large curing premises in Back Street: it came to nothing on the grounds of cost.[56] Not for nine years was another serious effort made then, in 1861, the Board approached a Mrs Pirie to see if she would set aside part of her property for the accommodation of paupers.[57]

By 1865 somewhere had at last been found. In Barrack Lane Elizabeth Troup agreed to act as matron for a lodging house in return for five shillings a week and an agreement that she be allowed to go to work at the herring gutting, or suitably compensated if she could not be spared.[58] By October 1865 there were twenty-one inmates at Barrack Lane. Elizabeth Troup, helped by her mother, dealt with all the washing and cooking and looked after ten paupers who could not cope with everyday chores.[59] The Board seemed quite pleased with the arrangement, reckoning that at least five of the paupers would have cost eight to ten shillings a week more if placed elsewhere. The Matron found herself far too busy to be able to work at the herring fishing. One pauper in particular proved to be 'very excited . . . and required attention by night as well as by day'.[60] Her wages were raised by two shillings and extra compensation was promised for her inability to earn extra from the fishing season. Yet in October 1866 Elizabeth Troup was dismissed after there had been several complaints about her.[61] Her replacement, Mrs Burnett, had herself been on the roll of paupers: now she became Matron at eight shillings a week, her children's school fees were paid and she was allowed to take on extra work outside if she wished to do so.[62] The Barrack Lane lodgings were abandoned in the summer of 1872 for the Board now had places in a proper Poor House at its command.[63] Even so there were soon grumbles being voiced that Fraserburgh still needed lodgings for casual poor, and in 1876 the Board made a halfhearted and unsuccessful effort to take over the Links Hospital for the purpose.[64]

A serious resolve to provide a proper Poor House was first voiced by the Parochial Board in 1865.[65] A series of meetings were held at Maud between delegates from the various Buchan parishes out of which emerged a scheme to provide a joint Buchan Combination Poorhouse. Fraserburgh Parochial Board borrowed £900 from the North of Scotland Bank to help pay for its share, insisting in return on a right to at least twenty-two beds in a very substantial building capable of accommodating at least a hundred paupers.[66] On February 1st, 1869, the Poor House opened up. Fraserburgh had already worked through its roll picking out the mentally deficient as its first choice for places at Maud, and adding a list of at least nineteen others.[67] Five people were initially selected, all of them in poor physical shape such as the elderly lady who was 'bed-rid and would be much better attended to in the House'. The solitary male among the initial selection was to be shifted to Maud in the hope of improving his 'dirty and intemperate habits'. The Board considered he would benefit both physically and morally from being placed at Maud.[68]

But the paupers offered places at the Poor House frequently refused to go; others went and then left. After a year's opening the Poor House contained but nine Fraserburgh paupers. Fourteen of those who had been asked to go simply refused and five had gone, only to withdraw very quickly without permission.[69] A further difficulty was presented by the Board's determination, that, if possible, paupers placed at Maud should have relatives who could help meet expenses.[70] For the rest of the century Fraserburgh was never able to fill the quota in the Poor House upon which it had originally insisted.[71] At Maud Fraserburgh tried to place those mentally incapable of coping with life, mothers of illegitimate children, widows with families and wives of prisoners.[72]

Paupers whose behaviour needed strict control were, if possible, sent there too. Not all of these were adults, one was a boy completely beyond the control of Mrs King with whom he boarded.[73] Other children placed there were being rescued from a life with their parents of utter poverty. The four children of a tin-case maker, for example, aged 3, 6, 9 and 10, were put to Maud after being found to live in such neglect that 'they are reported as having been seen taking pickings from the pails in the street'.[74] But the distrust with which the Poor House was regarded was irritating to the Board. They had found a sizeable sum to help pay for a large and soundly built property and were pleased with the food, bedding and general care given the paupers.[75] Their ability to threaten paupers that if they did not accept a place at Maud they would be denied all help may well have contributed to the falling assessment for supporting the poor in the later part of the century. Those still determined not to go could be forced to look for support to relatives, not the Board.

Other forms of aid

Regular payments in money or kind, and the provision of lodging and Poor House accommodation were not the only forms of help that Fraserburgh provided for its poor. Very severe winter unemployment was sometimes met by the provision of temporary work. In December, 1859, the degree of unemployment led to the offer of labouring work to the poor. They were to build a road through the Links for twopence an hour.[76] This method of tackling poverty required the co-operation of the Police Commissioners. The 1859–1860 winter road-building cost them fifty pounds.[77] In 1879 the Commissioners again agreed to provide work breaking up road metal for new streets.[78] Four years later, after a delegation of labourers had complained that so scarce was employment that they and their families were near starvation,[79] work was found for them on the town's new drainage scheme. Yet more stone-breaking work was offered to up to twenty men in February 1888 at a wage according to the work they completed up to a twelve shilling maximum for a week's labour.

Prior to the creation of the Parochial Board, Fraserburgh poor had, upon occasion, been helped by their better-off neighbours to buy food during especially severe winters. The practice continued after 1845. In December 1846, a soup kitchen opened for six days a week, serving people unable to support themselves and their families because of the high price of food.[80] So severe were the consequences of this winter, and of the failure of the potato crop, that soup distribution continued until early July and weekly sales of meal were added in February, providing the poor with the opportunity to buy it at two shillings and threepence a stone.[81] In 1861 a Clothing Fund was established providing apparel for the destitute from a fund built up by voluntary subscriptions and a little levied from the poor themselves at the rate of a penny a week.[82] Clothing distribution petered out leaving Lord Saltoun in control of the funds. When the provision of free, or subsidised food reappeared in the late nineteenth century, help from this Clothing Fund was sought to finance the scheme.[83] The severe 1885–6 winter led the Board to set up a committee to supply the poor with soup and also with coal. Eighty six families (with an average of four in the family) were supplied, but others in need proved too proud to accept charity.[84] The committee therefore announced themselves willing to sell for a penny sufficient soup to feed a family of six.[85]

By 1898 a scheme to provide poor children with hot dinners was in operation. So keen were fishermen to see it work that they offered to pay a two-pence a week levy should the £25 fund be insufficient.[86] The fund did indeed prove too little. By April 15, 636 hot dinners had been served to children since mid December: the cost – £74 – was met by a new collection of subscriptions.[87] The Clothing Fund money was drawn upon to provide books for needy children, from time to time, though even here there could be a crisis and a special effort – such as a concert – was required to buy enough footwear.[88]

In 1894 the Parochial Board became the Parish Council.[89] The Board of Supervision in Edinburgh congratulated Fraserburgh on its management of the poverty problem for the assessment had long been down to a level it found acceptable and the system ran with adequate efficiency.[90] The Board provided just enough to keep utter destitution at bay, to ensure poor children received schooling and that there was medical treatment for paupers too. Crises caused by disease, crop failure or poor fishing required special extra voluntary efforts by local people. What had been done was not necessarily regarded with gratitude by the poor themselves. Refusals to go to the Poor House, reluctance to use the soup kitchen, even occasional unwillingness to apply for financial relief all indicate that to some Fraserburgh people dire poverty was preferable to the shame of becoming a recognised pauper.

Chapter Six

EDUCATION

During the nineteenth century Fraserburgh equipped itself with a range of cultural amenities. By late Victorian times the town possessed a public library, a reading room paid for by subscriptions, a library run by the Church of Scotland and a circulating library organized by a book-shop proprietor.[1] Entertainments of varying cultural merit paid visits ranging from strolling players who put on performances in a granary, at the beginning of the century,[2] to silent-cinema shows at the end of the century like the one in January 1898 when 'Messrs Walker and Company of Aberdeen gave "Snow-balling" and "Pantomime" to a large and appreciative audience. Mr James Dunn, tenor, sang splendidly and Mr Nicholson presided at the piano with his customary skill and ability'.[3] Fraserburgh acquired a cricket club, the Links were used, increasingly, for golf, and bathing from the town's bleak but splendid sweep of sand took place. In 1879 the Police Commissioners introduced by-laws sternly separating male and female bathers on the beach.[4] A forty-yard no-man's land was marked out to divide the sexes; boys who reached the age of ten were strictly prohibited from bathing with females. The bathing by-laws were concerned with morality, not safety, the commissioners insisting that 'no male person above fourteen years of age shall be permitted to bathe without wearing drawers or other bathing costume after ten o'clock in the morning, except north of the Ballasthill'.

Schooling before 1872

Fraserburgh's formal system of education left much to be desired in the early nineteenth century. Around forty or fifty children[5] went to a recently built school on the Links[6] where they learned not only reading, writing and arithmetic but Latin, book-keeping and navigation.[7] However, until he was persuaded to depart in 1811, the schoolteacher seemed to the Kirk session to be far from competent. The children went to school when they felt like it, and, when there, played for excessively long periods. Most of them made negligible progress, sitting staring at problems set them with no kind of help, or perhaps writing utterly absurd compositions. Their ill-mannered behaviour was rarely checked – yet when discipline was enforced it was done with a violence that left children badly bruised.[8]

Once the teacher of these early years had been persuaded to depart (helped on his way with a permanent pension of ten pounds a year) the parish school improved. Lord Saltoun must have been relieved for he believed that decent schooling was vital to Fraserburgh's expansion: 'nothing can be a greater encouragement to people of small fortune settling in a Town' he wrote.[9] The school on the Links closed in 1838 and the pupils transferred to a new building in Saltoun Place – marching there in style, on the first day, led by a child skilled at flute playing.[10] The school numbers had, by the forties, more than doubled to around a hundred, and French, Geography and Mathematics had been added to the considerable burden born by the solitary schoolmaster in return for his £130 a year.[11] Poverty prevented a number of children from going to school. Not only were the school fees a problem, some children did not even possess clothing of sufficient respectability to venture out in. A handful of poor children were taught free of fees, paid for by the Milne Bequest, yet this still left forty to fifty unable to pay for an education.[12] In 1863 the Parochial Board attempted to tackle the issue, agreeing to pay the fees of the destitute, and furnish books too if necessary. The Inspector was soon busy identifying and trying to help such children.[13]

The education of the period did not necessarily seem sufficiently important to some working class parents to be worth their children's involvement. They preferred to keep their family to help at farming or fishing or to watch over infants whilst parents worked.[14] The town – and surrounding parish – also contained a number of small private 'venture' schools run by female teachers.[15] In the early seventies there were three such schools in the town itself at which over a hundred children were to be found.[16] Many parents liked to send their children to these schools when they were very young to prepare them for their work at the parish school, and also so that they would not roam the streets whilst both parents were working.[17] The Disruption produced a Free Church School in the Town whilst the Episcopal Church established St Peters as its own educational centre.[18] In Broadsea the Established Church set up a school for the children of the fisher families. The pupils who attended it were expected to take a lump of coal or peat with them every day and were made to feel very guilty were they to fail in this task.[19] A school aimed especially at poorer families opened in 1863, named after a Miss Strachan who provided the bulk of the £730 needed to build it and a further £500, the interest from which kept down fees to a very low level. The intention was to aid girls in particular, teaching them sufficient skills and appropriate manners to fit them to become domestic servants.[20]

Private generosity also provided the town with an Academy. In 1870 it opened its doors to boys and girls wishing to study more than the basic subjects. The benefactor – John Park – provided a £5,000 investment to enable a qualified teacher to be hired.[21] The Academy offered Latin, Greek, Mathemtics, Higher English, French, German, Music, Drawing, Physics, Needlework, Geography and History.[22] This was a range of subjects beyond any of the other schools. Strachan's and St Peter's offered Higher English, Broadsea Geography and English, the Free Church School English, Maths and French. Only the parish school of 1870 could approach the range of subjects found in the Academy. In Saltoun Place pupils could study Latin, Greek, Geography, Maths, German, Sewing, Music and French. All were being very capably taught, though of the two hundred plus pupils, whilst two thirds studied Geography and English, only thirty-four studied Latin, twenty-five Algebra and but two struggled with Greek.[23]

The cost of education was, inevitably, a major factor in shaping pupils' opportunities. Twenty-five to thirty children were educated free at the parish school,[24] but far more were still, in 1870, not going to school at all. An attempt to measure the size of this problem in 1872 put the number permanently absent from school in the whole parish as high as two hundred and twenty.[25] Strachan's only charged around one and six per quarter and this, despite the school's limitations, was enough to attract well over 350 children in the early seventies. It thus contained far more children than the parish school where fees ranged from two and six in Standard I up to five shillings in Standard VI, with extra charges for higher level subjects up to two and six. Academy fees discriminated sharply between the seventy-four boys there in 1872, who were charged four and six a quarter, and the sixty-three girls for whom the fee was sixteen shillings. Broadsea kept the fees for its seventy odd pupils down to one and nine: the Episcopal and Free Church schools both charged three shillings.[26]

The School Board years

Before the 1872 Education Act Fraserburgh had already built up a considerable range of schools, some of which operated with vigour and efficiency. But a large number of children were not attending school and not all the schools worked as well as the parish school under its energetic head, John Sutor. The Fraserburgh School Board first met in April 1873, surveyed available accommodation in so far as it could (Mr Macgill, the Academy's head would not co-operate) and proceeded, in October, to announce it was going to insist upon the attendance at school of all children between five and thirteen years of age.[27] The school rate it levied – at first fourpence but soon sixpence – was gathered in by the Parochial Board along with other rates.[28]

In the following years the Board attempted to develop a more systematic education that all children would experience. One of the obstacles that had to be tackled was provided by the buildings themselves. The Free Church School was taken over and, at first, run as a second Board School.[29] But this proved both expensive and inefficient. The former Free Church School in School Street attracted criticisms from Inspectors who felt its head teacher was giving insufficient time to reading, writing and arithmetic, so eager was he to prove his competence at teaching the higher branches.[30] In November 1875 the Board decided to turn School Street into a department for Infants and the first standards, juggle with the teaching staff and thus save £70 a year.[31] This was but an interim measure. Whilst the Academy and St Peters had considerable areas of under-used space, the 'Fraserburgh Public School' (as the parish school was now known) was cramped and either new classrooms would have to be tacked on to an existing site, or a completely new building put up.[32]

The building of a new school was bound to be costly, estimates suggested it would be over £6,000, but the sale of existing sites could help keep the cost down.[33] The reports that flowed in from Inspectors encouraged the Board to feel a fresh start would be best for the School Street premises were criticised as unsuitable for teaching and unhealthy too.[34] Though Saltoun Place was slightly better, its playground was so tiny the children played in the road and were in frequent danger of injury from passing traffic.[35] Yet no sooner had the Board made up its mind than, in July 1878, one of its number rallied opposition to the project arguing a new school would be an unnecessary extravagance.[36] A two-year battle followed before, in 1880, plans for the new school finally went ahead.[37]

The estimates for the new school came to almost £6,000, the bulk of this was borrowed from the Public Works Commissioners at $3\frac{3}{4}\%$.[38] By now the need for new premises was urgent as numbers pressed in, partly from population increase and partly from the Board's drive to insist upon attendance.[39] The sole surviving small private school run by Miss Taylor in a highly informal fashion operated in a single room fourteen feet by thirteen but fell below the Board's requirements. Its pupils were, from 1879, to be added to the Public Schools and to be regarded as absentees if they still attended Miss Taylor's classes.[40] There was, then, a need for accommodation for around 550 children. The new school opened in September 1882.[41] Inspectors looked approvingly upon its size, its construction and the moderate size of its rooms, a great advance (they felt) upon 'unwieldy rooms where two or three teachers have to shout each other down'.[42] Yet it was soon under pressure as the school roll soared to a nominal figure of 890 in 1887 and over 1,000 in the early nineties.[43] By 1890 the Board was planning to spend a further £1,000 to extend its new school on top of the final bill of almost £8,000 the original structure had actually cost.[44]

The accommodation crisis was slightly eased in 1894 when the Academy finally allowed itself to be linked to the Board School structure and to be run by a governing body drawn from the School Board and the Town Council.[45] This move solved the problem that had been developing of where to focus a determined effort to develop a centre for higher education in the town.[46] The Board had in 1890 started to push the claims of its Public School. It stressed the presence of two capable graduate teachers already providing Latin, Maths, Greek and French to classes of sixty odd in the first two subjects, forty odd in French though a mere single-figure handful in Greek. The latter subject never proved popular with Fraserburgh parents. Boys in the Latin class generally refused to do Greek 'as their parents do not wish to send them to University'.[47] John Sutor, still serving as Head, instructed students preparing for advanced Science, Law Agents and Pharmaceutical examinations.[48]

One of the Academy's functions was to provide evening classes. Here, too, it built on foundations laid by John Sutor in the Public School in the 1870s.[49] Classes ran through the winter in science, sewing, cookery and laundry work enlivened by the occasional visit from a lecturer offering curious topics like 'The Relation of Christianity to Agriculture'.[50] In the 1890s short-hand classes, Maths classes, lectures in Hygiene, in English and, especially, a Navigation course were all on offer. Although the latter class was capably conducted by teachers who are very well qualified, one on the practical and the other on the theoretical side, it did not attract very many men.[51] It operated in the winter when seamen were least likely to be busy.

Despite its role as Fraserburgh's centre for teaching children wishing to go beyond Standard VI levels, the Academy did not really flourish. Perhaps in part this was due to a head who finally left in 1898: certainly the Inspectorate felt his successor had done much to raise the status of the school.[52] The behaviour of the older pupils was raised above its 1895 level when they had talked excessively instead of working, attempted to cheat during tests, were scarcely audible when answering questions and 'when a class was summoned to the floor it came creeping out in disorder, the boys usually with their hands in their pockets'.[53] Despite the new head's efforts the school of 1900 still had unsatisfactory furnishings (including seats without backs) poor equipment, and a playground that was too small.[54]

Poverty continued to interfere with the Board's efforts to persuade all pupils to attend school regularly. Winter after winter inadequately clad children stayed off school: repeatedly funds had to be raised to find enough to purchase boots for destitute scholars.[55] Yet the cost of schooling itself was cut. The Board inherited a system in which children were charged for the coal that kept their schoolrooms warm and the pens and ink they occasionally used for work for which slates were less appropriate: in 1876 these charges were abolished.[56] The fees were adjusted in 1882 so that they proved a smaller burden in so far as younger children were concerned. A penny a week was required from Infants and Standard I, the fees then rose to sixpence for Standard VI but this high figure covered Latin, Greek and Maths too, for which there had formerly been an extra levy.[57] Despite these charges, the attendance officer still found himself faced with families too poor to send children to school. One fisherman told the Board 'he had been unsuccessful in the fishing for some time past and therefore had been unable to provide the children with proper clothing to attend school, but that he had now obtained a berth in a sailing vessel and expected to be soon in a position to put the children to school'. Cases like this were by no means rare.[58]

Not only poverty kept pupils from school. The fishing season had its impact in other ways too, indeed the local newspaper grumbled that the School Board foolishly failed to face the inevitable absenteeism the season brought.[59] The 'Fraserburgh Herald' published the Board's warnings that skippers should not hire boys under fourteen who hadn't passed the fourth standard:[60] it also observed that waiting until July 8th to close for a vacation was to make absenteeism inevitable. Once the season was under way it dominated town life. The school playground at Strachan's was taken over by curers who piled up barrels there that excluded children even when the holidays were over.[61] John Sutor noted in his logbook on July 10th 1874 that his pupils would not concentrate. They thought only of the holidays and the fishing. 'The Compulsory Officer has visited their parents but I must add that he has done so in vain for they flatly refuse to send their children to school as they are now almost into the stir of the herring fishing'.[62] Pupils began to stay away to prepare for the fishing season about a month before the school closed officially. Not till well into October were they back again in large numbers.[63] Some served on boats, others were employed to run errands or keep an eye on infants whilst parents worked.[64]

Although the fishing season brought about the greatest absenteeism, farm work too pulled away pupils. In particular there were parents who took their children to help them in the potato fields[65] and other pupils who went to the country to herd cattle in spite of pressure put upon their parents to keep them at school till after the Inspection.[66]

In general the Inspectorate thought well of John Sutor's work. He coped with an expanding roll, with the distractions posed by the fishing season, but was not quite so afflicted by the constant to and fro of pupils that made teaching in country schools such a difficult task. At times he despaired of pupils like the boy questioned as to where a Scottish monarch had fallen from his horse when fleeing from a battle – 'Please Sir, he fell upon the "Grun" '.[67] He organized special events – like paper chases[68] and tried to bring in science in the early seventies to the extent of carrying a sheep's heart to school and dissecting it before attentive senior pupils.[69] One rather hostile colleague complained that Sutor's interest in areas other than the basic subjects could be excessive and that, in particular, he was quite likely to teach Hygiene for over an hour every day.[70] His staff at times gave him problems that ranged from an over-lax attitude that allowed children to wander from school, running errands[71] to a discipline so physically violent that considerable numbers of parents came to protest.[72]

Between the Head and the School Board an unfortunate tension built up. Board affairs were a real source of excitement; one child was even moved to another school because his father's side had lost at the School Board Election.[73] The clash of the late seventies over the issue of new buildings certainly excited both teachers and pupils.[74] But it was the Board's attempts in the eighties to interfere in detailed running of the school that led to the biggest difficulties. They believed their role allowed them to organize classes and teaching to such an extent that the Head felt highly resentful and wrote indignant letters to the local press. In return the Board complained that school discipline was too fierce, 'the lashing of lessons into a child being injurious to health and progress'[75] and that John Sutor was arrogant, 'an old parochial teacher, he felt the School Board only useful for raising money'.[76] Some of the Board's attempts to cut costs produced bizarre results such as crowding ninety children into one room where their teacher could not hear them all read,[77] and expecting the Head himself to teach over ninety older children.[78] For a time the Board tried to back a teacher with whom Sutor was on poor terms, creating a position of independence for him that the Head found intolerable. When he intervened to reclaim control the offending teacher refused to teach yet remained whilst his superior taught, reading books and newspapers.[79] After an unpleasant three months Sutor's authority was finally accepted.[80] The Board turned down his appeals for spending on a School Library and for a Music Teacher, and tried to insist that drawing be taught without facing the problem that the cost of material was beyond many children.[81]

After over a decade of tussling with one another, the Board and the Head settled down to a somewhat less abrasive relationship. John Sutor had been used to his own ways before 1872; each found the other was not to be easily bullied and it cannot be said that the transformation of parish school into Board School ever operated entirely smoothly during the nineteenth century. Nevertheless the growth of the town in the nineteenth century had been matched by a growth in educational provision and a far more professional attitude to teaching.

Appendix 1

Fraserburgh Toll Bar, amount raised from annual roup
(Source, Treasurer's Accounts, Ellon, Peterhead and Fraserburgh Road)

Year	Amount £	Year	Amount £	Year	Amount £
1812	40	1831	113	1850	136
1813	61	1832	112	1851	148
1814	61	1833	75	1852	152
1815	61	1834	80	1853	144
1816	61	1835	75	1854	148
1817	60	1836	75	1855	153
1818	60	1837	75	1856	168
1819	60	1838	75	1857	155
1820	60	1839	80	1858	148
1821	80	1840	75	1859	168
1822	91	1841	79	1860	170
1823	123	1842	99	1861	160
1824	90	1843	100	1862	151
1825	120	1844	92	1863	141
1826	No roup	1845	119	1864	132
1827	90	1846	112	1865	142
1828	80	1847	100	1866	60
1829	80	1848	121		
1830	80	1849	121		

Appendix 2

Occupations in 19th century Fraserburgh

(Sources, Pigot's Directory 1837, Slater's Directory 1867, Worrall's Directory 1877, Slater's Directory 1903)

Occupations	1837	1867	1877	1903
Professional				
Accountants	–	–	–	2
Notaries and Solicitors	3	4	5	10
Surgeons	3	2	4	3
Veterinary surgeons	1	–	–	1
Services				
Auctioneers	2	1	2	1
Banks	2	4	4	4
Bill posters	–	–	–	2
Building Societies	–	–	–	2
Coastguard	1	1	1	1
Fire and office agents*	4	20	19	14
Horse hirer	–	–	2	–
Midwife	–	–	–	3
Reporters	–	–	–	1
Shipbroker	–	2	8	2
Shipowners	–	2	8	2
Shopkeepers and dealers				
Bakers and confectioners	4	10	9	21
Booksellers and stationers	3	3	3	2
Chemists	–	2	2	4
Coal dealers	–	3	3	7
Cycle agent	–	–	–	2
Dairymen	–	–	–	8
Drapers	5	7	12	17
Eating house keepers	–	2	–	1
Fish salesmen	–	–	–	9
Flesher and butchers	3	5	5	14
Fried fish dealer	–	–	–	1
Fruiterer and greengrocers	–	3	4	5
Glass, china and earthenware dealers	4	4	3	5
Grocer and spirit dealers	19	17	21	31
Hairdresser	1	–	1	5
Innkeeper and hoteliers	1	1	2	11
Ironmongers	–	3	3	7
Manure merchants	–	–	5	1

Occupations	1837	1867	1877	1903
Shopkeepers and dealers cont'd				
Photographers	–	–	2	2
Salt merchants	–	–	2	1
Shopkeepers	–	7	11	19
Tobacconists	–	–	3	4
Toydealers	–	1	2	1
Crafts and trades				
Artificial teeth fitter	–	–	–	1
Basketmakers	–	–	–	1
Blacksmiths	5	3	6	3
Blockmakers	1	1	2	2
Boatbuilders	4	2	2	4
Boot and shoe makers and repairers	15	14	20	22
Brewers	–	2	1	2
Cabinet makers	–	3	3	6
Carpenters and cartwrights	12	5	7	8
Carters	–	–	3	17
Coachbuilders	–	–	–	1
Coopers	6	12	} 58 {	5
Fish curers	25	18		69
Distillers	1	–	–	–
Dyers	–	–	1	–
Engineers	–	–	–	2
Grain merchants	6	4	2	1
Granite workers	–	–	1	1
Masons and builders	1	3	8	4
Milliners and dressmakers	–	6	8	5
Painters	2	2	2	3
Plasterers	–	–	1	2
Plumbers	–	–	1	4
Printers	–	1	2	1
Rope and sailmakers	2	3	2	2
Saddlers	4	2	2	1
Saw millers	–	–	3	2
Slaters	1	–	1	3
Tailors	8	12	17	12
Timber merchants	4	3	7	2
Tinsmiths	1	2	3	1
Turners	1	–	–	–
Vintners	15	11	10	6
Watch and clockmakers	3	3	3	4

* Denotes number of companies. Some agents represented more than one company.

Appendix 3

Offences dealt with in 1882 in Fraserburgh Police Court

(Source, Fraserburgh Police Court Book 1881–96)

Distribution during the year:

Month:	Jan.	Feb.	March	April	May	June
No. of offences:	22	12	13	18	26	39
Month:	July	Aug.	Sept.	Oct.	Nov.	Dec.
No. of offences:	53	48	52	11	3	3

Occupations of offenders	*Number of offences*
Labourers	72
Fishermen	44
Pedlar or vagrant	24
Vagrants	18
Seamen	15
Carters	15
Coopers	10
Tailors	4
Sawyers	4
Housekeepers	3
Apprentice carpenters	2
Domestic servants	2
Watchmakers	2
Millworkers	2
Grocers	2
Innkeepers	2
Shoemakers	2
Plumbers	2

plus a number of other occupations providing one offence each.

Appendix 4

Rates raised by the Fraserburgh Police Commissioners
(Source, Minute books of the Police Commissioners, 6 Vols.)

Year	Total Rate	Police	Drainage and sewage	Water	Health*
1840–46	1/–	1/– (for lighting)			
1846–49	1/–½	1/– (for lighting and ½ watching)			
1850–52	1/6	1/–¼	2¼	3½	
1853–61	1/6	9d	2½	4d	≠
1862–70	1/–	*			
1871	2/–	1/–		1/–	
1872	2/2	1/2		1/–	
1873	2/3	1/6		9d	
1874	2/–	1/2		10d	
1875	2/–	1/2		10d	
1876	1/7	9d	4d	6d	
1877	1/7	7d	4d	8d	
1878	1/11	10d	4d	8d	1d
1879–80	2/–	10d	4d	9d	1d
1881–83	2/5	10d	4d	1/2	1d
1884	2/4	10d	4d	1/2	–
1885	2/4	1/–	4d	1/–	
1886	2/3	11d	4d	11d	1d
1887–89	2/5	11d	4d	1/–	2d
1890	2/2	9d	4d	11d	2d
1891–97	2/–	9d	4d	10d	1d

* The break-down of the total rate is not always indicated in earlier volumes of Minutes.
≠ Where the total rate is more than its elements, the additional amount was devoted to debt reduction and interest payments.

Appendix 5

Poverty in the 1850s
(Source, Register of Poor Persons on the Roll of the Parish of Fraserburgh 1846–59)

	1854	*1855*	*1859*
(i)			
Total	90	83	97
Number of males	19	15	18
(Trades) Servant	11	5	5
Herds cattle	1	–	–
Dress maker and seamstress	1	1	2
Sailor	1	–	–
Labourer	2	2	5
Outdoor work	–	–	3
Mason	1	–	1
Wright	1	1	1
Domestic servant	2	–	1
Shoemaker	1	1	3
Cooper	1	–	–
Lodging house keeper	1	–	–
Blacksmith	1	–	–
Fisherman	1	2	2
Weaver	–	1	–
'Able bodied'	10	9	14
Hawker	–	1	1
Sells fish	–	–	1
Bookbinder	–	–	1
Knitting	–	–	1
(ii) *Cause of Poverty*			
Blind	4	1	1
Lame	3	3	–
Weakness	2	2	2
Asthma	2	1	2
Liver complaint	1	–	–
Cripple and old age	4	2	–
Old age	26	25	39
Deafness	2	1	1
Weakness	4	2	2
Rheumatism	4	6	5
Cripple	2	2	2
Weak intellect and silly	4	3	3
Bedrid and debility	5	6	6

	1854	1855	1859
(iii) cont'd			
Gravel	1	1	1
Imbecile	–	1	2
Rupture	–	1	–
To support children	6	–	8
Bronchitis	–	–	1
(iii)			
Number of males who also had wives	7	8	3
Number of children dependent on an adult	66	58	57
Number getting some family support	1	3	–
Number getting help with rent	17	29	45
Number getting help with meal	15	17	15
Number getting help with shoes and clothes			10
(iv) *Part time occupations of the poor*			
Herring gutting	1	–	–
Spins hemp	2	2	1
Selling bread	1	2	1
Out work	4	2	4
Knits stockings	6	12	13
Washing	2	1	–
Fishing in summer	1	2	2
Collecting eggs	1	1	–
Shoe making	1	1	2
Street scavenger	1	–	–
Sells peats	1	–	–
White fishing	1	–	–
Hawking	–	1	–
Dressmaking	–	1	2
Helps innkeeping	–	1	–
Going to the country with fish	–	1	2
Knits and sews	–	1	1
Weaving	–	2	–
Sells eggs	–	1	1
Farm work	–	1	1
Labourer	–	–	1
Mends and weaves herring nets	–	–	3
Mason	–	–	1
Selling small toys	–	–	1

(The registers for these years were kept in a rather haphazard fashion and these figures can give no more than impressionistic view.)

Appendix 6

Occupation of applicants for poor relief, 1894–1902

(Source, Record of Applications for Parochial Relief Fraserburgh 1894–1902)

Occupation	No.	Occupation	No.
General labourer	83	Ship-master	2
Fishworker	27	Hairdresser	1
Child	21	Soldier	1
Widow (no occupation)	19	Fancy-wool shopkeeper	1
Hawker	15	Plumber	1
Fisherman	13	Garener	1
Woman caring for children	13	Butcher	1
Cooper	10	Groom	1
Fishmonger	10	Doctor	1
Housewife	10	Chimney sweep's wife	1
Pedlar	7	Carter's wife	1
Labourer's wife	7	Engine fitter	1
Fisherwoman	7	Railway labourer	1
Shoemaker's wife	6	Travelling musician	1
Tailor	5	Ship's carpenter	1
Seaman	5	Stoker	1
Insane or incapable	5	Confectioner	1
Outdoor worker	4	Tailoress	1
Sells fish	4	Housekeeper	1
Tramp	4	Aerated water 'manie'	1
Knitting	3	Scavenger	1
Labourer's wife	3	Printer	1
Shoemaker	3	Besom maker	1
Domestic servant	3	Watchmaker	1
Tinsmith	3	Factory worker	1
Blacksmith	3	Cutler	1
Sewing	2	Cook	1
Mason	2	Umbrella maker	1
Farmworker	2	Vagrant	1
Former crofter	2	Shepherd	1
Baker	2	Gas worker	1
Keeps lodgers	2	Joiner	1
Hawker's wife	2	Sawmiller	1
Millworker	2	Post boy	1
Sells coal	2	Sailmaker	1
Fisherman's wife	2		
Washerwoman	2		

Steam threshing, Tarland, 1900

CONCLUSION

Conclusion

The development of a number of small towns and large villages was a marked feature of nineteenth century Scottish history. Modern Aberdeenshire provides many examples of this process which was, in its way, as significant a feature for the North East as was the growth of industrial communities for the central belt. The solid granite housing, the schools, civic and ecclesiastical buildings of these places today are visible signs of processes in the past which brought increased affluence and greater leisure to the area's population. The character of these communities varies according to their location and purpose. Several of the fishing places which prospered in the nineteenth century still consist of tightly packed huddles of houses built with their gables towards the sea. South of Fraserburgh the villages of Inverallochy and St Combs are particularly impressive examples of a type of settlement whose appearance suggests the battle with the sea which created them. Inland villages felt freer to sprawl out; whether their shape then follows rigid geometrical lines or a meandering form is likely to show the degree of interest and determination of local lairds bent on bringing in improvement regardless of tenants' wishes. A long and wearisome battle to win wealth from land and sea generated the work and income that created the smaller communities. The massive properties of the great landowners of the nineteenth century which still dot the Aberdeenshire landscape are reminders of one of the powerful forces that contributed to change.

The nineteenth century functions of communities can still be detected. Market squares for ordinary trading are found in many – including Inverurie and Fraserburgh. Some, such as the village of Tarland, still contain much larger open spaces where once great gatherings of animals were assembled by traders. Blacksmiths' workshops, water-powered meal mills, warehouses, fish-smoking sheds, distilleries and massive Victorian hotels are all examples of survival from a once busy past. The crucial transport developments that shaped community fortunes can be seen in the shape of turnpike toll houses, bridges (sometimes – as at Ellon – now bypassed) railway track and the many miles of former railway now empty of metal. Communities still serve their localities. Many of the shops being visited today were first built in Victorian times. In 1842

Insch shopkeepers dealt in 'groceries, cloth, hard and software, drugs etc. There are also two watchmakers, a baker, a saddler and other trades-men. Most of the shops and dwelling houses have been for some years lighted with gas'.[1] The watchmakers have long gone, gas lighting has been replaced with electricity, yet otherwise Insch still serves its local people today in much the same fashion.

The success of Aberdeenshire communities in coping with the prob-lems posed by growth is also still detectable. School and hospital building, small rows of poorhouses, the Buchan Poorhouse and council offices can all be observed. Less obvious is the network of piping and the associated works which brought in safe water supplies and cleared away sewage from these concentrations of population.

As to what it was like to live in an Aberdeenshire village in Victorian times, James Milne's memories of New Pitsligo in the 1880s exemplify existence in many country communities.[2] Most of the little but-and-ben cottages were still thatched; re-building and slating were usually the sign of a more successful mason or tradesman whilst the few grander pro-perties were inhabited by the doctor, the church ministers, the banker and the schoolmaster. Simple locally-made furniture filled the rooms. The walls were whitewashed and, at night, the dwellings illuminated by the flickering light of paraffin lamps. The inhabitants fetched their water from pumps in the street. No home possessed a bathroom and houses therefore adjoined patches of ground at the rear where dry closets were located. The village was well supplied with shops and services. There were six general merchants selling groceries, sweets, and serving as drapers too. A druggist served also as a newsagent and there was an ironmonger, a dealer in crockery, two butchers and two bakers. People bought their clothes from one of the four tailors' shops where they were made and their boots from one of the four shoemakers – though here the factory-made product was beginning to challenge the village craftsmen's efforts. In addition there were wandering salesmen and visiting fishwives with creels on their backs. Village craftsmen also included two joiners, two blacksmiths, two thatchers and a slater. The villagers worked not only in these shops and crafts but in the fields and in the nearby quarries. Women worked at making-up clothes and on New Pitsligo's speciality of bobbin lace. People lived on a limited and repetitive diet centred round porridge, brose, potatoes, sowens, soups and, occasionally, fish or boiled beef. If they wanted milk they bought it from feuars who kept cows and if they decided to lavish money upon tinned food, only salmon and corned beef were available. The quiet of the village was disturbed by children playing safely in the streets, by horse-drawn vehicles and, very occasion-ally, by travelling fairs and menageries that set up business in the square.

But by nine at night the village in winter was generally in darkness and silence. Glimpses of a changing world came to the village in the shape of cyclists from Fraserburgh, steam traction engines, and even a reaping machine. But in general the villagers' lives were filled with long hours of work for pay too low to permit travel or lavish treats.

The burghs of Inverurie and Fraserburgh were two of the most successful of nineteenth century Aberdeenshire communities. They enjoyed advantages which enabled them to outgrow most other burghs and villages. Inverurie rapidly outpaced its once grander neighbour, Old Meldrum, whilst Fraserburgh narrowed the gap in size with its closest competitor, Peterhead. For both places geographical location played a part in bringing expansion. Inverurie's site on a main route, by a river crossing amid potentially fertile fields was matched by Fraserburgh's location on a sea route used by coasting traffic and close to the herring shoals which swarm by in the summer. A promising site was not, however, enough. Kincardine O'Neil was well placed at a crossroads – river crossing point, Ellon's site bore similarities to Inverurie's, yet neither place grew as rapidly. Growth depended upon local readiness to exploit a favourable situation.

Getting growth to accelerate, especially in the early nineteenth century, depended a great deal upon the attitude of the major local landowners. The Earl of Kintore played a leading part in inspiring the bridging of the Don at Inverurie and contributed substantially to the creation of the Inverurie turnpike. He owned almost half the burgh lands,[3] attended important events and encouraged education. His near neighbours the Elphinstones, were also active. When the Aberdeenshire Canal Company was created the Earl of Kintore took up 22 shares, Robert Elphinstone took up 28. No other founder-member put in as much. James Elphinstone played an important part in the creation of the Aberdeen-Huntly line for the Great North of Scotland Railway. Fraserburgh owes its early emergence and original harbour to the Frasers of Philorth. In the early nineteenth century Lord Saltoun encouraged harbour and town improvement and led the way in subscribing to funds for these purposes. In 1805, for example, he provided £800 of the £2,000 raised for harbour works. In the later nineteenth century, with increased government activity, access to favourable loans and the emergence of a number of well-to-do men of affairs the lairds' attitudes were less crucial though their example and influence remained important.

It was evident to such landowners that the encouragement of better travel was vital to the communities whose expansion they wished to see. The turnpike road and bridge building activities of the late 1790s and early 1800s swept through the County with impressive force. Fraserburgh was one of the later places to benefit; Inverurie was but one of many communities connected into the system. The improved roads brought regular coach and carrier services and a great growth in private traffic but they did not, on their own, contribute to the particular success of Inverurie and Fraserburgh. It was the growth of water-born traffic that brought these two places advantages. A writer of 1837, trying to account for Inverurie's expansion, believed it was due to bridges and the canal which 'have imparted a new stimulus to industry and Inverurie is now becoming a thriving town'.[4] The burgh was the most distant inland place in Aberdeenshire reached by barge loads of fuel, building materials and fertilizers. People from more distant parts were drawn to its basin to do business, warehouses sprang up and milling businesses thrived. By comparison Kintore, though on the canal, did less well. It did not grow dramatically in the canal age, suffering from being a wayside halt, not the terminus. Moreover the lime, bone dust and other fertilizers so aided farming improvement in the Garioch, (and especially that development so crucial to cattle-rearing – turnip growing) that Inverurie was set well on its path as a centre for the cattle trade. Inverurie outgrew other inland places that lacked its canal-traffic advantage. It began to overhaul Huntly which, in the 1790s had been well over five times as heavily populated as Inverurie. Whereas contemporaries were struck by the way traffic was drawn into Inverurie from many miles around, Huntly in 1837 'is now a place of no particular manufacturers and the trade is merely local and confined to the immediate neighbourhood. The town appears to be rapidly declining but derives some assistance from its being situated on the road betwixt Aberdeen and Inverness'.[5] When the canal went out of business Inverurie continued to enjoy transport advantages. It was one of the first places north of Aberdeen to be linked to that city by rail. The G.N.S.R. network spread, with Inverurie enjoying a focal position on it. By comparison Old Meldrum merely lay at the end of a short spur of branch line. Businessmen who had congregated around the canal basin easily made the short move to the railway station. The G.N.S.R. confirmed the importance to it of Inverurie at the end of the century by building a large new station and locating nearby the locomotive works that had once been in Aberdeen.

Fraserburgh lay on the outer fringe of the transport network, never contemplated canal-building and was linked in late to the railway system. Nevertheless here too transport improvements were crucial to success. Fraserburgh's efforts were concentrated upon the costly and seemingly endless process of improving the harbour to make it appropriate to the shipping of the period. In this way it kept itself open to the schooner and steamer traffic that brought in items for building, fuel, farm improvement etc. and exported not only barrels of fish but the produce of the north Buchan countryside. Peterhead made similar efforts to increase and deepen its harbour. No other Aberdeenshire ports, other than the City's, spent so heavily on harbours. The result was that Fraserburgh and Peterhead steadily squeezed out fishing and trading business from smaller ports and absorbed it themselves. John Cranna, a harbour official himself, reckoned that total expenditure on Fraserburgh harbour by 1900 amounted to £308,000: an estimate of 1885 put Peterhead's total harbour bill by that date at nearly £300,000.[6] The huge Balaclava project that gave Fraserburgh such a vast fourteen acre increase in harbour space and much improved shelter for boats may well have given the town the edge over Peterhead for some years. The increase in population for the last forty years of the century, 6,000 in all, far exceeded Peterhead's increase for the same period of a little over 2,000. Fraserburgh's efforts meant that the harbour could accommodate a thousand boats, double the number able to squeeze into Peterhead's two canal-linked areas. It is not surprising that by 1900 Peterhead was about to go ahead with a huge new project to be executed by convict labour. Estimates of 1902, showed that Fraserburgh's revenue from harbour dues slightly exceeded Peterhead's (around £18,000 as opposed to £13,000).[7]

Both Inverurie and Fraserburgh benefited from and contributed to the economic growth of the area around them. Both housed specialist services to aid local farmers and shops and markets to serve local people. The increased concentration on farming and fishing and the increased profits yielded by these activities brought in wealth to be spent in the local communities on various goods and services. Each place had a particular speciality to serve – Inverurie provided for the cattle trade and Fraserburgh for the herring boom.

No other small Aberdeenshire town served the cattle trade as effect- ively as Inverurie. In 1877 the burgh contained ten butchers, Old Meldrum and Turriff a mere four and Huntly five (at the same date the Aberdeen district contained 118 butchers). Inverurie's cattle markets were 'largely attended by both buyers and sellers of stock, large quant- ities of meat in carcase is forwarded to the London market weekly, the tanning of leather is extensively carried on'.[8] The compilers of nineteenth century directories, guides and gazeteers repeatedly stressed Inverurie's importance as a cattle-dealing centre; no other small com- munity in the County attracted such comment. Inverurie's advantage sprang from its convenient position on transport systems, from its early importance as a centre of a cattle rearing area, and from the growth of expertise there inspired by the impact of the canal. One of the most important of late nineteenth century cattle dealers, Alsops, had their headquarters in Inverurie. The railway enabled it to share in the booming dead-meat trade of the later nineteenth century. In December 1901 Inverurie sent 500 carcases to the Christmas markets. Until the seventies the farming boom brought benefits to Inverurie; even the agricultural uncertainties of the later nineteenth century were not most severely felt in the meat trade. In any case, by 1900, Inverurie had managed to attract a new source of employment in the railway works, and possessed a large paper mill and Hays lemonade factory. Inverurie never quite overhauled Huntly, despite the latter's lack of a role of similar importance in the cattle trade. In the later nineteenth century Huntly recovered from its early textile industry setbacks. By 1900 it had four woollen mills, a hosiery factory and a large agricultural implements manufacturer. It served a wide area as a market and shopping centre, attracted many holiday visitors, and enjoyed the patronage of the Dukes of Richmond and Gordon. But Old Meldrum, Turriff and Ellon lagged well behind Inverurie.

The decline of Old Meldrum compared to its near neighbour is particularly striking. In the 1790s it was three times Inverurie's size, a centre for the stocking trade and a focus for a very fertile farming area. Its weekly markets were far more important than anything offered by Inverurie, easily-worked quarries lay nearby and the inhabitants in-cluded many tradesmen and craftsmen. The town developed further in the early nineteenth century helped by the completion in 1804 of the Aberdeen-Banff turnpike and the building of a good road to the port to Newburgh. Yet by 1841 Inverurie had outgrown Old Meldrum, the days 'when the town near the mouth of the Ury used to depend almost entirely on Old Meldrum for its grocery and other provisions'[9] were soon forgotten. Old Meldrum lacked the impetus provided by the Canal, its hosiery trade collapsed and its 1856 railway connection put it at the end of a short branch line running off the main route north. Though its distilleries continued to prosper Old Meldrum failed to find a fresh impetus to growth, reached its highest population in 1851 and thereafter declined slowly back to a size in 1901 little bigger than that of 1821. Its inhabitants in 1900 provided the kind of services commonly found in bigger villages like Strichen and New Pitsligo. Given the success of Inverurie as a centre for services to farmers it would have been surprising if the Garioch could have supported a second sizeable place as close by as Old Meldrum.

Turriff sustained growth for somewhat longer, declining only in the last decade of the nineteenth century. By 1841 Inverurie had outgrown Turriff, the latter's expansion being at a far more sluggish rate. The

Old Meldrum Occupations, 1900 (Source, Slater's Directory)	
2 banks	1 saddler
2 coal dealers	2 watchmakers
3 hotels	3 tailors
1 auctioneer	3 bakers
1 hairdresser	2 blacksmiths
1 engine driver	1 photographer
7 grocers	1 distiller and brewer
1 grocer and draper	1 joiner
1 draper	1 painter
1 ironmonger	2 boot and shoemakers
4 accountants and insurance agents	1 surgeon
2 chemists and booksellers	2 traction engine drivers
1 fishmonger	3 slaters
1 butcher	

community grew to serve the surrounding improving farmland, linked first by turnpike and then by rail to other parts of the North East. Turriff was slow in developing weekly markets, lagging behind Old Meldrum, Inverurie and Huntly in this respect and it too suffered from the decline of textiles; hosiery work, flax dressing, spinning and bleaching were all in a sad state by 1842. By the 1880s textile work had almost vanished 'and the pickled pork trade is now the staple industry'.[10] Turriff lay in an area of Aberdeenshire served by several modest communities, none of which really developed to dominate the rest. The failure to find an effective replacement for textiles left them as shopping, service and craft centres where farming and a few professional folk lived. By the time of the textile collapse the better roads and (before long) the railways meant the pull of Aberdeen probably prevented such places from developing into much more than very local service centres.

Fraserburgh, even more than Inverurie, leaned upon the business of a particular group. Herring fishing proved a more volatile activity than the cattle trade and the curers and coopers who depended upon it probably experienced more severe swings in fortune than Inverurie's cattle-trade specialists. But the Balaclava project enabled Fraserburgh to out-strip Peterhead in the herring business. Before it was built, in the early 1850s, the value of boats, nets and lines at Peterhead was more than double Fraserburgh's.[11] By 1902 Fraserburgh possessed 551 boats with a total tonnage of 10,306: Peterhead's 375 vessels came to 6,772 tons. Around a thousand more local men and boys gained employment from fishing in Fraserburgh than in Peterhead.[12] In that year Fraserburgh's herring exports were valued at £291,659; Peterhead's came to £147,716. Both places had, by now, created fish markets and had built similar lengths of docking areas (around 10,000 feet) where boats could tie up and discharge. Peterhead's ability to remain larger than Fraserburgh stemmed from its greater diversity of activities. It was never quite so wholly dependent upon the herring fisheries. Though its days as a holiday resort did not last long, it did enjoy a period of importance in whaling and sealing. Its 3 quarries were of greater significance than Fraserburgh's quarry and led to granite exports and the creation of stone-polishing works in the town. A comparison between the two towns using Worrall's Directory of 1877 shows Peterhead's greater volume of general business. It possessed 34 shipowners to Fraserburgh's 8, 9 coal dealers to Fraserburgh's 3, 21 drapers to 12 in Fraserburgh, 12 bakers to 9 in Fraserburgh, 45 grocers to 21 in Fraserburgh. In category after category Peterhead figures show more numerous groups of businessmen, craftsmen and shopkeepers.

The rapid expansion of Inverurie and Fraserburgh produced two communities that differed greatly in appearance. Inverurie sprawled along the major roads and round the canal basin, Fraserburgh's more compact shape remained; even though it grew it stayed hunched around its vital harbour. There were obvious differences in the occupations of the inhabitants stemming from the importance to them of different activities. Yet the two towns contain strong similarities. Both were re-built in stone with a market place at the centre and with re-built churches, civic buildings, schools and shops. Both came to contain the banking, tailoring, shoemaking, baking and legal skills that served their localities. Each built up its range of grocers, drapers, druggists and other shops as Aberdeenshire people came increasingly to look for expertly-made goods for use, wear and consumption rather than the simpler products of the part-time specialists of the old townships. Inhabitants of 1800 would have found it hard to recognise the streets of these towns, and the people who walked them, by the end of the period. Children went regularly to school throughout the year, shops had specially built windows and well-furnished interiors, gas lighting illuminated the streets and many of the properties. Goods on sale came not only from other parts of Britain but from many distant regions of the world.

But growth brought its problems too. The more comfortable life of 1900 had been made possible, in part, by a number of costly improvements. Matters of health, safety and organization had once been coped with rather casually in an overwhelmingly rural environment; the concentration of people even in places as small as the towns of Aberdeenshire posed problems that required more systematic solutions. Both communities experienced the pressure for change brought by new national legislation, by new bodies of officials and by the growth of more representative government. These problems and pressures proved too

much for the old unrepresentative burgh councils. Inverurie was a royal
burgh. Its self perpetuating council was ended by municipal reform in
1833 and turned into a body chosen by £10 householders. Its meagre
income from customs, rents and feus was wholly inadequate for the tasks
that faced it. Fraserburgh was a burgh of barony and regality and reform
in 1833 did not alter its character. Lord Saltoun remained as perpetual
provost with the right to fill council places as he thought best. It was the
adoption of Police Acts that drastically altered government in both
places. In Inverurie this did not take place until 1867 but the elective
character of the council meant that the same group of men could carry
out both functions. The merging of the two bodies at the end of the
century was little more than a formality. But in Fraserburgh the adoption of the Police Acts in 1840 led to the setting up of a body quite distinct
from the Town Council. Until the later nineteenth century three of the
Police Commissioners were nominated by the Town Council, but the
majority – twelve – were elected by £10 householders. In the mid
nineteenth century Lord Saltoun abandoned his title of hereditory
provost, but his council lived on till 1892. When it was finally extinguished it left behind a group elected by feuars to continue to manage the
'common good'.

The Police Commissioners' powers were increased by the various
Police Acts of Victorian times. Using money raised from the rates and
loans borrowed on the strength of this income, the Commissioners of
Inverurie and Fraserburgh set about tackling the problems of water
supply, drainage and sewage, street cleaning and lighting, and law and
order. They were not always eager to act. The prospect of rate increases
did not fill them with enthusiasm and both had to be nagged by officials
from Edinburgh. The picture is clearer in Inverurie's case since the clerks
keeping the Police Commissioners' Minutes often copied in not only the
Commissioners' decisions but the complaints to which they were reacting. Fraserburgh commissioners employed more circumspect minute-
keepers who rarely did more than note decisions. Gas lighting in the
streets spread speedily, probably because private companies produced
the supply and rates could be easily adjusted to meet the bills. But the
provision of an adequate supply of clean water was a different matter for
it involved quite heavy outlays of capital. Peterhead and Huntly installed satisfactory water supplies in the sixties, Fraserburgh and
Inverurie waited till the seventies. Fraserburgh acted more readily than
Inverurie, no doubt because of the need for water in the herring industry;
the inland burgh only moved after a long period of argument with
Edinburgh officialdom. Both fishing and cattle trade activities produced
filth in parts of the burghs that added to the routine street cleaning and

cesspool and privy emptying. Even the installation of sewers did not remove the problems, for these ran down main streets leaving many residents with no connection to the system. The slaughterhouses of Inverurie, being located amid housing, were an even bigger menace to health than the curing areas of Fraserburgh which were increasingly concentrated in the north east of the town. But whereas the building of the public slaughterhouse transformed the situation in Inverurie, the peculiar problems for health brought about by the seasonal influx of several thousand folk for the herring season were still plaguing Fraserburgh with accommodation and sewage-disposal difficulties in 1900. At least both places had, by then, adopted regular year-round scavenging systems instead of the inadequate and occasional clearing work of earlier years.

Concern over health problems helped bring about all these improvements. Both places were troubled by cholera scares and by outbreaks of typhoid and other illnesses. Fraserburgh was the more sensitive to cholera panics since, being a port, it feared importing illnesses from elsewhere. It is not surprising that Fraserburgh obtained a hospital twenty years before Inverurie. Till a charitable gift in Fraserburgh and joint action with other places in Inverurie provided the money for proper hospitals, both places managed with short-term arrangements, reacting to crises then permitting their hospital accommodation to fade into disuse.

Law and order posed greater problems for Fraserburgh too. Again it was the seasonal factor of herring fishing that brought the difficulties, but both places persistently grumbled about the costs of regular policing and about the inadequacies of the service they received. The police were essential to control the vagrants attracted into communities, especially in winter. The regulation of lodging houses where many vagrants gathered troubled both places. It added an extra dimension to dealing with poverty which, though supposedly tackled by the Parochial Boards of each parish from 1845, still left serious deficiencies in winter that local charity had to attempt to solve. Fraserburgh joined the move to create a Buchan Poorhouse; Inverurie was smaller and near enough to Aberdeen to manage with a few cottages for housing some of the poor.

The effort at improvement inevitably pushed up the rates. The biggest jump was caused by the addition of water and sewage works to the earlier ones of lighting and 'watching'. Fraserburgh rates were slightly higher than Inverurie's running at over two shillings in the eighties and at two shillings in the nineties, whereas Inverurie held down rates to just under the two shilling mark. But Fraserburgh had to cope with the very costly herring season and with a need for water greater than

Inverurie. Both places found numerous local residents appealing against their assessments but at least Inverurie was free of Fraserburgh's extra difficulty – that of a strong preference for trying not to pay rates until the herring season.

The experiences of these two towns shows a struggle to create a decent community life that was just as serious to the inhabitants as the similar struggles in industrial areas. It did not require large-scale factory building for there to be health hazards and water shortages in Scotland's towns and villages. Towns like Inverurie and Fraserburgh were a vital part of Scottish nineteenth century development. Whether they can enjoy a similar role in the later twentieth century is far less certain. Inverurie is sufficiently close to Aberdeen to attract commuters and to acquire businesses, but the slump in fishing has hurt Fraserburgh badly. Once more its rival, Peterhead, has proved better at diversifying and has attracted oil-industry business. Fraserburgh's dependence on fishing which brought such a surge of expansion in the nineteenth century now seems to be far less of an asset.

Today, more than ever before, other communities in Aberdeenshire feel the dominance of the City. The City's influence in 1800 was limited by the transport system of the time. The turnpikes were expensive to use and ill-suited to cheap bulk transport, nevertheless the way they focussed around Aberdeen was an ominous sign for other communities hoping to sustain a diversity of occupations. The railway system too centred on the City enabling its products and its services to be used by far more people in the County. Moreover, through the excellent harbour in Aberdeen, as well as along the rail network, the products of other parts of Britain and of the wider world came increasingly to challenge locally-made goods. By 1840 the textile industry of Aberdeenshire was in decline as a result of outside competition; by 1900 even tailors, shoemakers and wrights were feeling the impact of factory-made goods and were having to look to repair work as a way of off-setting the declining demand for their products. The nineteenth century saw Aberdeenshire being firmly tied into a much wider economy; the effects of this continue to exercise a vital influence today.

Station Road, Ellon

The circus comes to town in late victorian Huntly

REFERENCES

Part 1. The shaping of Aberdeenshire communities
1. The growth of smaller communities
1. The communities of the late eighteenth century

1. J. B. Caird, *Patterns of Rural Settlement* in C. M. Clapperton (ed) *Scotland, A New Study* Newton Abbot 1983 pp. 129
2. J. Milne, *New Pitsligo 70 Years Ago* in *Transactions of the Buchan Field Club* Vol 17 1955 pp. 53
3. K. Walton, *Population Changes in North East Scotland 1696–1951. Scottish Studies* Vol 5 1961
4. R. Paddison, *The Evolution and Present Structure of Central Places in North East Scotland* Aberdeen PhD 1969 pp. 87–8
5. J. Sinclair, *Analysis of the Statistical Account of Scotland* Edinburgh 1831 pp. 74
6. O.S.A. XI pp. 126
7. O.S.A. XV pp. 451
8. O.S.A. V pp. 102
9. I. Carter, *Farm Life in North East Scotland 1840–1914* Edinburgh 1979 pp. 53
10. See A. R. B. Haldane, *The Drove Roads of Scotland* Edinburgh 1952
11. J. Anderson, *A General View of the Agriculture and Rural Economy of the County of Aberdeen* Edinburgh pp. 70
12. O.S.A. XVI pp. 606–7
13. J. B. Caird, op. cit. pp. 130
14. J. Anderson, op. cit. pp. 35
15. J. R. Coull, *Fisheries in the North East of Scotland before 1800* in *Scottish Studies*, Vol. 13 1969
16. J. Taylor, *Rosehearty, its History as a Fishing Town* Rosehearty 1982
17. O.S.A. V pp. 98–9
18. O.S.A. V pp. 99
19. See A. R. Buchan, *The Port of Peterhead*, Peterhead 1980, pp. 17–37
20. O.S.A. XVI pp. 606–7
21. W. Laing, *An Account of Peterhead, its mineral well, air and neighbourhood* London 1793 pp. 23–6
22. W. Murray, *Peterhead a Century Ago* Peterhead 1810 pp. 29
23. W. Laing, op. cit. pp. 56
24. O.S.A. XXI pp. 97
25. J. Anderson, op. cit. pp. 22
26. *Report by the Committee on the Turnpike & Commutation Roads* in *Aberdeen* Aberdeen 1857, pp. 4–5
27. *James Beattie's Day Book*, 1773–1798, Aberdeen 1948 pp. 172
28. O.S.A. XIX pp. 389
29. O.S.A. VI pp. 474
30. W. Alexander, *Notes & Sketches Illustrative of Northern Rural Life in the 18th century* Aberdeen 1980 re-print pp. 42–4

31. J. Anderson, op. cit. pp. 20–21
32. Aberdeen University Department of Geography, *Royal Grampian Country* Aberdeen 1969 pp. 48–52
33. J. Minty, *Reminiscences of a 40 years residence in Turriff*, Banff 1865 pp. 4
34. Burnett of Kemnay MSS. Bundle 267
35. W. Diack, *The Rise and Progress of the Granite Industry in Aberdeen* Aberdeen 1949 pp. 77
36. Ibid. pp. 35
37. R. Michie, *Trade & Transport in the Economic Development of North East Scotland in the 19th Century, Scottish Economic and Historical Review* Vol 3 1983 pp. 68
38. J. P. Shaw, *The New Rural Industries, Water Power and Textiles* in M. L. Parry and J. R. Slater, *The Making of the Scottish Countryside* London 1980 pp. 293–4
39. J. B. Caird, op. cit. pp. 144
40. J. P. Shaw, op. cit. pp. 296
41. O.S.A. XI pp. 127–8
42. O.S.A. IV pp. 322
43. O.S.A. XI pp. 472
44. O.S.A. XVI pp. 451
45. O.S.A. III pp. 154
46. O.S.A. VI pp. 223
47. O.S.A. VI pp. 55
48. R. Dinnie, *The History of Kincardine O'Neil* Aberdeen 1885 pp. 55–63

2. *Factors shaping community growth*

49. A. Harvey, *Agricultural Statistics of Aberdeenshire* Aberdeen 1859 pp. 5
50. G. Skene Keith, *A General View of the Agriculture of Aberdeenshire* Aberdeen 1811 pp. 604
51. A. Harvey, op. cit. pp. 11
52. N.S.A., pp. 536
53. A. Murray, op. cit. pp. 11
54. E. J. T. Collins, *The Age of Machinery* in G. E. Mingay, *The Victorian Countryside* Vol I, London 1981 pp. 201
55. J. Pirie, *The Parish of Cairnie and its early connections with Strathbogie* Banff 1906 pp. 62
56. N.S.A. XII pp. 816
57. J. Pirie, op. cit. pp. 63–4
58. A. Smith (ed) *A New History of Aberdeenshire* Vol I, pp. vi
59. N.S.A. XII pp. 639
60. A. Smith, op. cit. pp. 578
61. Ibid. pp. 20
62. S. G. E. Lythe and J. Butt, *An Economic History of Scotland 1100–1939* Glasgow 1975 pp. 208
63. W. McCombie, *Cattle and Cattle Breeders* Aberdeen 1886 pp. 71–2
64. Ibid. pp. 72
65. *The Hatton Estates* Banff 1887 pp. 3–11
66. G. Skene Keith, op. cit. pp. 140
67. J. Sinclair, *Analysis of the Statistical Account of Scotland* Edinburgh 1831 pp. 170–178
68. The *Aberdeen Journal* 27.3.1798
69. C. Smout, *The Landowner and the Planned Villages in Scotland 1730–1880* in N. J. Phillipson and R. Mitchison (ed) *Scotland in the Age of Improvement* Edinburgh 1970
70. D. G. Lockhart, *The Evolution of the Planned Villages of North East Scotland 1700–1900* (unpub PhD, University of Dundee 1974)
71. O.S.A. VI pp. 129–131
72. N.S.A. XII pp. 724–5

73. N.S.A. XII pp. 412
74. D. G. Lockhart, *The Planned Villages of Aberdeenshire: the Evidence from Newspaper Advertisements* S.G.M. Vol 94, No 2, pp. 98
75. A. Smith, op. cit. pp. 1254
76. N.S.A. XII pp. 781
77. K. Walton, op. cit. 169

Transport
78. C. H. Lee, *British Regional Employment Statistics* 1841–1971, Cambridge 1979 pp. 3–4
79. Charleston T.M.B. 22.1.1801
80. G. Skene Keith, op. cit. pp. 535–7
81. Charleston T.M.B. 20.1.1802 and 6.2.1809
82. Old Meldrum T.M.B. 62.1809 and Ellon T.M.B. 9.12.1800
83. G. Skene Keith, op. cit. pp. 535–7
84. *Report by the Committee on the Turnpikes* etc 1857 pp. 7
85. Ellon T.M.B. 2.5.1800
86. Ibid.
87. Ibid. 1.4.1816
88. G. M. Fraser, *The Old Deeside Road, its course, history and associations* Aberdeen 1921 pp. 135
89. *Aberdeen Journal* 15.4.1812
90. G. M. Fraser, op. cit. pp. 158
91. *Report by the Committee on Turnpikes* pp. 8
92. N.S.A. XII, pp. 160, 202 and 438
93. *Aberdeen Journal* 31.3.1800
94. *Report by the Committee on Turnpikes* pp. 6
95. *Old Meldrum Past and Present* Banff 1893 pp. 11
96. J. Pirie, op. cit. pp. 84–6
97. *Aberdeen Journal* 22.3.1819
98. Ibid. 30.11.1808
99. G. Gray, *Recollections of Huntly as it was 70 years ago* Banff 1892 pp. 22–3
100. N.S.A. XII pp. 1004
101. J. Wilken, *Ellon in Bygone Days* Ellon 1926 pp. 30
102. *The Bon Accord Directory* Aberdeen 1842 pp. 184–9
103. Aboyne Census Schedules, 1841 and 51
104. *Aberdeen Journal* 13.9.1865
105. *Bon Accord Directory* 1842 pp. 186
106. *Kemnay Bazaar Book* 1896, Aberdeen 1896 pp. 25
107. A. S. Morris, *The Nineteenth Century Scottish Carrier Trade: Patterns of Decline* S.G.M. Vol 96 No 2, pp. 78
108. A. Everitt, *Town and Country in Victorian Leicestershire. The Role of the Village Carrier.* In A. Everitt (ed) *Perspectives on English Urban History* London 1973
109. *Old Meldrum Past and Present* pp. 11
110. *Report by the Committee on Turnpikes* pp. 6
111. *Aberdeen Journal* 13.9.1865
112. N.S.A. XII. pp. 128
113. Ibid. pp. 586
114. Ibid. pp. 69
115. Ibid.
116. See H. A. Vallance, *The Great North of Scotland Railway* Dawlish 1965
117. *Journal of the Stephenson Locomotive Society* XXX No 352 1954 pp. 290
118. Ibid.

119. A. Smith, op. cit. pp. 857
120. *Journal of the Stephenson Locomotive Society* pp. 280
121. *Peterhead Sentinel* 25.7.1856
122. A. Smith, op. cit. pp. 223
123. Ibid. pp. 501
124. *Aberdeen Journal* 4.10.1865
125. J. Pirie, op. cit. pp. 66
126. J. Minty, op. cit. pp. 13
127. *Royal Grampian Country* pp. 53
128. *Aberdeen Journal* 2.3.1899
129. R. R. Notman, *A Letter to the landed proprietors of Deeside* Aberdeen 1850 pp. 2–15
130. *Aberdeen Journal* 7.7.1852
131. R. Gordon, *The Early Days of the Deeside Railway Deeside Field* 1927
132. J. Coutts, *A Dictionary of Deeside* Aberdeen 1899 pp. 226
133. *Aberdeen Journal* 2.3.1899
134. R. C. Michie, *Trade and Transport in the Economic Development of North East Scotland in the 19th Century. Scottish Economic and Social History* Vol 3 1983 pp. 66–85

Industry and commerce

135. M. Gray, *The Fishing Industries of Scotland*, Oxford 1978
136. M. Gray, *Fishing Villages 1750–1880* in (ed) A. C. O'Dell and J. Mackintosh, *The North East of Scotland* Aberdeen 1963 pp. 103
137. A. Smith, op. cit. pp. 942–3
138. Pigot & Co, *National Commercial Directory of Scotland* London 1837 pp. 211
139. J. Worrall, op. cit. pp. 166
140. R. C. Michie, *The Northern Whale Fishing 1752–1893* in *Northern Scotland* Vol III No 1, 1977–8
141. P. Thomson, T. Wailey and T. Lummis, *Living the Fishing* London 1983 pp. 17
142. Ibid. pp. 91
143. M. Gray, *The Fishing Industries of Scotland* pp. 166
144. Slaters *Directory* 1903
145. N.S.A. XII pp. 159
146. Ibid. pp. 695
147. W. H. K. Turner, *The Localisation of Early Spinning Mills in the Historic Linen Region of Scotland* S.G.M. Vol 98 No 2, pp. 77–80
148. J. P. Shaw, *The Rural Industries, Water Power and Textiles* in M. L. Parry and J. R. Slater, op. cit. pp. 300
149. K. Walton, *Population Changes* etc pp. 174
150. Ibid.
151. D. Bremner, *The Industries of Scotland, Their Rise, Progress and Present Condition* 1869 republished Newton Abbot 1969 pp. 477
152. J. Worrall, op. cit. pp. 185
153. G. Mingay, Vol 1, op. cit. pp. 7
154. H. Hamilton, *Industries and Commerce* in A. C. O'Dell and H. Mackintosh op. cit. pp. 154
155. J. Worrall, op. cit.
156. Ibid.
157. J. N. Bartlett, *Investment for Survival, Culter Mills Paper Company Ltd., 1865–1914 Northern Scotland* 1982
158. *The Vale of Ythan* pp. 38
159. J. A. Chartres and G. L. Turnbull *Country Craftsmen* in G. E. Mingay, op. cit. pp. 321
160. W. A. Armstrong, *The Flight from the Land* in G. Mingay, op. cit. pp. 125

161. W. Diack, *The Rise and Progress of the Granite Industry in Aberdeen* Aberdeen 1949 pp. 78
162. A. Smith, op. cit. pp. 781–2
163. Burnett of Kemnay M.S.S. Leases to J. Fyfe
164. Kemnay School Logbook 10.5.1889
165. Burnett of Kemnay M.S.S. Leases to J. Fyfe
166. J. Worrall op. cit. pp. 139–140
167. *Kemnay Bazaar Book* 1896 pp. 10
168. J. Slater, 1903 Directory
169. Ibid.
170. O.S.A. XII pp. 1045
171. Ibid. pp. 389
172. Ibid. pp. 761
173. C. W. Munn, *The Scottish Provincial Banking Companies 1747–1864* Edinburgh 1981 pp. 195
174. R. Cameron, *Banking and Industry in Britain in the nineteenth century* in (ed) A. Slaven & D. H. Aldcroft, *Business, Banking and Urban History* Edinburgh 1982
175. S. G. Checkland, *Scottish Banking. A History 1695–1973* Glasgow 1975 pp. 196–8
176. Ibid. pp. 108
177. S. Lythe and J. Butt, op. cit pp. 139
178. A. Murray, op. cit. pp. 52
179. N.S.A. XII pp. 198
180. N.S.A. XII pp. 1005
181. J. Minty, op. cit. pp. 14–15
182. J. Wilken, *Buchan in Grandfather's time and today* Ellon, n.d. pp. 44
183. Lythe and Butt, op. cit. pp. 227–8
184. *Old Meldrum Past and Present* pp. 12
185. J. Minty op. cit pp. 19
186. J. A. Chartres, *Country Tradesmen* in G. E. Mingay, op. cit. pp. 304
187. Pigots Directory 1837, pp. 205
188. Ibid. pp. 206
189. G. Gray, op. cit. pp. 17–18
190. J. Wilken, *Ellon in Bygone Days* pp. 35
191. J. Wilken, *Buchan in Grandfather's time* etc p. 66
192. *Peterhead Sentinel* 5.9.1856
193. J. Pirie, op. cit. pp. 141
194. A. Smith, op. cit. pp. 562
195. Ythan Wells School Logbook 28.4.74
196. Ibid.
197. *Aberdeen Journal* 19.7.1865
198. *Aberdeen Journal* 23.8.1865
199. A. Smith, op. cit. pp. 474
200. *Aberdeen Journal* 14.4.1898
201. Slater's Directory Ltd, *The Royal National Directory of Scotland* Manchester 1903 pp. 147
202. *The Vale of Alford Past and Present* Aberdeen 1896 pp. 9
203. Ibid. pp. 10
204. *Aberdeen Journal* 17.5.1865
205. Draft Report by a Subcommittee of Rural Police of Aberdeen County, Aberdeen 1853
206. N.S.A. pp. 1046
207. W. Watson, *Remarks on the Bothie System and feeing markets* Aberdeen n.d. pp. 4
208. J. B. Pratt, *Buchan* Aberdeen 1858 pp. 25

209. Ythan Wells School Logbook 24 July and 7 August 1875
210. M. J. Mitchell, *The Cruden Bay Hotel and Its Tramway* in *Great North Review* Vol 16, No 63, 1979
211. A. I. McConnachie, *Cruden Bay* in A. I. McConnachie (ed) *The Book of Ellon* Ellon 1901 pp. 130
212. Slater, op. cit. pp. 134
213. A. Smith, op. cit. pp. 674
214. *Aberdeen Journal* 17.11.1800
215. N.S.A. XII 781
216. *Aberdeen Journal* 16.8.1865
217. *Aberdeen Journal* 10.7.1867
218. *Guide to the Highlands of Scotland* Edinburgh 1902 pp. 40–46
219. Ibid. and *Furnished Lodgings in Districts served by the G.N.S.R.* Aberdeen 1912 pp. 31–3
220. A. I. McConnachie, *Deeside* Aberdeen 1900 pp. 14
221. Ibid. pp. 197

3. Different communities

222. J. Taylor, op. cit.
223. T. McWilliam, *Sketch of a quiet Buchan Parish* Banff 1899 pp. 20–81
224. N.S.A. XII pp. 843
225. J. Wilken, *Ellon in Bygone Days* pp. 5
226. Ellon S.B.M. 1984
227. *The Vale of Ythan, Book of the Bazaar of Logie Buchan Bridge Scheme* Aberdeen 1895 pp. 38
228. 1851 Census, Vol 7, *The Population of Scotland* pp. 71
229. C. W. Chalklin, *Country Towns* in G. E. Mingay, Op. Cit. pp. 276
230. Ibid. pp. 277

2. Problems of growth

The problems

1. J. B. Pratt, op. cit. pp. 80
2. A. Smith, op. cit. pp. 578
3. J. Minty, op. cit. pp. 11
4. G. Gray, op. cit. pp. 17
5. Ibid. pp. 45
6. Ibid. pp. 9
7. O.S.A. XI pp. 467
8. G. Gray, op. cit. pp. 19
9. A. Murray, op. cit. pp. 13–14
10. T. Ferguson, *Scottish Social Welfare 1864–1914* London 1958 pp. 1
11. J. Watt, *Annual Report upon the Health and Sanitary Conditions of the various districts of the County of Aberdeen* Aberdeen 1892 pp. 14–15
12. Report of the Inspector of Prisons in Scotland 1837 pp. 39
13. Ibid. 1835 pp. 63
14. Ibid.
15. Ibid. 1837 pp. 36
16. Ibid. pp. 37
17. Ibid. pp. 36

National legislation
18. I. H. Adams, *The Making of Urban Scotland* London 1978 pp. 131
19. D. O. Dykes, *Scottish Local Government* Edinburgh 1907 pp. 17
20. I. H. Adams, op. cit. pp. 157
21. J. R. Shaw, *Local Government in Scotland, Past, Present and Future* Edinburgh 1942 pp. 16
22. See A. E. Whetstone, *Scottish County Government in the 18th and 19th Centuries* Edinburgh 1980
23. D. O. Dykes, op. cit. pp. 47
24. T. Ferguson, op. cit. pp. 11
25. Ibid. pp. 294

Improvement in Aberdeenshire Communities
26. *Aberdeen Journal* 11.4.1898
27. *Proceedings of the County of Aberdeen for the establishment of a rural police*
28. *Regulations and Instructions to be observed by the constabulary force in the County of Aberdeen* Aberdeen 1840
29. Huntly P. C. M. Vol 1, 23.3.60
30. County of Aberdeen, Police Report 1894
31. Regulations and Instructions etc. pp. 6
32. N.S.A. XII pp. 1013–4
33. County of Aberdeen Police Report
34. Report of the Rural Police to the Commissioners of Supply 1853 pp. 5–6
35. Huntly P. C. M. Vol 1, 12.12.1847
36. Kincardine O'Neil P.B.M. Vol 12, 12.11.1870
37. Ibid. 29.5.1878
38. Ibid. 15.12.1888
39. Old Meldrum P.B.M. Vol 2, 18.11.1864 and 27.1.1870
40. Ibid. 31.3.1870
41. Huntly P.C.M. Vol 1, 17.12.1847
42. Ibid. 10.8.1854
43. T. Ferguson, op. cit. pp. 168
44. Kincardine O'Neil P.B.M. Vol 2, 20.2.1883
45. J. Pirie, op. cit. pp. 62
46. A. Murray, op. cit. pp. 6
47. Ythan Wells School Logbook 21.5.1874
48. Ibid.
49. Ibid. 28.5.1874
50. Ibid. 7.12.1877
51. Report of Inspector for Prisons in Scotland 1837 pp. 36
52. N.S.A. XII pp. 211
53. *Catalogue of the Huntly Circulating Library* Peterborough 1886
54. *Aberdeen Journal* 5.4.1898
55. Kemnay Parish Council Minutes, Vol 1895–1915, 9.8.1897
56. J. Minty, op. cit. pp. 11
57. J. Valentine, *The People of Aberdeenshire* Aberdeen 1871 pp. 6
58. Detail based on the 1901 Scottish census
59. J. P. Watt, op. cit. pp. 61
60. J. P. Milne, *New Pitsligo 70 Years Ago* Trans. Buchan Field Club, Vol 17 pp. 54–5
61. J. P. Watt op. cit. pp. 7
62. J. P. Watt, 2nd Report 1892 pp. 8

63. J. P. Watt, 1st Report 1891 pp. 54
64. J. P. Watt, 4th Report 1894 pp. 16
65. J. P. Watt, 1st Report pp. 4
66. Tarland Drainage Board Minutes 1875
67. J. P. Watt op. cit. pp. 4, 17 and 18
68. Ibid. pp. 45
69. 4th Report pp. 24
70. 2nd Report pp. 16
71. 1st Report pp. 18
72. 4th Report pp. 24
73. 10th Report pp. 17
74. 7th Report pp. 10
75. Huntly P.C.M. Vol 3.3.1893
76. T. Ferguson, op. cit. pp. 173
77. J. Milne *New Pitsligo* etc., op. cit. pp. 56
78. Ibid. pp. 5
79. J. P. Watt, 1st Report pp. 19
80. Old Meldrum P.C.M. Vol 11, 4.3.1895, 1.3.1897
81. Tarland and Migvie P.B.M. Vol 2, 20.1.1872
82. Ellon District Committee Minutes December 1892
83. J. P. Watt, 1st Report pp. 2 and 52

The problems of poverty

84. See J. Lindsay, *The Scottish Poor Law, its operation in the North East from 1745 to 1945* Ilfracombe 1975
85. Ibid. pp. 40
86. Ibid. pp. 45
87. G. Skene Keith, op. cit. pp. 597
88. Poor Law Enquiry Appendix II pp. 680
89. Ibid. pp. 758
90. Ibid. pp. 771
91. O.S.A. VIII pp. 155
92. J. Lindsay, pp. 118
93. Ibid.
94. Ibid. pp. 143
95. Ibid. pp. 170
96. Ibid. pp. 172
97. J. Wilken, *Buchan in Grandfather's Time* pp. 60
98. G. Gray, op. cit. pp. 49
99. I. Levitt & C. Smout, *The State of the Scottish Working Class in 1843* Edinburgh 1979
100. Poor Law Enquiry Appendix II pp. 710
101. Ibid. pp. 566
102. Ibid. pp. 715
103. Ibid. pp. 718
104. Ibid. pp. 562
105. Ibid. pp. 712
106. C. Scott, *Remarks on the Circumstances and Claims of the Indigent Poor with reference to the Town and Parish of Peterhead* Aberdeen 1841 pp. 26
107. Ibid. pp. 23–29
108. Poor Law Enquiry Appendix II pp. 718
109. A. Paterson, *The Poor Law in 19th century Scotland* in D. Fraser, *The New Poor Law in the 19th century* London 1976

110. Ibid. pp. 181
111. J. Milne, New Pitsligo etc. op. cit. pp. 62
112. Kincardine O'Neil P.B.M. Vol 12, 26.7.1869
113. Huntly P.B.M. Vol 12, 4.3.1864
114. T. Ferguson, op. cit. pp. 309
115. Ibid. pp. 249
116. Huntly P.B.M. Vol 2, e.g. 6.1.1865
117. Old Deer P.B.M. 25.6.1888
118. New Pitsligo P.B.M. 8.6.1871
119. New Deer P.B.M. 6.7.1897
120. Tyrie P.B.M. 3.11.1879
121. New Deer P.B.M. 12.12.1878

The Buchan combination poorhouse
122. New Deer P.B.M. 12.12.1878
123. Ibid. 2.2.1878
124. Banffshire Journal, 10.1.1888
125. Annual Report of the Board of Supervision 1850 pp. 1–3
126. New Pitsligo P.B.M. 30.3.1871
127. Buchan Combination Poorhouse Minute Book Vol 1886–1905, 11.5.1895
128. Agreement between the Buchan Combination Poorhouse and originally combined
     boards and the Parochial Boards of the new parishes
129. Buchan Combination Poorhouse Minutes, 8.5.1886 and 12.11.1887
130. Poorhouse Offences Book 1869–70
131. Poorhouse Minutes, 12.2.1886
132. Poorhouse Patients report Book 1869–1917, 28.5.1869
133. Poorhouse, Register of Lunatics 1869–1900
134. Poorhouse Minutes, 9.11.1889
135. Ibid. 13.11.1886
136. Ibid. 22.8.1891
137. Poorhouse Register of Attendance, pp. 28
138. Ibid. pp. 28
139. Patients Report Book, 28.5.1869
140. Ibid. 22.10.1875
141. Governor's Journal, 5.7.1900
142. Poorhouse Minutes, 13.2.1892
143. Patients Report Book, 3.4.1871
144. Poorhouse Minutes, 10.2.1899
145. Ibid. 11.5.1900
146. Ibid. 12.8.1905
147. Land Accounts of the Poorhouse 1879–1949

Part II. A country community – Inverurie

1. Unimproved Inverurie

1. The spelling of 'Inverurie' as it is today was adopted in 1866. The reason for the
   change from 'Inverury' was recorded in the Burgh Minutes of 5.2.1866 as being due
   to 'the many annoyances and delays caused to the Merchants, Traders and Inhabitants generally by the name of the Town not appearing in the list of the General Post
   Office as a Post Town, and their correspondence being thus frequently sent to
   Inverary'.

2. J. Anderson, op. cit. pp. 19.
3. *The Aberdeenshire Poll Book* 1696 pp. 354–8.
4. See Roy's Military Survey and the Canal Map of 1796.
5. From '*Letters on a Tour through various parts of Scotland in the Year 1792*' quoted C. B. Davidson, *The Burgh of Inverurie A Retrospect* Inverurie 1888 pp. 37.
6. O.S.A. VII pp. 332.
7. Alexander Bisset, *Memories 1855* (A privately produced recollection held in the N. E. of Scotland Library, Aberdeen) pp. 1.
8. '*Letters on a Tour*' etc., C. B. Davidson, op. cit. pp. 37.
9. Ibid.
10. O.S.A. VII pp. 332.
11. Ibid. pp. 334.
12. A. Bisset, op. cit. pp. 12–13.
13. Ibid.
14. J. Anderson, op. cit. pp. 19.
15. O.S.A. VII pp. 332.
16. A. Bisset, op. cit. pp. 10–11.

2. Factors affecting Inverurie's growth

1. O.S.A. XII pp. 90.
2. See Illustration No. 2.
3. O.S.A. VIII pp. 332–3.
4. Quoted in Tawse & Allen, *The Old and New Bridges over the River Don at Inverurie 1791 and 1924*, Aberdeen 1925 pp. 113.
5. Ibid. pp. 20.
6. Quoted Ibid. pp. 120.
7. Ibid. pp. 34.
8. O.S.A. VIII pp. 332–3.
9. Tawse & Allen. pp. 28.
10. Ibid.

The turnpike road

11. Inverurie T.M.B. 1798–1822 pp. 15–16.
12. Inverurie T.M.B. pp. 45–6.
13. Inverurie Turnpike Trust Accounts Book.
14. Ibid.
15. See A. J. Patrick. *The Coming of Turnpikes to Aberdeenshire* Aberdeen n.d.
16. Inverurie T.M.B. pp. 45–6.
17. Ibid.
18. Aberdeen Turnpike Trustees T.M.B. 1823 pp. 102–4.
19. Ibid.
20. Inverurie T.M.B. pp. 108–9.
21. Ibid. 6.4.1819.
22. Pigot & Cos. *Directory* 1837 pp. 204–5.
23. J. Davidson, *Recollections Forty Years On.* 1885 Inverurie. (A series of un-numbered leaflets.)
24. Ibid.

The canal

25. Quoted in J. Lindsay, *The Canals of Scotland* Newton Abbot 1968 pp. 104.
26. *Aberdeen Journal* 29.10.1805.
27. Inverurie T.M.B. pp. 184–5.

28. Burgh Court Minute Book 25.5.1835.
29. Quoted in *The Royal Burgh of Inverurie*, 1902 Aberdeen.
30. L. S. Morgan, *The Aberdeenshire Canal* (M. A. Thesis, Aberdeen).
31. J. Davidson, *Recollections*.
32. O.S.A. VII p. 333.
33. G. Skee Keith, op. cit. pp. 543.
34. N.S.A. XII pp. 664.
35. Ibid. pp. 683–4.
36. J. Davidson, *Recollections*.
37. N.S.A. XII pp. 664.
38. Burgh Scroll Minute Book 1842–59 pp. 48.

The railway
39. Scroll Minute Book 3.10.1845.
40. Ibid. 2.2.1852.
41. *Journal of the Stephenson Locomotive Society* Vol. XXX No. 352.
42. Scroll Minute Book 7.2.1853.
43. Ibid. 14.10.1853.
44. Slater's *Directory*, 1867 pp. 317.
45. Burgh Minutes 28.10.1869.
46. Ibid. 14.12.1876.
47. Ibid. 3.6.1892.

Agricultural improvement
48. A. Bisset *Memories* pp. 5–12.
49. Ibid.
50. *The Municipal Corporations of Scotland* (British Parliamentary Papers) pp. 49.
51. J. Davidson, *Recollections*.
52. J. Davidson, *Inverurie and the Earldom of the Garioch*, Edinburgh 1878 pp. 383.

3. The growth of Inverurie

1. C. B. Davidson, op. cit. pp. 38 and F. H. Groome, *Ordnance Gazeteer of Scotland*, Edinburgh 1883, pp. 319.
2. Scroll Minute Book 1842–59, 10.1.1842.
3. Burgh Court Book 1797–1805, 3.7.1799 and 20.7.1799.
4. Ibid. 5.3.1803.
5. G. Skene Keith, op. cit. pp. 53 and 139.
6. G. Shaw, *The Content and Rehability of Nineteenth Century Trade Directories* in *The Local Historian* Vol. 13 No. 4 pp. 205–8.
7. G. Timmins, *Measuring Industrial Growth from Trade Directories*, *The Local Historian* Vol. 13 No. 6 pp. 349–52.
8. F. H. Groome, op. cit. pp. 318–19.
9. This section is based on J. Pigot & Cos. 1837 Directory pp. 204–5. Worrall's Directory of 1877, I. Slater's Directory of 1867 pp. 317–320, and I. Slater's 1903 Directory pp. 138–9. See Appendix B.
10. I. Slater's Directory of 1903, pp. 138–9.
11. N.S.A. XII pp. 683–4.
12. Ibid.
13. J. Davidson, op. cit.
14. A. L. Gray, *A. W. Gray Ltd., Bakers. The Story of an Aberdeen Bakery*. Inverurie 1975.
15. J. Davidson, op. cit.

16. *The Royal Burgh of Inverurie*, 1902 Aberdeen.
17. Scroll Minute Book. 10.1.1843.
18. Burgh Court Book 1797–1805. 7.5.1798.
19. *Aberdeen Journal* 3.7.1798.
20. Ibid.
21. O.S.A. VII pp. 332.
22. N.S.A. XII pp. 685.
23. Burgh Court Book 31.1.1800.
24. Ibid. Vol.
25. Ibid. 1.11.1887.
26. Burgh Court Book 8.10.1824.
27. Scroll Minute Book 2.2.1852 and Burgh Minutes 4.5.1870.
28. Burgh Court Book 17.2.1834.
29. Scroll Minute Book 11.11.1844.
30. Burgh Minutes 13.9.1871.
31. Scroll Minute Book 13.10.1840.
32. Burgh Court Book 12.11.1823.
33. O.S.A. VII pp. 333.
34. Quotations from *The Municipal Corporations of Scotland, British Parliamentary Papers* Vol. 9 pp. 121–2.
35. A. Smith, op. cit. pp. 750.
36. *The Royal Burgh of Inverurie* 1902 pp. 11.
37. Burgh Court Book 1797–1805, 10.1.1801.
38. Ibid.
39. Ibid. 28.5.1804 and 1.6.1804.
40. Ibid. 4.10.1820.
41. A series of entries for 1857 in the Scroll Minute Book.
42. Burgh Court Book 5.6.1861.
43. Ibid. 10.7.1862.
44. Ibid. 27.2.1871.

4. The problems of growth

The town council
 1. Council Minutes 12.9.1874.
 2. Inverurie P.C.M. 8.4.1878.
 3. e.g. Burgh Court Book 4.6.1835 and Scroll Book 11.1.1859.
 4. Scroll Book 2.4.1847.
 5. Illnesses all noted in Inverurie P.C.M. for these years.
 6. Inverurie P.C.M. 30.3.1895 and 15.3.1897.
 7. Council Minutes 12.1.1880.
 8. Inverurie P.B.M. 20.3.1866.
 9. Ibid. 28.6.1866.
10. Ibid. 21.8.1866.

The Police Commissioners and matters of health
11. Inverurie P.C.M. 4.3.1867.
12. Ibid. 9.5.1867.
13. Ibid. 10.6.1867.
14. Ibid.
15. Ibid.
16. Ibid. 7.5.1877.

17. Ibid. 1.1.1868.
18. Ibid. 20.3.1899.
19. Ibid. 27.2.1868.
20. Ibid. 6.4.1868.
21. Ibid. 22.2.1871.
22. Ibid.
23. Ibid. 1.9.1868.
24. Ibid. 13.5.1872 and 13.2.1873.
25. Ibid. 4.7.1871.
26. Ibid. 22.2.1871.
27. Ibid. 4.7.1871.
28. Ibid. 11.12.1871.
29. Ibid. 4.7.1871.
30. Ibid. 8.2.1872.
31. Ibid. 1.12.1873.
32. Ibid. 13.4.1874.
33. Ibid.
34. Ibid.
35. Ibid. 14.5.1874.
36. Ibid. 16.10.1874.
37. Ibid. 10.11.1874.
38. Ibid. 22.2.1875.
39. Ibid. 24.2.1875.
40. Ibid. 22.3.1875.
41. Ibid. 22.3.1875.
42. C. B. Davidson, op. cit. pp. 11.
43. Inverurie P.C.M. 13.5.1876 and 14.4.1879.
44. Ibid. 6.1.1899 and 5.10.1899.
45. Ibid. 10.11.1876.
46. Ibid. 8.4.1878.
47. Ibid. 30.5.1895.
48. Ibid.
49. Ibid. 1.7.1895
50. Ibid. 1.3.1897.
51. Ibid. 3.7.1899.
52. Ibid. 20.12.1898, 5.10.1899, 5.2.1900.
53. Ibid. 11.1.1892.
54. Ibid. 20.12.1898.

Lighting and Paving
55. Burgh Court Book 17.7.1834.
56. Ibid. 3.11.1834.
57. N.S.A. XII pp. 685.
58. Scroll Minute Book 10.1.1842.
59. Inverurie P.C.M. 10.10.1870.
60. Ibid. 25.9.1867.
61. Ibid. 14.10.1867.
62. Ibid. 11.10.1886.
63. Scroll Minute Book 31.8.1849.
63. Scroll Minute Book 31.8.1949.
64. Inverurie P.C.M. 7.8.1899.
65. Ibid. 2.10.1891.

66. Ibid. 20.11.1882.
67. Ibid. 8.4.1878 and 10.11.1882.
68. Ibid. 3.12.1889.
69. Ibid. 3.12.1889 and 18.4.1890.
70. Ibid. 9.4.1894.
71. Ibid. 30.5.1895.
72. Ibid. 18.1.1897.
73. Ibid. 15.3.1897.

Law and order
74. Burgh Court Book 20.10.1797.
75. Ibid. 10.1.1842.
76. Council Minutes 12.11.1886.
77. Scroll Book 16.3.1854.
78. Ibid. 5.8.1856.
79. Ibid. 7.2.1853 and series of entries 1857.

5. Caring for the poor and the young

Coping with poverty before 1845
1. O.S.A. VII pp. 335.
2. N.S.A. XII pp. 686.
3. Ibid.
4. Poor Law Enquiry (Scotland) 1848. Appendix Part II pp. 754–5.
5. Ibid.
6. Ibid.

After 1845
7. This section is based on the Poor Law Enquiry (Scotland) Appendix IV and on I. Levitt and C. Smart, op. cit. pp. 60–62.
8. Inverurie P.B.M. e.g. 29.12.1859.
9. Ibid. 14.4.1860 and 9.9.1863.
10. Ibid. 20.1.1863.
11. Ibid. 10.12.1864.
12. A. Smith, op. cit. pp. 752.
13. Inverurie General Register of the Poor 1865–1912.
14. As shown in the volumes of Inverurie P.B.M. 1859–72 and 1872–95. See Appendix C.
15. Inverurie P.B.M. 26.3.1863.
16. Council Minutes 9.1.1888.
17. Minutes of the Inverurie Coal Fund 1854–82.

Schooling before 1872
18. O.S.A. VII pp. 335.
19. Inverurie S.B.M. 17.9.1895.
20. Ibid.
21. J. Davidson, Recollections of 40 Years.
22. Inverurie S.B.M. 17.9.1895.
23. Court Book 10.2.1834.
24. N.S.A. XII pp. 685.

25. Scroll Minute Book 17.2.1859.
26. Inverurie S.B.M. 7.4.1873.
27. Aberdeen Almanac & Northern Register, Aberdeen 1863, pp. 183.
28. Court Book 6.10.1821 and N.S.A. XII pp. 685.
29. Inverurie S.B.M. 7.4.1873.
30. A. S. Crichton, Annals of a Disruption Congregation pp. 7–12.
31. Inverurie S.B.M. 7.4.1873.
32. Council Minutes 30.7.1870 and 27.3.1871.
33. Ibid. 8.8.1871.
34. 3rd S.A. Aberdeen County pp. 524.
35. Council Minutes 30.8.1900 and William Clark's Mortification Book.
36. Inverurie S.B.M. 8.6.1873 and 7.7.1873.
37. Ibid. 7.7.1873, 27.8.1874, 19.10.1874.
38. Ibid. 9.6.1873.
39. Ibid. 5.5.1873 for this and following quotes.
40. Ibid. 21.2.1876 and 13.10.1879.
41. Ibid. 8.5.1876.
42. Ibid. 13.3.1889 and 1.7.1890.
43. Ibid. 3.12.1891.
44. Market Place (Infants) Logbook 17.9.1895.
45. Inverurie S.B.M. 27.12.1894.
46. Ibid. 11.5.1882.
47. Ibid. 8.5.1888.
48. Ibid. 4.4.1893.
49. Ibid. 30.7.1894
50. Ibid. 17.9.1895, 16.10.1895, 23.12.1895.
51. Ibid. 29.8.1896.
52. Ibid. 11.7.1898.
53. Ibid. 26.9.1898.
54. Ibid. 17.11.1875 and 7.7.1873.
55. Ibid. 16.2.1891 and 12.4.1897.
56. Ibid. 28.3.1894, 17.9.1895.
57. Ibid. 16.10.1895.
58. Ibid. 18.12.1893, 7.11.1894.
59. Ibid. 11.7.1899
60. Market Place (Infants) Logbook 13.11.1895.
61. Ibid. 5.12.1896.
62. Ibid. 22.8.1898.
63. St. Mary's Logbook pp. 14–57.
64. Ibid. pp. 14.
65. Market Place (Infants) Logbook 27.5.1896.
66. Ibid. 27.5.1898.
67. Ibid. 20.4.1896.
68. Ibid. 14.8.1899.
69. Scroll Minute Book 10.1.1842.
70. Aberdeen Almanac & Northern Register 1858, pp. 278.
71. Scroll Minute Book 1859.
72. Council Minutes 8.2.1871.
73. Ibid. 3.3.1884.
74. Ibid. 24.4.1877, 5.2.1889, 20.7.1894 and 21.2.1884.

Part III. A fishing town – Fraserburgh

1. Fraserburgh before the nineteenth century

1. Fraser of Philorth M.S.S. Vol. 189. *Memoranda concerning the feudal rights of Lord Saltoun in Fraserburgh.*
2. J. Cranna. *Fraserburgh Past and Present.* Aberdeen 1914 pp. 17–19.
3. Ibid. pp. 19 and Fraser Vol. 189.
4. J. Stuart (ed.) *A List of Pollable Persons within the Shire of Aberdeen 1696* 1844 Aberdeen pp. 97–101.
5. Roy's Military Survey.
6. O.S.A. Vol. VI pp. 9.
7. Quoted J. Cranna, op. cit. pp. 27 and 317.
8. O.S.A. Vol. VI p. 3.
9. Fraser, Vol. 100. Estate book 1784–88 pp. 11.
10. O.S.A. Vol. VI pp. 5–6.
11. Fraser, Estate book pp. 6.
12. O.S.A. Vol. VI pp. 11.
13. Fraser, Estate book pp. 7–36.
14. *Minute Book and Ledger and of the Magistrates and Town Council of Fraserburgh.* 12.11.1804.
15. Quoted J. Cranna, op. cit. pp. 319.
16. O.S.A. Vol. VI pp. 13.
17. Ibid. pp. 12.
18. Ibid. pp. 10.
19. J. Cranna, op. cit. pp. 61.
20. Fraser, Estate book pp. 23.
21. O.S.A. Vol. VI pp. 4.
22. Ibid. pp. 12.
23. Minute book and Ledger. 12.11.1802.
24. Fraser, Vol. 189. *Notes for the information of the Committee of feuars and householders.*
25. J. Cranna, op. cit. pp. 45 and 52.

2. The improved economy

Fishing
1. O.S.A. Vol. VI pp. 3.
2. Fraser, Vol. 100, Estate book pp. 7.
3. G. T. Sheves, *Fishing, Development and Spatial Change – Fraserburgh 1800–1974* pp. 7.
4. O.S.A. Vol. VI pp. 13.
5. J. Cranna, op. cit. pp. 56–9 and D. Fraser (ed.) *The Christian Watt Papers* Edinburgh 1983 pp. 3–4 and 15.
6. O.S.A. Vol. VI pp. 12.
7. M. Gray, *The Fishing Industries of Scotland 1790–1914.* Oxford 1978 pp. 5–6.
8. J. Cranna, op. cit. pp. 237–9.
9. Aberdeen Journal 11.9.1805 and 31.10.1810.
10. Ibid. 2.9.1814.
11. D. Fraser (ed.) *The Christian Watt Papers*, pp. 16 and 88.
12. J. Cranna, op. cit. pp. 354–7 and I. Macleod, *To the Greenland Whaling*, Sandwick, 1979 pp. 3.

13. J. Cranna, op. cit. pp. 240, and 3rd S. A. Aberdeen pp. 329.
14. M. Gray, op. cit. pp. 83.
15. A. Smith, *A New History of Aberdeenshire* Vol. 1. Aberdeen and Edinburgh 1875 pp. 589.
16. F. H. Groome, Ordnance Gazeteer of Scotland Vol. III pp. 60.
17. M. Gray, op. cit. pp. 158.

Farming
18. O.S.A. Vol. VI pp. 5–6.
19. Pigot's Directory 1837, pp. 199.
20. D. Fraser (ed.) *The Christian Watt Papers* pp. 47.
21. N.S.A. XII pp. 252–3.
22. A. Smith, op. cit. pp. 592–3.

Travel
23. O.S.A. Vol. VI pp. 4–5.
24. Ibid. pp. 11.
25. Pigot, pp. 201.
26. Slater's Directory 1903 pp. 127–8.
27. Ellon Road Committee Book 1796–1823 pp. 1–5.
28. Ibid. pp. 11–12.
29. Ibid. pp. 93–106.
30. Ibid. pp. 107.
31. Ibid. pp 111.
32. Ibid. pp. 117.
33. Fraser, Bundle 401.
34. Ibid. Bundle 261.
35. Ellon Road Committee Book pp. 113–14.
36. Treasurer's Accounts, Ellon, Peterhead and Fraserburgh Road. The remainder of this paragraph derives from this source.
37. Fraser, Bundle 323. Report by Thomas Burnett.
38. Treasurer's Accounts and Pigot pp. 199.
39. Pigot pp. 201.
40. Worrall's Directors 1877 pp. 131.
41. Slater's Directory 1903 pp. 128 and *Fraserburgh Herald,* June 1897.
42. H. A. Vallance, *The Great North of Scotland Railway* London 1965 pp. 61.
43. Fraser, Vol. 193, Papers concerning Lord Saltoun and guarantees to the Formartine and Buchan Railway.
44. e.g. *Fraserburgh Herald,* 30.6.1885.
45. Ibid. 29.3.1898.
46. O'Dell Miscellany Vol. 13. Light Railways in North East Scotland.
47. D. Fraser (ed.), op. cit. pp. 92.
48. *Fraserburgh Herald,* 18.1.1898.

3. The improved town

Business growth
1. N.S.A. XII pp. 252 and F. H. Groome, op. cit. pp. 60 and J. Cranna, op. cit. pp. 445.
2. O.S.A. Vol. VI pp. 9–11.
3. A. Smith, op. cit. pp. 604.

4. *A Description of the Formartine and Buchan Railway*, Banff 1865 pp. 59.
5. Groome, op. cit. pp. 59.
6. Minute Book and Ledger of Fraserburgh Town Council 25.3.1816.
7. *Fraserburgh Herald*, January 1897.
8. This section is based on Pigot pp. 199–200. Slater (1867) pp. 307–9, Worrall (1877) pp. 129–34, and Slater (1903) pp. 126–131. Firms entered separately are counted separately even when one man is responsible for several businesses.
9. Fraserburgh Police Commissioner's Minutes 25.8.1880.
10. Ibid. 9.4.1888.
11. *Aberdeen Journal* 29.6.1808.
12. Ibid. 26.8.1807.
13. See Directories listed above.
14. Cranna op. cit. pp. 46.
15. Ibid. pp. 25.
16. See Directories listed above.
17. *Fraserburgh Herald* 25.1.1898.
18. D. Fraser, *The Christian Watt Papers*, pp. 95.
19. Fraserburgh Herald 4.1.1898.
20. G. T. Sheves, op. cit. pp. 19.
21. Ibid. pp. 23.
22. See Directories listed above and 6″ O.S. maps 1874 and 1902.
23. Sheves op. cit. pp. 23.
24. Cranna op. cit. pp. 16.
25. Sheves op. cit. pp. 16.
26. *Fraserburgh Herald* 30.6.1885.
27. Pigot and M. Gray op. cit. pp. 64.
28. M. Gray op. cit. pp. 64.
29. Slater's Directory 1867.
30. M. Gray op. cit. pp. 64.
31. Slater 1903.
32. M. Gray op. cit. pp. 71.
33. Cranna op. cit. pp. 275.
34. *Fraserburgh Herald* 30.6.1885.
35. M. Gray op. cit. pp. 72.
36. *Fraserburgh Herald* 17.11.1885.
37. Slater 1903.
38. *Aberdeen Journal* 16.3.1899.
39. Ibid. 17.6.1898.
40. N.S.A. XII pp. 252.
41. Cranna op. cit. pp. 293.
42. *Fraserburgh Herald* 7.7.1885.
43. Worrall pp. 129 and D. Fraser op. cit. pp. 97.
44. *Fraserburgh Herald* 30.6.1885.
45. Police Commissioners' Minutes 3.9.1885 and 24.7.1882.
46. Ibid. 9.6.1868, 25.7.1879 and 25.8.1880.

Managing the town
47. O.S.A. Vol. VI pp. 10 and N.S.A. XII pp. 254.
48. Police Commissioners' Minutes 11.8.1845.
49. *Description of the Formartine and Buchan Railway* pp. 58.
50. Cranna op. cit. pp. 46.

51. Police Commissioners' Minutes 31.1.1868 and 10.6.1891.
52. Ibid. 1.10.1868.
53. Ibid. 15.2.1872.
54. Ibid. 18.3.1890.
55. *Fraserburgh Herald* 31.5.1898.
56. Police Commissioners' Minutes 29.4.1875.
57. A. Gammie, *Church Life in Fraserburgh, past and present*. Aberdeen 1908 pp. 1–57.
58. A. Smith, op. cit. pp. 601.
59. Cranna op. cit. pp. 386.
60. *Fraserburgh Herald* 17.11.1885.
61. Ibid. 17.5.1898.
62. O.S.A. VI pp. 12.
63. N.S.A. XII pp. 254–5.
64. Minute Book and Ledger of the Town Council 21.4.1809.
65. Fraser, Vol. 189, Answers to the Commissioners of Burghs of Barony.
66. Ibid. Memoranda concerning the feudal rights of Lord Saltoun.
67. 3rd S. A. Aberdeen County pp. 326.
68. P.C.M. 2.5.1840.
69. Fraser, Estate Book pp. 23.
70. P.C.M. 7.5.1883.
71. Fraserburgh Police Court Book 1881–96.
72. P.C.M. 9.11.1866.
73. Ibid. 5.10.1849.
74. Ibid.
75. J. Wilken, *Ellon in Bygone Days*. Ellon 1926 pp. 33.
76. This section is based on Fraser, Bundle 470, Letters to Lord Saltoun from Alexander Anderson.
77. e.g. P.C.M. 10.6.1858.
78. Ibid. 19.2.1861.
79. Ibid. 2.6.1862.
80. Ibid. 2.9.1873 and 12.11.1868.
81. A. Smith op. cit. pp. 603.
82. P.C.M. 8.1.1841.
83. Ibid 4.12.1842.
84. Ibid. 26.3.1841 and 11.5.1841.
85. Ibid. 18.8.1856.
87. Ibid. 11.9.1863.
88. 3rd SA., Aberdeen County pp. 331.

Improving the harbour
89. O.S.A. VI pp. 11.
90. Ibid. pp. 12.
91. Fraser, Estate book, 1784–8, pp. 6.
92. Fraser, Bundle 401, Harbour subscriptions.
93. Minute book and Ledger of the Town Council 14.1.1805
94. Ibid. 22.1.1807.
95. Ibid. 12.11.1808 and 21.4.1807.
96. Fraser, Bundle 401, Letter from William Kelman to Lord Saltoun.
97. Ibid, Account of Expenditure on the New Pier.
98. N.S.A. XII pp. 255.
99. Cranna op. cit. pp. 321.
100. Slater, 1867, pp. 307 and Cranna op. cit. pp. 334.

101. Cranna op. cit. pp. 322–4.
102. N.S.A. XII pp. 255.
103. Cranna, op. cit. pp. 324.
104. Ibid. pp. 376.
105. Worral, pp. 129.
106. Cranna op. cit. pp. 327.
107. Worrall, pp. 129.
108. M. Gray, op. cit. pp. 75–7.
109. Cranna op. cit. pp. 330.
110. Worrall pp. 130.
111. Cranna op. cit. pp. 332–3.
112. F. H. Groome, op. cit. pp. 60.
113. Slater, 1903, pp. 126.
114. Ibid.
115. Cranna, op. cit. pp. 342.

4. Improved health

Coping with illness

1. Cranna, op. cit. pp. 80.
2. Fraser, Bundle 468.
3. Fraserburgh Parochial Board Minutes 3.12.1849.
4. Ibid. 19.12.1849.
5. Ibid.
6. Ibid. 8.10.1849.
7. P.C.M. 31.7.1849.
8. Ibid.
9. P.B.M. 8.10.1849.
10. P.C.M. 30.7.1866.
11. Cranna, op. cit. pp. 82.
12. P.C.M. 9.10.1874.
13. Ibid. 17.5.1872.
14. Ibid. 4.8.1866.
15. Ibid.
16. Ibid. 7.9.1866.
17. Fraser, Bundle 440. Address by Lord Saltoun to the inhabitants of Fraserburgh 1867 pp. 14.
18. P.C.M. 10.8.1866.
19. Ibid. 30.7.1866 and 4.8.1866.
20. Fraser, Bundle 440. Address by Lord Saltoun pp.2.
21. Ibid. Bundle 338 Broadsea Rentals.
22. Ibid. Bundle 440 Address by Lord Saltoun pp. 5.
23. P.C.M. 17.5.1872.
24. e.g. Ibid 5.8.1873; 19.5.1871.
25. Ibid. 9.8.1875.
26. Ibid. 12.6.1877.
27. Ibid. 14.5.1878.
28. Ibid. 30.9.1878.
29. Ibid. 17.2.1879.
30. Ibid. 31.5.1882.
31. Ibid. 28.8.1879 and 12.9.1887.

Water supplies
32. Cranna op. cit. pp. 448–9 and O.S.A. VI pp. 12.
33. N.S.A. XII pp. 254.
34. 3rd S.A. County of Aberdeen pp. 330.
35. P.C.M. 5.5.1851 and 13.7.1851.
36. Ibid. 24.12.1864 and 30.5.1865.
37. e.g. Ibid. 10.7.1853.
38. Fraser, Bundle 440, Address by Lord Saltoun, pp. 6.
39. P.C.M. 21.6.1869.
40. 3rd S.A. County of Aberdeen pp. 330 and P.C.M. 11.11.1875.
41. P.C.M. 3.6.1881.
42. Ibid. 14.8.1871.
43. Fraser, Bundle 468, Report by Dr Littlejohn.
44. P.C.M. 21.12.1880.
45. Ibid. 3.6.1881 and 4.9.1882.
46. 3rd S.A. pp. 330 and Fraserburgh Herald 15.3.1898.
47. Cranna, op. cit. pp. 450.
48. P.C.M. 25.2.1896.
49. Ibid 11.3.1895.

Housing
50. Fraser, Bundle 468, Dr Littlejohn's Report.
51. Ibid. Bundle 388, Rental of Broadsea 1855–65.
52. Ibid. Bundle 468, Dr Littlejohn's Report.
53. Ibid. Letter from Sir Alexander Anderson, 1873.
54. Ibid. Broadsea Rentals, 1878.
55. Ibid. Bundle 469, Broadsea tenants.
56. Fraserburgh Herald 15.3.1898.
57. Fraser, Bundle 338, Remarks on Broadsea tenants.
58. Ibid. Bundle 440, Address by Lord Saltoun.
59. P.C.M. 10.6.1891.
60. Ibid. 9.4.1874.
61. Ibid. 23.10.1879.
62. Ibid. 17.8.1891.
63. Ibid. 8.9.1866.
64. Ibid. 8.2.1892.
65. Ibid. 15.6.1868.
66. Ibid. 21.9.1882.
67. Ibid. 29.9.1881.
68. Ibid. 24.7.1882.
69. Ibid. 12.9.1887.
70. Ibid. 1.4.1888.
71. Ibid. 28.9.91. The rest of the paragraph is based on this source.

Cleansing
72. Minute book and ledger of the Town Council 8.8.1811.
73. Ibid. 18.10.1822.
74. Ibid. 12.11.1831.
75. Ibid. 12.11.1829, 11.11.1826. 12.11.1828.
76. P.B.M. 13.11.1848.
77. Ibid. 4.12.1848.
78. Ibid. 3.12.1849.

79. P.C.M. 3.10.1849.
80. P.B.M. 19.9.1853.
81. Ibid. 21.10.1853.
82. P.C.M. 8.10.1853.
83. Ibid. 11.2.1859.
84. Ibid.
85. e.g. Ibid. 17.2.1851, 29.8.1863.
86. Ibid. 29.6.1877. £7.14.0d was raised from 1 month's sales.
87. Fraser Bundle 440, Address by Lord Saltoun pp. 14.
88. P.C.M. 8.9.1866.
89. Ibid. 15.9.1866.
90. Ibid. 22.11.1866, 12.6.1867.
91. Ibid. 9.9.1871.
92. Ibid. 11.12.1871.
93. Ibid. 5.5.1875 and 8.5.1876.
94. Ibid. 3.1.1868.
95. Ibid. 12.11.1868, 16.10.1871, 17.5.1872.
96. Ibid. 30.5.1875.
97. Ibid. 2.8.1870.
98. Ibid. 29.4.1875, 11.11.1875, 1.3.1876.
99. Ibid. 11.11.1875.
100. Ibid. 17.2.1851 (when work began in Broad Street).
101. Ibid. 26.11.1875.
102. Ibid. 18.3.1890.
103. Ibid. 15.2.1872.
104. Ibid. 29.6.1877.
105. Ibid. 1.3.1876.
106. Ibid. 7.9.1881.
107. Ibid. 18.10.1883.
108. Ibid. 19.10.1883.
109. Ibid. 13.10.1887.
110. Ibid. 13.10.1887 and 27.1.1896.
111. Ibid. 14.1.1896.
112. Ibid. 28.9.1891.
113. Ibid. 25.5.46.
114. The section is based on the rates assessments noted throughout the Police Commissioners' Minutes.

5. Poverty

Before 1846
  1. O.S.A. VI pp. 7.
  2. Fraser, Estate Book, pp. 23.
  3. Poor Law Enquiry, 1843. Appendix II pp. 709.
  4. Ibid. pp. 706.
  5. O.S.A. VI pp. 7.
  6. Fraser, Estate Book, pp. 15.
  7. Ibid., Bundle 474.
  8. Poor Law Enquiry 1843, II, pp. 706.
  9. Ibid. pp. 708.
  10. Ibid. pp. 707.

11. Ibid.
12. Ibid. pp. 706.
13. Ibid. pp. 707.
14. Ibid. pp. 706.
15. Ibid. pp. 708.
16. Ibid. and D. Fraser, *The Christian Watt Papers*, pp. 16.
17. Ibid. pp. 709.

The parochial board
18. Parochial Board Minutes 13.12.1845.
19. Ibid. 12.2.1846.
20. Ibid. 13.12.1845.
21. Registers of Poor Persons on the Roll of the Parish of Fraserburg 1846–59 and 1865–88.
22. Parochial Board Minutes 1.8.1876.
23. Ibid. 13.12.1845.
24. Ibid. 2.11.1846.
25. Ibid. 5.4.1869.
26. Registers of Poor Persons.
27. P.B.M. 11.8.1852.
28. Record of Applicants for Parochial Relief in Fraserburgh 1894–1907, pp.3.
29. Ibid. pp. 43.
30. Registers of Poor Persons.
31. Ibid.
32. Record of Applicants pp. 80.
33. Ibid. pp. 11.
34. Ibid. pp. 39.
35. P.B.M. 7.12.1859.
36. Ibid. 4.12.1894.
37. Ibid. 7.12.1863.
38. Children's Separate Register 1865–1914, of Fraserburgh Parochial Board pp. 3–77.
39. P.B.M. 1.2.1848.
40. Ibid. 28.5.1849.
41. Ibid. 3.12.1849.
42. Ibid. 21.9. 1863.
43. Ibid. 6.3.1848.
44. Ibid. 4.12.1894.
45. Ibid. 25.1.1847, 8.3.1847, 1.2.1848.
46. Ibid. 12.4.1847.
47. Ibid. 10.1.1899.
48. Fraser, Bundle 277, 1862 Inspection of Poor.
49. P.B.M. 16.4.1860.
50. Fraser, Bundle 277, 1862 Inspection of Poor.
51. P.B.M. 23.6.1863.
52. Ibid.
53. Detailed in P.B.M. 1860–1900.
54. Ibid. 1846–1900.
55. *Fraserburgh Herald*, 15.12.1885.

Accommodating the poor
56. P.B.M.

57. Ibid. 4.3.1861.
58. Ibid. 3.4.1865.
59. Ibid. 4.10.1865.
60. Ibid.
61. Ibid. 9.10.1866.
62. Ibid. 12.6.1868.
63. Ibid. 7.11.1871.
64. Ibid. 5.6.1876.
65. Ibid. 3.4.1865.
66. Ibid. 8.8.1865.
67. Ibid. 20.5.1868.
68. Ibid. 9.4.1869.
69. Ibid. 2.8.1870.
70. Ibid. 6.10.1873.
71. Noted in P.B.M. 1869–1900.
72. Ibid. 5.2.1878.
73. Ibid. 6.2.1882.
74. Record of Applicants pp. 11.
75. P.B.M. 4.5.1885.

Other forms of aid
76. P.C.M. 8.1.1883.
77. Ibid.
78. P.B.M. 6.1.1879.
79. P.C.M. 8.1.1883.
80. P.B.M. 21.1.1847.
81. Ibid. 15.2.1847.
82. *Fraserburgh Herald* 4.1.1898.
83. Ibid.
84. Ibid. 15.12.1885.
85. Ibid.
86. Ibid. 4.1.1898.
87. Ibid. 5.4.1898.
88. Ibid. 4.1.1898.
89. P.B.M. 4.12.1894.
90. Ibid.

6. Education

1. A. Smith, op. cit. pp. 610.
2. Fraser, Estate Book, pp. 36.
3. *Fraserburgh Herald*, 18.1.1898.
4. P.C.M. 29.3.1879.

Schooling before 1872
5. O.S.A. VI pp. 8.
6. Fraserburgh S.B.M. 6.6.1873.
7. O.S.A. VI pp. 8.
8. Cranna, op. cit. pp. 224–6.
9. Fraser, Estate Book, pp. 17–18.
10. Cranna, op. cit. pp. 228.
11. N.S.A. XII pp. 257.

12. P.B.M. 20.3.1854.
13. Ibid. 7.12.1863.
14. Poor Law Enquiry 1843, App. II, pp. 708.
15. N.S.A. XII pp. 257.
16. S.B.M. 1.5.1874.
17. N.S.A. XII pp. 257.
18. Slater's Directory 1867, pp. 307.
19. Ibid. and D. Fraser, *The Christian Watt Papers*, pp. 5.
20. A. Smith, op. cit. pp. 610.
21. Ibid. pp. 609.
22. S.B.M. pp. 22.
23. Ibid. pp. 19–22.
24. Ibid. pp. 15.
25. Ibid. 1.5.1874.
26. Ibid. pp. 14–22.

The school board years
27. Ibid. 23.4.1873 and 3.10.1873.
28. P.B.M. 3.2.1874.
29. S.B.M. 3.4.1874.
30. Ibid. 6.8.1875.
31. Ibid. 4.11.1874.
32. Ibid. 15.2.1877.
33. Ibid.
34. Ibid. 22.6.1878.
35. Ibid.
36. Ibid. 5.7.1878.
37. Ibid. 7.5.1880.
38. Ibid.
39. Ibid. e.g. 2.3.1880.
40. Ibid. 26.11.1878.
41. Ibid. 12.9.1882.
42. Logbook of Fraserburgh Central School 4.6.1883.
43. S.B.M. 1.11.1887, 25.2.1890.
44. Ibid. 4.7.1890.
45. Slater's Directory 1903 pp. 127.
46. S.B.M. 29.7.1890.
47. Logbook of Fraserburgh Central School 21.3.1884.
48. S.B.M. 29.7.1890.
49. Ibid. 3.10.1873.
50. Ibid. 4.11.1876.
51. Logbook of Fraserburgh Academy 17.11.1893.
52. Ibid. 24.7.1899.
53. Ibid. 4.6.1895.
54. Ibid. 2.9.1901.
55. *Fraserburgh Herald* 4.1.1898 and 1.3.1898.
56. S.B.M. 6.7.1876.
57. Ibid 1878–1882.
58. Ibid 3.g. 1889 reports by attendance officer.
59. *Fraserburgh Herald* 5.7.1898.
60. Ibid. 30.6.1885.
61. Hector Barclay, *The Penny Schoolie*, Peterhead n.d.

62. Logbook of Fraserburgh Central School 10.7.1874.
63. Ibid. 11.6.1875 and 15.10.1875.
64. Ibid. 717.1882.
65. Logbook of Broadsea School, e.g. 23.10.1903.
66. Logbook of Fraserburgh Central School 25.5.1877.
67. Ibid. 13.2.1874.
68. Ibid. 6.11.1874.
69. Ibid. 18.12.1874.
70. S.B.M. 4.12.1891.
71. Fraserburgh Central School Logbook 28.9.1877.
72. Ibid. 19.10.1878.
73. Ibid. 28.4.1876.
74. Ibid. 24.4.1879.
75. S.B.M. 18.12.1884.
76. Ibid 27.1.1885.
77. Fraserburgh Central School Logbook 14.11.1884.
78. Ibid. 28.9.1885.
79. Ibid. 21.12.1891.
80. Ibid. 5.2.1892.
81. Ibid. 27.11.1885 and S.B.M. 4.7.1883.

REFERENCES

Conclusion

1. N.S.S. XII pp. 758
2. J. Milne, *New Pitsligo* etc., op. cit.
3. N.S.A. XII pp. 682
4. Pigot, op. cit. pp. 24
5. Pigot. op cit. pp. 203
6. F. Groome, op. cit. V pp. 203
7. Slater's Directory 1903, pp. 126–7 and 153–4
8. J. Worrall, op. cit. pp. 148
9. Banffshire Journal, 12.12.1893
10. F. H. Groome, op. cit. pp. 456
11. *The Imperial Gazeteer*, Vol I pp. 698, Vol II pp. 610
12. Slater's Directory pp. 126–7 and 153–4

SOURCES

1. Manuscripts

(a) At the Grampian Regional Archives
Burgh Minutes for Inverurie, including Burgh Court Books and Scroll
Minute Book
Coal Fund Minutes Inverurie
Drainage and Water Supply District Minutes, Ballater
Minute Book and Ledger of the Magistrates and Town Council of Fraserburgh
Parish Council Minutes for Kemnay
Parochial Board Minutes for Ellon, Fraserburgh, Glenmuick, Inverurie, Kemnay,
Longside, Methlick, Monquhitter, New Deer, New Pitsligo, Old Deer, Tarves,
Tyrie, Udny, Huntly, Tarland, Kincardine O'Neil, Old Meldrum
Parochial Board Registers for Fraserburgh and Inverurie; Children's Separate
Register for Fraserburgh
Police Court Book, Fraserburgh
Police Commissioners' Minutes for Fraserburgh, Old Meldrum, Huntly, Turriff
and Inverurie
School Board Minutes for Fraserburgh, Glenmuick, Inverurie, Kemnay,
School Log books for Ballater, Broadsea, Ellon, Fraserburgh, Inverurie, Kemnay,
Maud and Ythan Wells
Turnpike Trust Minutes for the Inverurie Road, the Ellon and Fraserburgh Road,
the Deeside and Charleston Road
Turnpike Trust Treasurer's Accounts for the Ellon and Fraserburgh Road
William Clark's Mortification Minute Book (Inverurie)
(b) At the Grampian Health Board Archives
The Minutes, Land Accounts, Registers and Governor's Journal of the Buchan
Combination Poorhouse
(c) At the University of Aberdeen Archives
Fraser of Philorth MSS
(d) At Kemnay House
Burnett of Kemnay MSS

2. Maps
The Aberdeenshire Canal 1843.
A Arrowsmith's Map of Scotland 1807.
Ordnance Survey, 1″, 6″, 25″, first and second surveys.
Parliamentary Boundaries Maps 1832.
Roy's Military Survey.
The Turnpike Roads of Aberdeen 1865.
Turnpike and Junction Roads, Fraserburgh.

3. Photographs
The A. Norrie Collection, Arbuthnott Museum, Peterhead.
The North East of Scotland Museums Collection, Arbuthnott Museum, Peterhead.

The Washington Wilson Collection, University of Aberdeen.

4. Newspapers

The Aberdeen Journal.
The Banffshire Journal.
The Buchan Observer.
The Fraserburgh Herald.
The Peterhead Sentinel.

5. Periodicals

The Agricultural History Review.
The Buchan Field Club.
The Deeside Field.
The Great North Review.
The Journal of Transport History.
The Local Historian.
Northern Scotland.
Scottish Economic and Social History.
The Scottish Geographical Magazine.
Scottish Studies.
The Journal of the Stephenson Locomotive Society.
The Scottish Vernacular Buildings Group Magazine.

6. Pamphlets

M. Aitken, *Six Buchan Villages*, 1977, Cruden Bay.
J. Anderson, *Charity to the Poor*, 1823, Peterhead.
H. Barclay, *The Penny Schoolie*, n.d., Peterhead.
A. Bisset, *Memories* (typescript in N.E. of Scotland Library).
I. M. Black, *The Story of Inverurie South Parish Church*, 1942, Inverurie.
J. Black, *Report on the Cottage Accommodation in Buchan*, 1851, Edinburgh.
The Catalogue of the Huntly Circulating Library, 1886, Peterborough.
J. Cruickshank, *Observations on the Scotch System of Poor Laws*, 1813, Aberdeen.
J. Davidson, *Recollections of Forty Years*, 1887–8, Inverurie (privately printed and distributed).
A Description of the Formartine and Buchan Railway, 1865, Banff.
Draft Report by a sub-committee of the Committee of Rural Police of the County of Aberdeen on the causes of the recent increase of vagrancy and crime 1853, Aberdeen.
Furnished Lodgings in Districts served by the Great North of Scotland Railway 1912, Aberdeen.
A. Gammie, *Church Life in Fraserburgh*, Past and Present 1908 Aberdeen.
The Garioch Farming Club, 1882, Banff.
A. L. Gray, *A. W. Gray Ltd., Bakers, The Story of an Aberdeenshire Bakery*, 1975, Inverurie.
G. Gray, *Recollections of Huntly as it was seventy years ago*, 1892, Banff.
A Guide to the Highlands of Scotland, 1902, Edinburgh.
The Hatton Estates, 1887, Banff (re-printed from the Banffshire Journal).
A. Harvey, *The Agricultural Statistics of Aberdeenshire*, 1859, Aberdeen.
Hits and Kicks – the Book of the Peterhead Recreation Park Bazaar, 1891, Peterhead.
Kemnay Bazaar Book, 1896, Aberdeen.
W. Laing, *An Account of Peterhead, its mineral well, air and neighbourhood*, 1793, London.
R. M. Lawrence, *In Coaching Days*, 1927, Aberdeen.
T. McWilliam, *Sketch of a quiet Buchan Parish*, 1899, Banff.
J. Milne, *The Early History of Turriff*, 1890, Banff.
J. Minty, *Reminiscences of a Forty Years Residence in Turriff*, 1865, Banff.
W. A. Mitchell, *Or Was it Yesterday?*, 1847, Aberdeen.

A. Murray, *Peterhead a century ago*, 1910, Peterhead.
R. R. Notman, *A Letter to the Landed Proprietors of Deeside*, 1850, Aberdeen.
The Official Guide to Fraserburgh and Rosehearty, n.d., Peterhead.
Old Meldrum Past and Present, 1893, Banff (Articles re-printed from the Banffshire Journal).
The Past and Present Policy of the Directors of the G.N.S.R. 1862, Aberdeen.
W. Paterson, *The History of the Free Church of Fraserburgh*, 1885, Edinburgh.
W. Paul, *The Past and Present of Aberdeenshire*, 1801, Aberdeen.
J. Peter, *The Peat Mosses of Buchan*, 1876, Aberdeen.
Peterhead in 1840. 1840 Aberdeen (An enlarged version of the entry in Encyclopaedia Brittanica).
Police Report for the County of Aberdeen, 1894, Aberdeen.
Proceedings of the County of Aberdeen for the establishment of a rural police force, 1840, Aberdeen.
Prospectus for the Gordon Schools, Huntly, 1909, Huntly.
Regulations and Instructions to be observed by the Constabulary Force for the County of Aberdeen, 1840, Aberdeen.
Report of the Rural Police Committee to the Commissioners of Supply for Aberdeen, 1853, Aberdeen.
Report by the Committee appointed by the County of Aberdeen on the Turnpike and Commutation Roads in the County, 1857, Aberdeen.
The Royal Burgh of Inverurie in the Coronation Year, 1902, Aberdeen.
The Royal Route to the Highlands, the Great North of Scotland Railway, 1912, Aberdeen.
C. Scott, *Remarks on the Circumstances and Claims of the Indigent Poor with reference especially to the Town and Parish of Peterhead*, 1841, Aberdeen.
J. Taylor, *Rosehearty, Its History as a Fishing Town*, 1982, Rosehearty.
The Vale of Alford Past and Present, 1896, Aberdeen.
The Vale of Ythan, 1895, Aberdeen.
J. Valentine, *The People of Aberdeenshire*, 1871, Aberdeen.
W. Walker, *Nineteenth century progress in the North*, 1908, Aberdeen.
W. Watson, *Remarks on the Bothie System and feeing markets*, n.d., Aberdeen.
J. Wilken, *Ellon in Bygone Days*, 1926, Ellon.
J. Wilken, *Buchan in Grandfather's time*, n.d., Ellon.
F. Wyness, *Let's Look Around the Fraserburgh Area*, n.d., Aberdeen.

7. Theses

M. B. Anderson, *The Aberdeenshire Livestock Industry*, 1962, BSc Aberdeen.
J. W. Cameron, *The Historical Geography of Two Parishes – Aberdeen and Tyrie*, 1979, BSc Aberdeen.
D. G. Lockhart, *The Evolution of the Planned Villages of North East Scotland*. 1974, PhD Dundee.
F. McKichan, *Stirling 1780–1880: the response of burgh government to the problems of urban growth*, 1972, MLitt Glasgow.
L. S. Morgan, *The Aberdeenshire Canal. A Study in Transport History*, 1973, MA Aberdeen.
J. Mutch, *Inverurie; a study in a changing agricultural environment*, 1964, MA Aberdeen.
P. Nuttgens, *Settlements and Architecture of the North East Lowlands of Scotland*, 1959, PhD Edinburgh.
R. Paddison, *The Evolution and Present Structure of Central Places in North East Scotland*, 1969, PhD Aberdeen.
G. T. Sheves, *Fishing Development and Spatial Change – Fraserburgh 1800–1974*, 1975, MA Aberdeen.
J. Stephen, *The Development of Inverallochy and Cairnbulg: a systems framework*, 1976, MA Aberdeen.
A. G. Stopani, *Fraserburgh; the Evolution of the Town and Spatial change*, 1978, MA Aberdeen.

8. Books

(a) *Recently published works*

  (i) *General works on local history*

      M. Aston & J. Bond, *The Landscape of Towns*, 1976, London.

      N. Cossons, *The BP Book of Industrial Archaeology*, 1975, Newton Abbott.

      A. Everitt (ed), *Perspectives in English Urban History*, 1973, London.

      A. Henstock (ed), *Early Victorian Country Town*, 1978, Ripley.

      W. G. Hoskins, *Local History in England*, 1972, London.

      A. Rogers, *Approaches to Local History*, 1977, London.

      T. Rowley, *Villages in the Landscape*, 1978, London.

  (ii) *General Works on British and Scottish History*

      I. H. Adams, *The Making of Urban Scotland*, 1978, London.

      R. H. Campbell, *Scotland since 1707. The Rise of an Industrial Society*, 1965, Oxford.

      O. Checkland, *Philanthropy in Victorian Scotland*, 1980, Edinburgh.

      O. Checkland and M. Lamb (ed), *Health Care as Social History*, 1982, Aberdeen.

      S. G. Checkland, *Scottish Banking. A History 1695–1973*, 1975, Glasgow.

      C. M. Clapperton (ed), *Scotland. A New Study*, 1983, Newton Abbott.

      T. Devine (ed), *Lairds and Improvement in the Scotland of the Age Enlightenment*, 1978, Glasgow.

      I. Donnachie, *A History of the Brewing Industry in Scotland*, 1979, Edinburgh.

      A. J. Durie, *The Scottish Linen Industry in the 18th century*, 1979, Edinburgh.

      A. Fenton, *Scottish Country Life*, 1976, Edinburgh.

      T. Ferguson, *Scottish Social Welfare 1864–1914*, 1958, Edinburgh.

      M. Flinn (ed), *Scottish Population History from the seventeenth century of the 1930s*, 1977, Cambridge.

      D. Fraser (ed), *The New Poor Law in the Nineteenth Century*, 1976, London.

      G. Gordon and B. Dicks (ed), *Scottish Urban History*, 1983, Aberdeen.

      M. Gray, *The Fishing Industries of Scotland*, 1978, Oxford.

      A. R. B. Haldane, *The Drove Roads of Scotland*, 1952, Edinburgh.

      P. Horn, *The Rural World 1780–1850*, 1980, London.

      J. R. Hume, *The Industrial Archaeology of Scotland* Vol II, 1977, London.

      C. H. Lee, *British Regional Employment Statistics 1841–1971*, 1979, Cambridge.

      B. Lenman, *An Economic History of Modern Scotland*, 1977, London.

      I. Levitt & C. Smout, *The State of the Scottish Working Class in 1843*, 1979, Edinburgh.

      J. Lindsay, *The Canals of Scotland*, 1968, Newton Abbott.

      M. Lindsay, *Lowland Scottish Villages*, 1980, London.

      S. G. E. Lythe & J. Butt, *An Economic History of Scotland 1100–1939*, 1975, Glasgow.

      R. N. Millman, *The Making of the Scottish Landscape*, 1975, London.

      G. E. Mingay (ed), *The Victorian Countryside*, 2 vols, 1981, London.

      C. W. Munn, *The Scottish Provincial Banking Companies, 1747–1864*, 1981, Edinburgh.

      M. L. Parry & T. R. Slater, *The Making of the Scottish Countryside*, 1980, London.

      P. L. Payne (ed), *Studies in Scottish Business History*, 1967, London.

      N. T. Phillipson & R. Mitchison (ed), *Scotland in the Age of Improvement. Essays in Scottish History of the eighteenth century*, 1970, Edinburgh.

      A. Slaven & D. H. Aldcroft (ed), *Business, Banking and Urban History*, 1982, Edinburgh.

      P. Thompson, T. Wailey & J. Lummis, *Living the Fishing*, 1983, London.

      A. E. Whetstone, *Scottish County Government in the 18th and 19th centuries*, 1981, Edinburgh.

(iii) *Works dealing with the North East*
P. Anson, *Fishing boats and fisher-folk on the East Coast of Scotland*, 1930, London.
A. R. Buchan, *The Port of Peterhead*, 1980, Peterhead.
I. Carter, *Farm Life in North East Scotland 1840–1914, The Poor Man's Country*, 1979, Edinburgh.
A. S. Chrichton, *Annals of a Disruption Congregation in Aberdeenshire*, 1943, Aberdeen.
A. D. Farr, *The Deeside Line*, 1968, Newton Abbott.
A. D. Farr, *Stories of Royal Deeside's Railway*, 1971 Knaresborough.
D. Fraser, *The Christian Watt Papers*, 1983, Edinburgh.
C. Graham, *Aberdeen and Deeside*, 1972, London.
S. J. Jones (ed), *Dundee and District*, 1968, Dundee.
J. Lindsay, *The Scottish Poor Law, its operation in the North East 1745–1845*, 1975, Illfracombe.
A. C. O'Dell and J. Mackintosh (ed), *The North East of Scotland*, 1963, Aberdeen.
I. J. Simpson, *Education in Aberdeenshire before 1872*, 1947, London.
H. A. Vallance, *The Great North of Scotland Railway*, 1965, Dawlish and London.
University of Aberdeen Department of Geography, *Royal Grampian Country*, n.d. Aberdeen.

(b) *Early Works*
(i) *Guides, gazeteers and directories*
Aberdeen almanac and Northern Register 1858 and 1863, Aberdeen.
The Bon Accord Directory 1842, Aberdeen.
W. Ferguson, *A Guide to the Great North of Scotland Railway*, 1881, Edinburgh.
F. H. Groome, *The Ordnance Gazeteer of Scotland*, 1884, Edinburgh.
Pigot & Co., *National and Commercial Directory of the whole of Scotland and of the Isle of Man*, 1825, London.
Pigot & Co., *National Commercial Directory of Scotland*, 1837, London.
Slater's Directory Ltd., *Royal National Commercial Directory and Topography of Scotland*, 1867, Manchester.
Slater's Directory Ltd., *Royal National Directory of Scotland*, 1900, Manchester.
Slater's Directory Ltd., *Royal National Directory of Scotland*, 1903, Manchester.
J. Worrall, *Directory for the Counties of Aberdeen, Banff and Kincardine*, 1877, Oldham.

(ii) *Parliamentary and Official Papers*
Annual Reports of the Board of Supervision for the Relief of the Poor in Scotland 1850–1900, Edinburgh.
Board of Agriculture for Scotland, *Agricultural Statistics 1912*, Vol I, 1913, London.
Census Reports and Appendices 1841, 1851, 1891, 1901.
Annual Reports of the Inspection of Prisons for Scotland 1835, 1838, 1839, 1849.
First Annual Report, General Board of Commissioners in Lunacy for Scotland, 1859, Edinburgh.
The Poor Law Enquiry Commission for Scotland 1843, Appendices II and IV, 1844, Edinburgh.

(iii) *Books*
W. Alexander, *Notes and Sketches Illustrative of Northern Rural Life in the eighteenth century*, 1870. Re-pub. 1980, Aberdeen.
J. Anderson, *A General View of the Agriculture and Rural Economy* of the County of Aberdeen, 1794, Edinburgh.

D. Bremner, *The Industries of Scotland, their Rise and Progress and Present Condition*, 1869, reprinted 1969, Newton Abbott.

J. Coutts, *A Dictionary of Deeside*, 1899, Aberdeen.

J. Cranna, *Fraserburgh Past and Present*, 1914, Aberdeen.

C. B. Davidson, *The Burgh of Inverurie, a retrospect, 1863–1888*, 1888, Inverurie.

J. Davidson, *Inverurie and the Earldom of Garioch*, 1878, Edinburgh.

W. Diack, *The Rise and Progress of the Granite Industry in Aberdeen*, 1949, Aberdeen.

R. Dinnie, *A History of Birse*, 1864, n.p.

R. Dinnie, *A History of Kincardine O'Neil*, 1885, Aberdeen.

D. O. Dykes, *Scottish Local Government*, 1907, Edinburgh.

G. M. Fraser, *The Old Deeside Road, its course, history and associations*, 1921, Aberdeen.

H. Hamilton (ed), *The Third Statistical Account of Scotland*, 1960, Glasgow.

A. Harvey, *Agricultural Statistics of Aberdeenshire*, 1859, Aberdeen.

H. O. Horne, *Savings Banks at Kintore and Inverurie*, 1937, Aberdeen.

A. Keith, *The North of Scotland Bank Ltd., 1836–1936*, 1936, Aberdeen.

A. I. McConnochie, *Deeside*, 1900, Aberdeen.

A. I. McConnochie (ed), *The Book of Ellon*, 1901, Ellon.

W. Paul, *The Past and Present State of Aberdeenshire*, 1881, Aberdeen.

J. Pirie, *The Parish of Cairnie and its early connection with Strathbogie*, 1906, Banff.

J. B. Pratt, *Buchan*, 1858, Aberdeen and Edinburgh.

J. Sinclair, *Analysis of the Statistical Account of Scotland*, 1825, Edinburgh.

J. Sinclair, *The Statistical Account of Scotland, 21 volumes, 1791–9*, Edinburgh.

G. Skene Keith, *A General View of the Agriculture of Aberdeenshire*, 1811, Aberdeen.

A. Smith (ed), *A List of Pollable Persons within the Shire of Aberdeen, 1696.* 1844, Aberdeen.

Tawse & Allan, *The Old and New Bridges over the River Don at Inverurie, 1791 and 1924*, 1925, Aberdeen.

J. F. Tocher (ed), *The Book of Buchan*, 1910, Peterhead.

W. Watt, *A History of Aberdeen and Banff*, 1900, Edinburgh.

J. Wilson, *Tales and Travels of a School Inspector*, 1928, Glasgow.

INDEX